Visit us at

Secrets Stolen, Fortunes Lost: Preventing Intellectual Property Theft and Economic Espionage in the 21st Century

Christopher Burgess
Richard Power

KEY	SERIAL NUMBER
001	HJIRTCV764
002	PO9873D5FG
003	829KM8NJH2
004	BPOQ48722D
005	CVPLQ6WQ23
006	VBP965T5T5
007	HJJJ863WD3E
008	2987GVTWMK
009	629MP5SDJT
010	IMWQ295T6T

PUBLISHED BY
Syngress Publishing, Inc.
Elsevier, Inc.
30 Corporate Drive
Burlington, MA 01803

Secrets Stolen, Fortunes Lost: Preventing Intellectual Property Theft and Economic Espionage in the 21st Century

Printed in the United States of America
Transferred to Digital Printing, 2010

ISBN 13: 978-1-59749-255-3

Publisher: Andrew Williams
Acquisitions Editor: Patrice Rapalus
Project Manager: Gary Byrne
Indexer: SPI

Page Layout and Art: SPI
Copy Editors: Judy Eby, Michelle Lewis, Mike McGee, Adrienne Rebello
Cover Designer: Michael Kavish

For information on rights, translations, and bulk sales, contact Matt Pedersen, Commercial Sales Director and Rights, at Syngress Publishing; email m.pedersen@elsevier.com.

Authors

Christopher Burgess is a 30-year veteran of the CIA, where he served as both a Chief of Station and Senior Operations Officer. He is now the Senior Security Advisor to the CSO of Cisco Systems.

Upon his retirement from the CIA, the CIA awarded Burgess the Distinguished Career Intelligence Medal. At Cisco, in addition to his advisor role, he also leads the Global Investigative Support element (forensic support) and the Government Security Office (National Industrial Security Office).

Richard Power is an internationally recognized authority on security and risk. He has delivered executive briefings and led professional training in over 30 countries.

Power has served as Director of Global Security Intelligence for Deloitte Touche Tohmatsu, where he developed programs in cyber security, personnel security, crisis management, awareness and education, and related areas. Prior to Deloitte, Power served as Editorial Director of the Computer Security Institute, where he developed the CSI/FBI Computer Crime and Security Survey. He is the author of four other books, including *Tangled Web: Tales of Digital Crime from the Shadows of Cyberspace*.

Contents

Introduction

Your Enterprise at Risk

Intellectual property is your enterprise's lifeblood; is it safe or are you in danger of being put out of business because a predator has shed that lifeblood? We have found two profound but common misconceptions about intellectual property theft and economic espionage.

One of the great misconceptions is that the threat of economic espionage or trade secret theft is a limited concern—that it is an issue only if you are holding on to something like the formula for Coca-Cola or the design of the next Intel microprocessor. The many real-world stories included in this book illustrate the fallacy of thinking that this threat is someone else's problem.

The other great misconception, held by many business leaders who do acknowledge the danger to their trade secrets and other intellectual property, is that the nature of this threat is sufficiently understood and adequately addressed. Often, on closer inspection, the information-protection programs these business leaders rely on are mired in Industrial Age thinking; they have not been adapted to the dynamic and dangerous new environment forged by globalization and the rise of the Information Age.

Consider the following all-too-true scenario.

You are the chief executive of a successful manufacturer. You have patents and trademarks appropriately registered around the globe. You are informed that there is a product strikingly similar to your own yet-to-be-released product, already on the shelves in the capital city of a far-off land, and you are asking yourself, Who could do this? How big is the hit going to be to the corporate brand? What other intellectual properties have left the enterprise?

A cursory examination of the product shows it is so close to your own, yet-to-be-released product, it is practically a clone. A more comprehensive inspection shows that there has been a clear infringement upon your patent and trade secrets.

Your soon-to-be-introduced product is now out in the wild of the marketplace, being sold under another company's name.

You realize that what you are looking at is a wholesale acquisition and monetization of your intellectual property. Even though the manufacturer of these items will be the subject of your legal department's attention, you need to determine how this happened, what the impact will be, and how you can prevent it from happening again (assuming your enterprise survives this attack). So you initiate your own damage assessment and internal fact-finding investigation.

Your first stop in your damage assessment is with your legal team; they are able to demonstrate to your satisfaction that they had dutifully registered your patents and trademarks, not only in your own country, but globally. They also are engaging in the appropriate legal actions to have these product items taken out of the global marketplace and are seeking a court order to halt further manufacturing of them.

You continue your internal investigation and note no rhyme or reason in the manner in which information is processed throughout your research and development team. When you inquire you receive blank stares of incredulity that you would even question the research and development team; after all, they simply use what the information technology department gives them.

The information technology department head is pleased to listen to your inquiries and answers them with an appreciation for your desire to track the loss of the company's intellectual property. He duly notes the lack of policies and capabilities within the information technology infrastructure. No audit trails exist. He leaves you with the realization that information technologically implementation, viewed as a cost center vs. business enhancement, was really costing the enterprise in a manner in which you never thought possible.

You continue your walk-about investigation and review your talent acquisition process.

You knew that your team had evolved from the start-up days, and that you no longer were able to meet all new hires prior to their arrival, in order to get your own measure of the individual. You discover the company has grown so rapidly, that in your current situation, your new hires are acquired via a third-party agency, and neither you nor your managers have any perspective or appreciation on what "the background checks out" really means, or for that matter should mean, and whether it means the same thing in the United States as it does in China, Singapore, or Finland.

A visit to the manufacturing division further illustrates the natural evolution of a fast-growing enterprise, and the movement from in-house to a hybrid of in-house and contracted manufacturers. When you inquire into the nuances of the various entities with respect to protection of designs, methodologies, and techniques, you are greeted with a blank stare, and instead of answers, you are hosted to a lively presentation on how the manufacturing division can really get those products assembled even more rapidly, and how the capacity of each of the lines is increasing monthly.

Your look into the sales and marketing team's preservation of your corporate differentiators is fruitless, because they simply move forward, but never look back. They are goal-oriented—bring the sales in, fill the order book, go-go-go—but you have no idea as to the amount of detrude they leave behind as they traverse the marketplace.

All in all, you simply don't know where to start to determine where the hemorrhage of your intellectual property occurred that allowed your product to be duplicated.

Your off-the-cuff, with-your-own-eyes damage assessment was a good start. But there is much to be done. First, it is important to get the big picture.

In the twenty-first century, everything is interdependent, connected, interpenetrating (see Figures 1 and 2). The global economy is breaking down trade barriers and bringing others in competition with you even though they are halfway around the world. Furthermore, cyberspace has evolved and expanded in the same time frame of this relentless globalization, and has provided unprecedented access not just to information about your enterprise, but literally to the information of your enterprise itself, including and especially that information that is confidential, secret, or otherwise sensitive.

Figure 1 As Global Economy and Cyberspace Evolve, They Interpenetrate

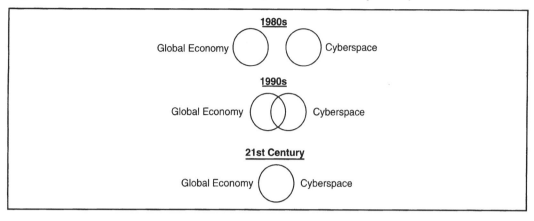

Figure 2 Global Economy and Cyberspace Occupy the Same Space and Share Many Risks and Threats

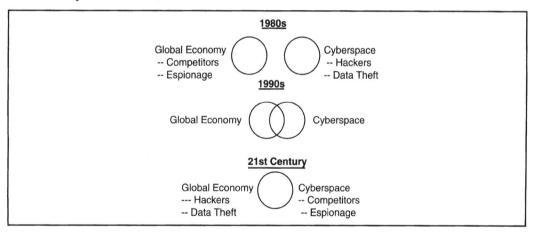

Whether you are Russian or French or German or Japanese or Brazilian or Indian or Chinese or American, what threatens your national economy threatens your enterprise, and whatever threatens your enterprise threatens the national economy.

Today, the U.S. economy, as just one example, faces many threats, including spiraling energy costs, corporate governance abuses, huge federal deficits, foreign ownership of the national debt, the loss of jobs to offshore outsourcing, and the impact of disasters (whether terrorist-related or environmental). And of course, there is the looming possibility of a bird flu pandemic or other global health emergency that could result in the closing of borders, the interruption of business, the cessation of travel, and the deaths of many thousands.

But as you can see from this overview, there is another threat, difficult to quantify or even detect, one that has not yet grabbed the headlines or captured the imagination, and yet is relentlessly and efficiently looting, pillaging, and plundering the U.S. and global economies of the magic ingredient—trade secrets.

Economic espionage and intellectual property theft are as real a threat as terrorism or global warming. But they are subtle, insidious, and stealthy. Even if the United States finds the will to come to grips with the many threats it faces, this silent, invisible hemorrhaging of intellectual know-how and trade secrets could deliver the death blow to the U.S.'s preeminent place in the global economic world before we even wake up to the magnitude of the danger.

According to the U.S. Commerce Department, intellectual property theft is estimated to top $250 billion annually (equivalent to the impact of another four hurricane Katrinas), and also costs the United States approximately 750,000 jobs. The International Chamber of Commerce puts the global fiscal loss at more than $600 billion a year. But both figures appear to be woefully underestimated; by some other estimates, there was over $251 billion worth of intellectual property lost or illegal property seized in August 2005 alone (http://www.goldsec.com/PR/05-10-05-2.htm).

In September 2006, the National Intellectual Property Law Enforcement Council reported to the U.S. President and Congress on the importance of intellectual property to the national interests. The report said, "Protecting intellectual property is vital to advances in science and industry and to creation of content enjoyed throughout the world and the failure to protect intellectual property has potentially serious health and safety consequences."

The U.S. government's focus on the threat to the intellectual property of U.S. industry has resulted in the funding of a myriad of studies on the insider phenomenon in the government's own efforts to raise the level of protection to U.S. government classified information.

Thus, while the U.S. government calls out the need to protect their data, it truly is the responsibility of every company to take appropriate steps to protect their company's assets. This must include the appropriate protection of intellectual property, be it patents, copyrights, trademarks, marketing plans, business-to-business methodologies, or others.

The United States, like other great nations, stands on three legs: military power, political power, and economic power. Arguably, economic power is the most vital of the three. Without economic power, the political elite would be bereft of the consultants and lawyers who insulate it; it would have nothing to bargain with at the geopolitical roulette table, and it would lack the bureaucratic muscle to impose its will domestically. Without economic power, the military would be unable to deploy advanced weapons systems, spy on its enemies from space, span the globe with bases, or even raise an army.

Secrets are the magic ingredient of power. When state secrets (i.e., political and military secrets) are stolen, governments fall and wars are lost, people are disgraced and people die. When trade secrets (i.e., scientific or engineering secrets) are stolen, corporations lose their competitive edge, small entities cease to exist, and whole sectors of the economy weaken and fall behind in the global marketplace; people lose their livelihood and their children's futures.

In other words, the United States could win the war on terrorism, overcome the hallenges of global warming, balance the federal budget, strengthen the United Nations, end global armed conflict, and restore our edge in science and engineering, and still end up behind China, India, Japan, Russia, or Brazil in several vital sectors of the economy, and at a serious, if not fatal, disadvantage within the global marketplace.

The threats of economic espionage, intellectual property theft, counterfeiting, and piracy are global, dangerous, and increasingly common.

It is within your power to decide for yourself if your enterprise is going to be a hard target or a soft target. The time for action is now. You can be prepared.

Secrets Stolen, Fortunes Lost: How to Prevent Intellectual Property Theft and Economic Espionage in the 21st Century is the guidebook.

It is organized and written in such a way that it can be both accessible and of practical use to a broad range of readers. In particular, these readers include not only executives who want to grow the enterprise, not preside over its pillaging, and the security and intelligence professionals empowered to protect the enterprise, but also lawyers seeking precedent and notions of due care, consultants who want to deepen their knowledge in this area of expertise, journalists searching for context and background, and government officials preparing briefing materials and developing public policy.

How to Read This Book

The book is organized into two main sections: *Part 1: The Challenge* and *Part 2: The Strategy*, and includes a collection of useful appendices.

Part 1: The Challenge provides an extensive analysis of numerous instances of intellectual property theft and economic espionage, and a comprehensive overview of the diverse vectors of attack. It includes examples of how insiders, competitors, state-sponsored agents, and organized crime entities target the intellectual property and trade secrets of enterprises throughout the world.

These real-world stories are based on open-source (i.e., not classified) intelligence. There is a compelling lesson in this fact. A decade ago, such stories rarely made it onto the news wire or into the courts. Today, they are commonplace. Unfortunately, the awareness and defenses required to thwart such damaging activities, although economical and effective, are far from commonplace. Our hope is to change that.

This section also includes an in-depth roundtable of subject matter experts who offer their answers to some of the toughest questions related to this risk and how to mitigate it.

Part 2: The Strategy introduces the concept of Holistic Security; in other words, a security program, in which all the elements (e.g., personnel security, physical security, and information security) are integrated (i.e., responsive to and reflective of each other), and which also benefit from a serious commitment to both awareness and education, to engage the work force, and intelligence, to enlighten decision-making.

To help you develop your own winning program, we have included three case studies related to the vital issue of awareness and education, and several information protection program assessment tools on different aspects of security (e.g., personnel, physical, and information security), which articulate questions to aid in the evaluation of your enterprise's current IP protection posture and give you clear guidance on how to strengthen it. We also have provided a presentation for selling IP protection upward, complete with a pitch, presenter's notes, and the background thinking you need to make a compelling and successful appeal for executive commitment.

As a further resource, a collection of appendices at the back of the book includes relevant information on leveraging your tax dollars, baseline controls mapped to ISO, notes on forensics, and a selection of relevant laws and treaties.

Upon the first read, *Secrets Stolen, Fortunes Lost* is intended to bring you not only up to speed, but ahead of the curve, on the full spectrum of problems and solutions related to intellectual property theft and economic espionage.

As an ongoing reference, *Secrets Stolen, Fortunes Lost* is intended to serve as an invaluable reservoir of ideas and energy to draw on as you move forward. When you need to develop a body of policies on new hire background checks, it will be there for you. When you need to document baseline information security controls, it will be there for you. When you need to tell some real-world stories to make your case to your colleagues, it will be there for you. When you need to identify the key elements of a powerful awareness and education program, it will be there for you. When you need to make the business case for the Board of Directors, it will be there for you. When you need to answer the hard questions like, "How did this happen? What do we have to do to prevent this from happening again? Are we safe? What do we have to do? Where do we begin?", this book will be there for you.

Portions of this book first appeared, in a condensed form, as a series of articles in *CSO Magazine*. We're grateful to have the opportunity to present this information to you in its full expression.

—*Christopher Burgess and Richard Power*

The Challenge

The challenge to you, as an executive charged with protecting your enterprise's information, is to confront a shape-shifting, stealthy menace that can (and probably will) come at you from multiple vectors, perhaps even simultaneously.

The truth is that there are no shortages of individuals (some skillful, others bumbling) and groups (some well-heeled, others fly-by-night) willing to go through a myriad of machinations and outwait you for many moons in order to acquire a competitive advantage at your expense and on your back.

To provide you with the full spectrum of threats, in vivid color and stark relief, in Part 1 of this book, we present you with five compelling pieces:

The first chapter, titled "The Tale of the Targeted Trojan," is an analysis of a startlingly example of how a successful twenty-first century effort in the illicit acquisition of intellectual property departs from some of the "conventional wisdom" (i.e., convenient clichés) of twentieth-century industrial espionage (e.g., "industrial espionage is done almost exclusively by the turning of insiders, and not by hacking," and "your industry competitors will not hack into your systems; it's too risky").

The next three chapters offer an exploration of the various points of origin from which attacks originate and real-world cases of how, why, and by whom economic and corporate lifeblood—that is, intellectual property—is spilt:

- When Insiders and/or Competitors Target Businesses' Intellectual Property
- When State Entities Target Businesses' Intellectual Property
- When Piracy, Counterfeiting and Organized Crime Target Businesses' Intellectual Property

"Part 1: The Challenge" concludes with a roundtable discussion held with a number of well-recognized security professionals. These subject matter experts share their perspectives on where we are now and where we are going. This discussion underscores the complexity of the mission at hand, as well as the variety of avenues available in achieving the common goal of protecting intellectual property.

Chapter 1

Introduction

The Greeks delivered a gift of a wooden horse to the people of Troy. The citizens of Troy accepted the gift, the city fell shortly thereafter, and the term "Trojan Horse" entered the popular lexicon.

The maturation of the information age has brought to us a plethora of network-based systems, a multitude of connectivity and information sharing methodologies, and a level of interconnectivity at the enterprise and individual level never experienced before. It is also likely to continue increasing in both scope and complexity (see Figure 1.1).

Figure 1.1 Trojan Horse Programs That Target Confidential Information Are Proliferating Rapidly. They Are Not Used Just for Phishing

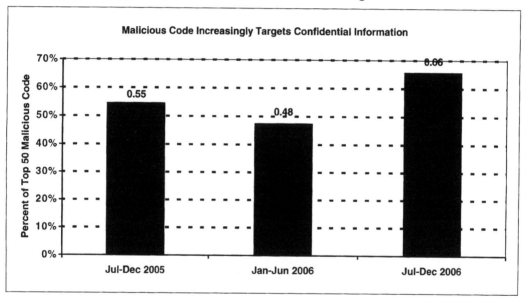

Source: *Symantec Internet Security Threat Report, 2007*

Without security programs installed and security features turned on, these systems and methodologies are clearly vulnerable. But the sad reality is that even when protected by such security programs, with their various security features activated, these systems continue to be vulnerable to carefully crafted low-profile attack software that will be undetectable by a multitude of defensive products, in part because the majority of these products are designed as signature-based rather than event-based.

For such products to be effective in maintaining the security of your system, three events must occur:

- The signature of the attack profile must match a known signature profile.

- The attack profile must have been seen before by the software manufacturer.

- The user must update the software to bring the signature of the attack profile to their system.

The Haephrati Case

This tale of the targeted Trojan—a.k.a., the Haephrati case—was active from 2003 to 2005 and came to the public light in January 2006.

At that time, we saw the extradition of Michael Haephrati along with his wife Ruth Brier-Haephrati from the UK to Israel, an event that under normal circumstances would not have garnered much attention had they not created, distributed, and utilized some of the most interesting and successful pieces of software specifically designed to steal the intellectual property of the target. Upon arrival in Israel, the couple pled guilty to the charges brought against them and were convicted. This case has turned out to be one of the most expansive and interesting cases of industrial espionage in many years.

In late-May 2005, the two Haephratis were arrested by British authorities in London, at the request of Israeli authorities, for having conducted he "unauthorized modification of the contents of a computer." Put more simply, they were charged with having created and placed a "Trojan" file on a computer, not their own, and having siphoned the contents from the computer. But this puts it too simply. What they really did was create their own cottage industry. They provided an "outsourced" technical capability that provided to the "business subscriber," a monthly compendium of illicitly obtained correspondence, documents, economic data, and intellectual property from the computer systems of firms targeted by the Haephratis' subscribers.

In essence, provisions of a sophisticated and highly effective outsourced industrial/economic espionage capability were made available to both individuals and enterprises. The Chief Superintendent of the Israel Police National Fraud Unit, Arie Edleman, describing the tool created by Michael Haephrati said, "It not only penetrated the computer and sent material to wherever you wanted, but it also enabled you to completely control it, to change or erase files, for example. It also enabled you to see what was being typed in real time." He continued, "This is not common software that anti-virus software makers have had to fix."

The When

- Initiated circa May 2003

- Discovered circa November 2004

- Neutralized circa May 2005

- Arrested in the UK and then extradited to Israel January 2006

- Convicted and sentenced March 2006

The How

The Hook

- Delivered via targeted personal e-mail.

- Received an e-mail from an address that looked like one of a known entity, such as the e-mail address gur_r@zahav.net.il, which was read as e-mail address gur-r@zahav.net.il.

- The bogus account was identified as being opened by a person who lived in London and charged the fees to their American Express card.

- Delivered via targeted commercial e-mail.

- Targets received an e-mail message offering a business opportunity.

- Those that responded to info@targetdata.biz would receive the Trojan.

- The domain targetdata.biz was registered to Haephrati.

- Delivered via targeted compact disc.

- Target received a compact disc offering a business opportunity.

- Those who responded to info@targetdata.biz would receive the Trojan.

The Mechanism

- While the exact code that Haephrati created and customized for each victim has not been released to the public, a review of relevant security bulletins provides a good indication of how the code functioned.

- The Trojan included a key-logger, a store-and-forward capability, and would send documents and pictures to FTP servers (file storage servers) located in Israel, the U.S. and other locales. The investigation turned up dozens of servers located around the globe. The program allowed for Haephrati to remotely control the computer of the unsuspecting victim. In essence, Haephrati was running a well-managed store-and-forward service. They were not relying on *botnets* or other illicitly acquired infrastructures. They had a business to support and leased their infrastructure. According to the Israeli police, items stolen included marketing plans, employee pay slips, business plans, and details on new products, all of which were passed to rivals. The data included over 11,000 pages of data, which consisted of thousands of pages of "confidential" data (more than 11 gigabytes of material).

The Who

Michael Haephrati is the computer programmer who created the original Trojan program, allegedly planted on his in-laws computer so as to provide him the means to harass his former in-laws. According to the press, Ruth Brier-Haephrati saw the business opportunity in selling the capability. In Israel, a number of private investigative firms were identified as being positioned between the Haephratis, the clients, and the victims. Haephrati began creating one-off programs for targeted delivery, based on information acquired about the victim—in other words, they were provided the specific information necessary to craft the tool that would undermine the security apparatus and/or techniques employed by the victim. According to the Israeli police, the capability was also sold to firms outside Israel, none of which have, as of mid-2007, been publicly identified. Thus, it is expected that firms outside Israel have also fallen victim to this type of methodology and specific technology.

The Why

As noted earlier, the initial motive was revenge. Haephrati resented his former in-laws and set about to defame them by manipulating information obtained from their computer. The recipient of the Haephratis' efforts had a simple motive: economic advantage over their competition.

The Cost

Haephrati charged each business customer the equivalent of US$3500 to create the customized program and make the initial install on the victim's computer, and another US$900/month to maintain the infrastructure used to collect, forward, store, collate, and deliver the illicitly acquired information on a monthly basis. The cost to the recipients was the fee they paid to the intermediary who contracted Haephrati's services. And what was the cost to the victims? Extreme. They lost their intellectual property, lost business opportunity, and lost the privacy of their employees' personal data. They also lost go-to-market plans, as well as customer requirements, and they potentially lost the trust of their customers. Table 1.1 lists various items traded on underground servers.

Table 1.1 Advertised Prices of Items Traded on Underground Economy Servers

Item	Advertised Price (US$)
U.S.-based credit card with card verification value	$1–$6
UK-based credit card with card verification value	$2–$12
An identity (including U.S. bank account, credit card, date of birth, and government-issued identification number)	$14–$18
List of 29,000 e-mails	$5
Online banking account with a $9,900 balance	$300
Yahoo Mail cookie exploit—advertised to facilitate full access when successful	$3
Valid Yahoo and Hotmail e-mail cookies	$3
Compromised computers	$6–$20
Phishing Web site hosting—per site	$3–$5
Verified PayPal account with balance (balance varies)	$10–$50
Unverified PayPal account with balance (balance varies)	$12
Skype accounts	$12
World of Warcraft accounts—one month duration	$10

Source: *Symantec Internet Security Threat Report, 2007*

The Discovery

Haephrati, the criminal, was undone by Haephrati, the vengeful. Haephrati's continued harassment of his former in-laws after having transitioned into the illegal provisioning to commercial companies of a criminal infrastructure was his undoing. His former father-in-law visited the law enforcement authorities in November 2004 complaining that his private work was showing up on the Internet in a manner designed to defame his person and character. The authorities suggested reformatting the hard drive, he did, and the problem persisted. The former father-in-law returned to the authorities, who looked deeper, using their forensic tools (not further identified) and noted a unique piece of malware had been installed. The authorities walked the path back and discovered Haephrati's cottage industry. When Haephrati sent his ex-wife an e-mail (see "The How:" section earlier), investigators and the ex-wife noticed the discrepancy in the e-mail address used and traced the bogus account to Haephrati. They discovered that Haephrati had paid for the account by using his American Express card, and the connection between the virtual criminal and the physical person behind the criminal activity was completed.

The Scope

The Superintendent of the Israeli Police, Peral Liat, told *Computer Weekly*, "We know Haephrati worked abroad. We assume that if he sold his Trojan horse to private investigators in Israel, he also offered it to companies abroad. That is why we have involved Interpol and the police in London, Germany, and the U.S." According to publicly available information, which should increase as the case proceeds through the Israeli court system, 18 individuals and numerous firms have been implicated. Those arrested in Israel were charged with uploading Trojan horses in targeted companies on behalf of their clients (the end-recipients). Most have been accused of "creating and distributing a computer virus, penetrating computer material, wiretapping, criminal conspiracy, aggravated fraud, and infringement of the Protection of Privacy Law (5741-1981 – Israeli penal code)."

Alleged Intermediary Clients

- Yitzhak Rath, CEO of Modi'in Ezrahi (Private investigation firm) and three of his employees.

- Zvi Krochmal, who heads Krochmal Special Investigations, and three of his investigators: Alex Weinstein, Yitzhak Dekel, and Ofer Fried.

- Eliezer Pelosoff and Avraham Balali, both of the Pelosoff-Balali investigative firm.

Alleged End-Recipients

- **Pele Phone Communications** The firm's Security Director, Shay Raz, allegedly ordered industrial espionage against Ran Rahav Communications and PR Ltd., who had as a client Partner Communications Co. Ltd.

- **Cellcom Israel Ltd.** Security Director, Ofer Reichman, is suspected of ordering industrial espionage against ad agency Reuveni-Pridan, which also had as a client, Partner Communications Co. Ltd.

- **Mayer Cars and Trucks** The CEO of the firm Uzi Mor is suspected of ordering espionage against Champion Motors of Israel.

- **Yes (an Israeli Satellite TV provider)** CFO Moriah Kathriel is suspected of ordering espionage against HOT, its cable competitor.

- **Hamafil Services (an office equipment and photocopy company)** CEO Yoram Cohen is suspected of ordering espionage against its rival Zilumatik, Ltd.

- **Tana Industries** Suspected of ordering industrial espionage upon its competitor Eden Springs (Maayanot Eden). No arrests as yet.

Companies Identified as Victims

- HOT

- Strauss-Elite

- I.M.C.

- Orange

- Champion Motors (Israel)

- Shalmor-Avnon-Aichay

- Young & Rubican

- Reuveni-Pridan

- Ran Rahav Communications

- PR Ltd.

- Eden Springs (Maayanot Eden)

- Shekem Electric

- Ace Marketing Chains (ACE Israel)

- Soglowek

- The Malam Group

- Zilumatik

- Globes

- Amnon Jackont, an Israeli mystery novelist and Tel Aviv University history professor (the former father-in-law)

- Natalya Wieseltier, Michael Haephrati's ex-wife

Related U.S./UK Advisories

UK – National Infrastructure Security Coordination Centre (NISCC)

On June 16, 2005, NISCC issued an advisory alert (NISCC Briefing 08/2005) that described in detail the capability created by Haephrati, without reference to Haephrati himself. The highpoints of the brief:

- A series of Trojaned e-mail attacks are targeting UK governmental offices and companies.

- The attackers' aim appears to be the covert gathering and transmitting of commercially or economically valuable information.

- Trojans are delivered either in e-mail attachments or through links to a Web site.

- The e-mails employ social engineering, including use of a spoofed sender address and information relevant to the recipient's job or interests to entice them into opening the documents.

- Once installed on a user machine, Trojans may be used to obtain passwords, scan networks, export information, and launch further attacks.

- Anti-virus software and firewalls do not give complete protection. Trojans can communicate with the attackers using common ports (for example, HTTP, DNS, SSL) and can be modified to avoid anti-virus detection.

On July 8, 2005 the NISCC issued a separate advisory (18/05 ID# 20050708-00561) with respect to the confirmed use of e-mail to deliver a Trojan attack.

- "Uniras has evidence that the horrific events of July 7th being used in the social engineering element of e-mail-borne Trojan attacks. Typically, the subject line of an e-mail, its content, and possibly a malicious attachment all make reference to the incidents in London. At this time, everybody is interested in keeping abreast of developments and will naturally be tempted to open e-mails of this nature. We urge security officers to take the opportunity to remind their staff that only reputable news sources should be used for this purpose and that e-mails relating to news events should be opened only if they are from a known and trusted source and are expected."

U.S. – The Department of Homeland Security (DHS)

On 21 December 2005, the DHS in conjunction with the Department of State issued a Joint Information Bulletin (JIB ID # 12212005) titled "Look Before You Click: Trojan Horses and Other Attempts to Compromise Networks." The key findings of the bulletin were:

- According to industry security experts, the biggest security vulnerability facing computer users and networks is e-mail with concealed Trojan horse software—destructive programs that masquerade as benign applications and embedded links to ostensibly innocent Web sites that download malicious code. While firewall architecture blocks direct attacks, e-mail provides a vulnerable route into an organization's internal network through which attackers can destroy or steal information.

- Attackers try to circumvent technical blocks to the installation of malicious code by using social engineering—getting computer users to unwittingly take actions that allow the code to be installed and organization data to be compromised.

- The techniques attackers use to install Trojan horse programs through e-mail are widely available, and include forging sender identification, using deceptive subject lines, and embedding malicious code in e-mail attachments.

- Developments in thumb-sized portable storage devices and the emergence of sophisticated keystroke logging software and devices make it easy for attackers to discover and steal massive amounts of information surreptitiously.

- Security experts believe the most important line of defense in computer security is the user. User training and awareness about social engineering attack techniques and safe Web browsing practices are integral to a sound computer security posture.

Haephrati's malware was active for a multiyear period, not detectable at that time by the many anti-virus programs available. Subsequent to the advisories, the fingerprint of the malware used by Haephrati was integrated into the anti-virus/anti-malware programs. The reality begs the question that we posited earlier: How many similar programs, written by more creative individuals with greater incentives not to be discovered, are currently attacking companies, and/or individuals' computer infrastructures—and what is the time lag between implementation, discovery, and remediation?

Lessons learned?

One lesson is that your competitors—or mercenaries and freebooters looking for something to peddle to them—are willing to attack you in cyberspace rather than just rely on the industrial-age method of turning insiders.

Another important lesson is that Trojans are not just used for phishing. Indeed, the proliferation of such programs is an indication of what lies farther out in deep water—that is, malicious code that targets enterprises and/or individual executives.

Those using targeted Trojans are more like frogmen carrying spear guns and riding mini-submarines, rather than fraudsters with big nets casting for the gullible and the naive. It may sound like something out of Ian Fleming, but it is nevertheless a reality.

Furthermore, when you couple the demonstrated capabilities of targeted Trojans with the intent and resources available to the organized crime entities in Russia and other former Soviet states, chilling scenarios abound (see Figure 1.2). Such threats are real, and not rare, although they certainly are rarely admitted by victimized enterprises or written about in the press. Indeed, the most unusual aspect of the Haephrati case is that it made it into print.

Figure 1.2 Russian Cyber Criminals Increasingly Use Trojans to Gather IP

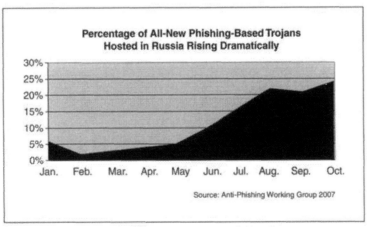

Source: *Anti-Phishing Working Group, 2007*

Chapter 2

When Insiders and/or Competitors Target a Business's Intellectual Property

Introduction

By definition, an insider can come in many forms, be it an employee, a member of the management team, a corporate board member, a vendor, a third-party contracted manufacturer, or a collaborative partner in a joint venture.

The newspapers are replete with countless examples of the damage an insider can do to a business.

The following is a selection of some particularly insightful cases, which serve to illustrate the various motivations of the offenders, as well as the damage done to the enterprises they undermined.

Lightwave Microsystems

Let us begin with the case of an employee at a privately held firm (Lightwave Microsystems), who occupied a trusted position within that company, that of Director of Information Technology, and who acted alone in his attempt to illegally share Lightwave's intellectual property. The individual, Brent Woodward of Oakland, CA, chose to exercise his venial needs, as well as obtain some solace via revenge when faced with circumstances that he believed were unjust—two very powerful motivators in an individual contemplating a malevolent act.

In late 2002, the owner of Lightwave Microsystems, a California firm, announced that the company would cease operations due to the firm's inability to make a profit, but Lightwave Microsystems was not without value—it owned patents and had evolved trade secrets that could be sold. (Lightwave was subsequently purchased by NeoPhotonics of San Jose, CA.) When faced with the prospect of unemployment and upside-down stock options, Woodward made copies of the company's trade secrets from the firm's backup tapes and created a plan to sell these secrets to a competitor. He would feather his own nest monetarily and get revenge for the abruptness of his CEO's actions.

No one at Lightwave Microsystems detected the unauthorized copy activity. Why would they? Woodward's access was both natural and unencumbered. Furthermore, as Director of Information Technology, it was Woodward's responsibility to protect this very data—to discover, neutralize, and mitigate any and all attempts to steal Lightwave Microsystems' intellectual property.

Admittedly, Woodward's methodology was very sophomoric, but worthy of sharing nonetheless. He created an alias name, "Joe Data," and also set up a Web-based e-mail account, lightwavedata@yahoo.com, from which he executed his crime. Woodward contacted JDS-Uniphase's (JDS) chief technology officer and offered to provide Lightwave Microsystems' data to JDS in return for a significant sum of money.

JDS did the absolute right thing: the firm immediately contacted the U.S. Federal Bureau of Investigation (FBI), and at their request, JDS consented to the monitoring of communications between JDS and "Joe Data," which was to occur via e-mail. The FBI, with a consensual monitoring permit provided by JDS, was able to observe the controlled negotiations between JDS and "Joe Data," as well as trace back these communications via the user's Internet protocol address to the e-mail service provider, Yahoo. The trace activity showed "Joe Data" was connected to the Internet from within Woodward's residence. This discovery enabled the FBI to execute a valid search warrant of the residence, which produced sufficient evidence to ultimately bring about Woodward's arrest. Ultimately, he was charged with one count of theft of trade secrets under 18 U.S.C. § 1832.

In August 2005, the United States Attorney's Office for the Northern District of California announced that Brent Woodward had pled guilty to the aforementioned charge. Though he could have been sentenced to ten years imprisonment and fined US$250,000, he received a $20,000 fine and was sentenced to two years in prison, plus three years of supervised release.

Though Woodward found that his vengeful attempt to obtain an illegal bonus to be very expensive in the end—in both defense fees as well as penalties adjudicated—it is important to note that Woodward was acting by himself, and for himself, and thus had no interests other than his own venial needs. What would have happened had Woodward offered the purloined data to a less ethical competitor? Perhaps that competitor would have taken the data and set up the equivalent of a parallel universe. Would the value of Lightwave Microsystems' intellectual property sold to NeoPhotonics have been jeopardized? What of NeoPhotonics, the purchaser of Lightwave Microsystems' technology? If the unscrupulous competitor had taken the trade secrets and capitalized on the technological advances, what recourse would NeoPhotonics have had to recoup their investment/payment to Lightwave Microsystems? Litigation would only be an option IF Lightwave Microsystems knew the intellectual property had been stolen. And this would have come to light when? The purchaser wouldn't have admitted to having purloined the intellectual property, and Woodward certainly wouldn't have advertised his sale. Only during the unscrupulous competitor's developmental, manufacturing, and/or marketing/sales processes would there have been the possibility that the technology acquisition might be revealed.

The best course would have been to initially establish a defense against Woodward's action. Lightwave Microsystems should have had in place multiple audit trails and either human or machine tracking of all users, including the super-user, so that a warning could have been sent that anomalous behavior had occurred.

America Online

Let's now move on to another case in which greed was the motivating factor, inducing an employee to steal his employer's private data. In April and May 2003, American Online (AOL) software engineer Jason Smathers, utilized a colleague's access codes to surreptitiously log on to the AOL server. Then, posing as the colleague, he used his colleague's access to acquire information from each of the then 30 million AOL customers. The data stolen by Smathers comprised 92 million records, which contained the personal identifying information of those 30 million customers. The data included e-mail addresses, screen names, ZIP codes, customer credit card types (not numbers), and telephone numbers associated with AOL customer accounts. Smathers sold the stolen AOL data to Sean Dunaway of Las Vegas. Dunaway paid Smathers US$27,000 for the addresses, and then utilized them to advertise his own online gambling Web site. Dunaway later resold the AOL data to online "spammers" for approximately US$52,000. Clearly, he was an early adopter of the concept of spamming.

The Department of Justice prosecuted this case under the (then new) federal law Can-Spam (Controlling the Assault of Non-Solicited Pornography and Marketing Act). Smathers had pled guilty in February 2005 to the crime. In October 2005, he was sentenced to 15 months in prison and fined US$84,000—triple what he had garnered through the sale of the data. Smathers clearly knew the data had value, but he grossly underestimated the value of the information. Though DOJ recommended to the presiding judge that Smathers be barred from the software profession, the judge noted Smathers' cooperation in the investigation and believed that his cooperation and Smathers' contrite behavior warranted leniency. Smathers noted to the court that AOL had said his theft and subsequent sale had cost the company at least US$400,000—and potentially millions of U.S. dollars.

At first glance, it would seem only AOL and their 30 million subscribers were exposed to unwanted spam. So where's the damage? The user can simply press the Delete key and get on with life. After all, spam is received by virtually every Internet user, and a variety of companies now specialize in filtering spam so only "good" e-mail arrives in their inbox. However, the loss of revenue to AOL was the loss of time each user experienced while deleting those unwanted e-mails—and time has value. But why was a crime that was committed in 2003 not prosecuted until early 2005? A very good question.

The delay in prosecution is largely due to the fact that until mid-2004, Smathers was still an employee of AOL and had not yet been identified as the source of the data breach. While AOL knew they had a problem and were cooperating with law enforcement, Smathers' use of a colleague's administrative logon was an effective method of bypassing the AOL corporate security apparatus. Smathers' colleague did have authorized access to the data, whereas Smathers did not. Had the colleague perhaps protected his passwords better (there is no evidence to suggest the unidentified colleague colluded or provided Smathers with his login passwords), this crime might never have occurred.

But the real damage may still be looming. What of the collation of e-mail addresses, usernames, and user telephone numbers? What malicious use could this data be to e-mail phishers or unscrupulous telemarketers? The answer: Priceless. That was 2003. Fast forward to 2007 where some spammed e-mail has evolved into what is known euphemistically as *phishing*.

AOL is advertised as a "family-friendly" environment—one where the customer doesn't have to be a technological marvel, nor think in bits or baud, to enjoy the pleasures of the Internet—and AOL works extraordinarily hard to exclude the seedier side of the Internet. As noted earlier, AOL admitted to having spent at least US$400,000 as a result of this incident, but the downside may be much greater as they continue creating software to mitigate the loss of customer data, while simultaneously working to regain the trust of their customer base.

According to the Privacy Rights Clearinghouse, in 2006 alone there were approximately 100,453,730 cases of personal identifying information revealed to those without a need to know. These revelations occurred in government entities, retailers, educational institutes, and consulting firms (www.privacyrights.org/ar/DataBreaches2006-Analysis.htm).

Casiano Communications

Let's look at another instance of personal greed—this in a separate industry where a worker was accused of stealing the intellectual property of his employer and setting up shop as a direct competitor. In mid-October 2005, Casiano Communications, Inc. (CCI), arguably the most prominent publisher within the Caribbean basin with respect to

Caribbean business and travel literature magazines, filed suit against a former employee, John Bynum. The suit alleged that Bynum stole intellectual property from CCI—specifically, CCI's databases, which Bynum then forwarded to his personal e-mail account from CCI's computers. According to the CCI complaint, Bynum stole client and advertiser information, violating CCI's Electronic Mail and Company Resources and Equipment policy, which is a condition of employment with CCI.

San Juan, Puerto Rico Superior Court issued a temporary restraining order against Bynum that required him to cease and desist from utilizing, transmitting, selling, or reproducing any form of database or other trade secrets obtained during the course of his employment with CCI. The injunction granted CCI the right to seize all materials contained in any computers, disks, or other information-technology items in the personal possession of the defendant. CCI alleged that Bynum had been selling a database of key island (Puerto Rico) business contacts to companies to market their products and services.

Again, this is an example of personal greed, motivated as much by circumstances as opportunity. It is not beyond the pale to assume your employees know who your competitors are and how to reach out to these firms to sell your intellectual property should the opportunity present itself and the competitor be unscrupulous enough to accept it (unlike the Lightwave Microsystems case).

Corning and PicVue

A case that hit the public eye in 2005, and that was settled in 2006, has these very circumstances present, where an opportunity presented to a low-level employee, coupled with the identification of an interested party, created a temptation for instant financial gain that was simply too great for a weak-willed employee to ignore.

This was the case of Corning Incorporated and PicVue Electronics, the latter a Taiwanese corporation. On October 20, 2005, the Department of Justice charged Jonathan Sanders, an employee of Corning's Harrodsburg, KY plant, with the theft of trade secret material belonging to Corning. Specifically, material pertaining to an "overflow down draw fusion glass-making process used to produce Thin Filter Transistor (TFT) Liquid Crystal Display (LCD) flat panel glass."

In the DOJ complaint, it is alleged that Sanders began his theft of Corning's IP in December 1999 and continued to perpetrate the crime through December 2001. Sanders allegedly took, without authorization, trade secret material belonging to Corning and subsequently sold that same material to PicVue Electronics Ltd., a Taiwanese corporation. This case of Economic Espionage, not only involved PicVue Electronics, the corporation, but also the former president of PicVue.

When arrested, Sanders waived his right to a preliminary hearing, was indicted, and pled guilty. He was sentenced to 48 months imprisonment and ordered to pay a fine of US$20,000 on April 18, 2006.

He told the FBI that he found blueprints containing the Corning trade secrets within a Corning warehouse in 1999. The blueprints were within a container of sensitive corporate material awaiting destruction. He said he simply took the blueprints instead of destroying them.

In December 1999, Sanders then traveled to California and met with PicVue's company president, Jacob Lin, as well as Yeong C. Lin, a consultant to PicVue. Sanders claimed he only described the fusion draw process, and did not show the drawings to the PicVue president nor his consultant. Subsequent to this meeting, Sanders was allegedly offered a job by PicVue, but declined the position.

Then around September 2000, Yeong C. Lin, the consultant, informed PicVue that Sanders was now offering Corning's blueprints/drawings via an oral description. PicVue authorized the payment of US$30,000 and wired the funds to a California bank account, where apparently the PicVue consultant took control of the funds. The consultant then enlisted the aid of a college roommate, Danny Price, who carried US$25,000 to a meeting with Sanders outside of Atlanta, GA, so as to obfuscate the connection between PicVue and Sanders.

Sanders met with Price as planned, outside of Atlanta, and accepted the money from Price. In exchange, he provided Price with the Corning blueprints he had stolen from the corporate sensitive data destruction bin. Price apparently gave the documents to consultant, Lin, who met with PicVue engineers in California. The PicVue engineers took digital pictures of the blueprint documents and transferred the images to a digital storage device. The engineers hand-carried the digital storage device back to Taiwan, and the blueprints were then, allegedly, destroyed.

Two months later (November 2000), engineers from PicVue traveled to Kentucky and met with Sanders directly to discuss the blueprints he had sold to PicVue. Sanders claims the conversations were centered on providing clarification to PicVue on details contained within the blueprints.

PicVue representatives then traveled to the offices of Saint-Gobain glass, Niagara Falls, NY in September 2001 to purchase a part specific to the fusion process. Given the prior commercial relationship between Corning and Saint-Gobain, the latter recognized the utility of the part as being only applicable to the fusion draw process and alerted Corning to the possibility that their trade secrets had been compromised to PicVue.

Corning representatives visited Saint-Gobain's offices, reviewed the specifications provided by PicVue and concluded that Corning trade secrets were involved. Corning contacted the FBI, who opened an investigation October 2001.

In this instance, Corning apparently had a set of procedures in place to destroy company confidential documents, but it would appear no mechanism existed to ensure that documents put into the "to-be-destroyed" bin were, in fact, subsequently destroyed. Again, the company was ignorant of the theft of their intellectual property until the recipient—PicVue, in this case—approached one of the few firms in the world able to create the parts necessary to make the purloined documents effective in the marketplace. If there is a bright side to the entire episode, it is the strength of the relationship between Corning and Saint-Gobain, which brought this illegal activity to light, not internal procedures.

Let us assume you have appropriate checks and balances in place to protect yourself against the opportunistic and greed-driven employee. What defense do you have to protect yourself when the theft of your technology is premeditated by individuals who are the leaders, and literally in the driver's seat of one of your main competitors? Can't happen, you say? Think again.

Avery Dennison and Four Pillars

Let's now review the well-documented and publicized instance of intellectual property theft that was encountered by Avery Dennison, the firm that makes labels, and by extension, the firm that spends a great deal of money on the research and development of adhesives. Unbeknownst to the company, they had had their intellectual property stolen from them from 1989 through 1997. The theft of their IP was literally a textbook example of the methodical harvesting of a firm's technological advances and research by a competitor.

Avery Dennison, whose headquarters is in Pasadena, CA, is one of the United States largest manufacturers of adhesive labels, and retains intellectual property for these formulas. The firm's adhesives and methodologies give Avery Dennison their market advantage within the global adhesive label market. Because of this, a competitor, Four Pillars Enterprise Limited of Taiwan, specifically targeted their research facility in Concord, OH.

Four Pillars is a manufacturer of pressure-sensitive products in Taiwan, with market share both in the United States and the Far East. Prior to 1989, Four Pillars CEO had identified his competition and had noted the competitive advantage held by market-sector leader Avery Dennison and so had set out as a corporate goal to capitalize on Avery Dennison's advance research in adhesives. A very determined individual, he was successful in stealing the formulas for Avery Dennison's adhesives—some might say very successful.

Successful that is, until 1997, when one of his Four Pillars' employees applied for work with Avery Dennison, and during the course of the interview(s) revealed that for the preceding eight years, Avery Dennison's adhesive formulas were being provided to Four Pillars by an employee of Avery Dennison.

Avery Dennison had not previously detected this theft of their IP. The firm took the correct action and contacted the FBI, and together with Avery Dennison, the two contrived a sting operation to identify the employee who was supplying Four Pillars with company secrets. The sting operation was fruitful and identified Mr. Ten Hong Lee—a.k.a., Victor Lee—a U.S. citizen and senior research engineer at Avery Dennison's Concord, Ohio research facility, who was stealing the intellectual property of his employer.

Lee was confronted and admitted his guilt, confessing to having stolen the formulas and methodologies of his employer from 1989 to 1997. He was later persuaded to act as a cooperative witness for the Department of Justice (DOJ), who wished to prosecute this theft of the intellectual property of a United States corporation by a foreign national, under the powers of the Economic Espionage Act (EEA) of 1996.

The ensuing investigation revealed Lee—who received his undergraduate degree at the National University of Taipei, his Masters degree in polymer science from Akron University, and his Ph.D. in chemical engineering from Texas Tech—had been invited to Taiwan by the Industrial Technology Research Institute to give a lecture at one of their conferences. While there, he was asked to present a technical lecture to Four Pillars by the company's technical director.

During this visit to Taiwan, Lee was enticed to covertly enter into a relationship with Pin Yen Yang—a.k.a., P.Y. Yang—President and CEO of the Taiwanese firm, Four Pillars Enterprise Company, Ltd as a "secret consultant." For this, he was paid $25,000 for his first year. Lee, Yang, and Yang's daughter, Hwei Chen Yang—a.k.a., Sally Yang—conspired to provide the Yangs with Avery Dennison's intellectual property and business methodologies. In exchange, Lee would be paid substantial sums of money—to be deposited with Lee's relatives, who were resident in Taiwan.

Following the discovery by Avery Dennison, the covert relationship continued under FBI scrutiny until early September 1997, when Lee provided to the Yangs proprietary information of Avery Dennison origin during a meeting monitored and controlled by the FBI in a room within the Holiday Inn located in Westlake, Ohio. Lee indicated on the video coverage of the meeting to the Yangs that the papers he was providing were the intellectual proprietary property of Avery Dennison. The Yangs acknowledged such, and following the meeting, the Yangs were observed cutting, with a knife, the headers and footers off the documents provided by Lee. Subsequently, the Yangs were arrested by the FBI as they attempted to board a plane and return to their corporate headquarters with the data.

The relationship between Lee and the Yangs' Four Pillars was a clear case of "economic espionage." During the prosecution of this case, it was learned that Lee was paid more than $150,000 over a period of eight years in exchange for sharing the intellectual property of his employer, Avery Dennison. In 1999, U.S. District Court Judge Peter C. Economus convicted both Yang and his daughter for stealing trade secrets and also convicted Four Pillars on economic espionage charges. Yang was sentenced to six months of home confinement and fined $250,000; his daughter was fined $5,000 and received a year's probation. The firm, Four Pillars, was fined $5 million for accepting the pilfered trade secrets. Lee pled guilty to wire fraud and defrauding his employer.

Avery Dennison's discovery of Four Pillars' illegal activity was due to a serendipitous event, the employment application by a former Four Pillars' employee and this employee's willingness to share information concerning Four Pillars' recruitment of an Avery Dennison employee for the sole purpose of compromising the intellectual property of Avery Dennison. In this instance, Four Pillars personnel targeted an individual with whom the Yangs could relate to on the basis of ethnicity, leveraging Lee's desire to help a fellow-countryman. The Yangs stroked Lee's ego, giving him "recognition" for his intellect, and providing him with remuneration in a covert manner—thus, keeping his skullduggery out of the view of the tax authorities, Avery Dennison lenders, or others who may question the increase/addition in Lee's income.

The Yangs' investment of approximately $150,000 resulted in an approximate $30 to 50 million loss to Avery Dennison. It is worth noting that Yang and his firm Four Pillars were acting in their own self-interest and not at the behest of any other entity.

Four Pillars ultimately appealed their conviction to the Supreme Court, hoping for a reduction in the sentence, but the convictions were upheld in October 2002. Four Pillars continues to be an active firm, involved in adhesive and label manufacturing.

Lexar Media and Toshiba

Let's move on to one of those ticklish situations that every company that has ever collaborated with another company encounters: *Is this a win-win scenario, or am I placing my company in a situation of inordinate risk?* The answer could be yes—*It could be a win-win situation*—but you must keep your eye on your property and monitor your partner's actions as well.

Now, let's review the litigation undertaken by Lexar Media (as of June 2006, a wholly owned subsidiary of Micron Technology) and their successful lawsuit in which they claimed the theft of their trade secrets by a foreign competitor and the competitor's U.S. subsidiaries.

In late March 2005, a California Superior Court jury found Toshiba Corporation (a Japanese company) guilty of the theft of trade secrets from Lexar Media and assessed damages of $381.4 million and punitive damages of $84 million for a total of $465.4 million. Lexar had alleged that Toshiba had utilized Lexar's trade secrets in Toshiba's product line, which included NAND flash chips, Compact Flash cards, xD-Picture cards, and Secure Digital cards. The jury agreed and the issuance of punitive damages by the jury indicated that the jury found Toshiba's actions to be oppressive, fraudulent, and/or malicious.

Toshiba petitioned the court in April 2005 to recognize the jury's award as an advisory verdict and asked that the monetary damages be reduced, while Lexar petitioned the court for an injunction against Toshiba so as to prevent the sale of any Toshiba products that incorporated Lexar's intellectual property. On October 14, 2005, the court ruled that the jury findings were not advisory but in fact final. The court also declined to issue an injunction against Toshiba. Lexar's Executive Vice President and General Counsel, Eric Whitaker, noted that Lexar will continue to pursue patent infringement litigation against Toshiba, and remains confident that once patent infringement has been confirmed, that an injunction against Toshiba preventing the sale of their products will be forthcoming. Then in April 2006, Lexar filed a petition with the U.S. International Trade Commission (ITC) to initiate a Section 337 investigation in which Lexar asked that Toshiba's NAND flash memory chips be barred from import into the United States. According to an ITC press release, in May 2006 the ITC voted to institute an investigation of certain flash memory chips, flash memory systems, and products containing the same. In October 2006, Toshiba and Micron (having acquired Lexar) reached a settlement, the details of which were omitted from the public Securities and Exchange Commission filings of November 2006.

A tremendous amount of legal wrangling was involved in the proceedings, and while a settlement occurred, it begs the question: How did it get this far? According to Lexar, in mid-1996 Lexar Media was created by employees of Cirrus Corporation, and its business plan centered on technology created by Cirrus. Prior to the creation of Lexar, Cirrus and Toshiba had been involved in discussions (1994 to 1995) on how Cirrus would collaborate with Toshiba in creating flash memory controllers in support of Toshiba's preferred flash memory technology. Upon creation of Lexar, discussions between Toshiba and Lexar increased in depth and frequency. Toshiba and Lexar's Toshiba—Toshiba America and Toshiba America Electronic Components (TEAC)—were given access to Lexar's intellectual property under a Non-Disclosure Agreement (NDA) signed on December 1, 1996, which had a five-year expiration date.

Following the signing of the NDA, in-depth discussion between the parties ensued, and Toshiba invested US$3 million in Lexar in May 1997. They also placed a member on the board of directors of Lexar. Throughout 1997, Lexar continued to share intellectual property with Toshiba. In April 1998, Toshiba and Lexar entered into a partnership so as to be competitive in the flash memory market. The joint relationship apparently prospered throughout 1998 and most of 1999. On October 6, 1999, Toshiba and SanDisk announced in a joint press statement that the two firms had entered into a joint agreement to develop and manufacturer Gigabit Scale flash memory. Interestingly, the Toshiba board member apparently missed the October 5, 1999 Lexar board meeting. Lexar felt that their "partner" had sold them out to their main competitor in the flash memory market—SanDisk. Not only had Toshiba been a partner in numerous joint development projects, but Toshiba's presence on the Lexar board of directors provided Toshiba with all the strengths and weaknesses of the firm.

The Lexar board requested an explanation from the board member representing their partner Toshiba. The board member provided assurances that the agreement between Toshiba and SanDisk did not involve Lexar technologies. The board member continued with his assurances, noting the publicized agreement between Toshiba and SanDisk involved a separate division within Toshiba than that involved with Lexar. Less than seven months later, SanDisk and Toshiba announced in a joint press statement that the two had signed a US$700 million deal to create a joint fabrication facility in Virginia to produce multilevel cell (MLC) flash memory chips. Lexar believed that their intellectual property, specifically the multipage write technology was being used in this, and that without this technology, the MLC flash memory initiative would not be financially viable.

Lexar believes that Toshiba and its subsidiaries have incorporated into their product line intellectual property which, when disclosed by Lexar to Toshiba, were not only considered proprietary trade secrets of Lexar, but also were covered under the subsequent NDA. Though suspicious, it was not until Toshiba published in 2001 the technologies used in their MLC smart memory application that proof was evident to Lexar that their IP had been used.

In this instance, Lexar was able to prove what they suspected when Toshiba published the technical specifications of the Toshiba product line. What makes this case especially noteworthy is the apparent brashness on the part of Toshiba. Toshiba had a seat on the board of the company whose intellectual property they would be purloining. In addition, Toshiba had a number of joint development projects, during which Lexar's intellectual property was fully disclosed to Toshiba, and which Toshiba then leveraged for their own benefit in their own product line.

So, would Lexar not have lost their intellectual property had they chosen their partners more carefully? Probably yes, but did they have a choice in choosing their dance partner? Lexar was a spin-out and a startup and thus required a rock-solid partnership to reduce the unremunerated burn rate and shorten the distance to profitability. The preexisting Lexar/Toshiba relationship at first appears to have given Toshiba the impetus to take advantage of the startup's perceived lack of attention to the protection of their intellectual property, when in reality the importance of the intellectual property was not lost on the Lexar executive team, being that they did pay attention and did notice it, albeit after the theft had occurred and the IP had been incorporated into a competitor's product.

SigmaTel and Citroen

Which brings us to two situations of alleged IP theft involving companies from two separate industries—automotive and audio entertainment devices. So what's the similarity? Both companies allege that their patented methodologies were copied by a competitor located within China and then marketed within the Chinese market—thus, the companies in each case apparently ended up competing against their own product designs, manufactured by companies that had little or no research costs associated with the development of the product design, allowing the companies to market the product for a cost considerably less than the company owning the patent. So, is that the price of doing business in China? The government of China claims to be improving their intellectual property rights protection methodologies, but as we noted earlier, they have a long row to hoe. There will be repeated instances where individual corporations will be victimized. Unscrupulous business practices will always arise when intellectual property protection is lax.

In January 2005, SigmaTel, a developer and manufacturer of audio devices, filed suit against Actions Semiconductor Company of Zhuhai, Guangdong, China (Actions Semi), alleging that Actions Semi's integrated circuits, which are within Action Semi's MP3 players, infringe upon multiple patents related to SigmaTel's portable audio devices. SigmaTel followed in March 2005, with the filing of a complaint with the

U.S. International Trade Commission (ITC), requesting that the ITC initiate a Section 337 investigation on Actions Semi. In the ITC complaint, SigmaTel identified the specific patents that they believe had been infringed upon and requested that the ITC grant a permanent exclusion order, banning the importation into the U.S. of the infringing products and issuing a cease-and-desist order halting sale of these same products. The ITC opened an investigation, and the trial began in November 2005.

Actions Semi claimed no infringement of SigmaTel's patents has occurred. In September 2006, the ITC found that Actions had infringed upon SigmaTel's patents and rendered judgment in favor of SigmaTel. The ITC issued a limited exclusion order protecting SigmaTel in the U.S. market from Actions Semi's importation of products that were found to contain certain identified components. Thus, SigmaTel had their U.S. market protected.

The second case, which occurred in October 2005, involves Citroen's joint venture in China: Dongfeng Peugot Citroen Automobile. Citroen alleged that Shanghai Maple used Citroen's core chassis technology in producing a series of Shanghai Maple models. According to the Chinese press, Shanghai Maple claimed their automobiles were created from their own designs. Citroen, however, claimed their patent on "special chassis technology" had already been filed with the world IP rights organization and had not been licensed to Shanghai Maple. Shanghai Maple, a subsidiary of Geely Automobile, claimed no knowledge of any infringement, stating that they had never received any documentation from Citroen.

Interestingly, the unlicensed use of technology apparently is not an unusual occurrence within the Chinese automotive manufacturing sector. In May 2005, General Motors Daewoo alleged that Cherry QQ copied its "Spark" sedan design and so demanded 80 million RMB (approximately US$10 million) as compensation for patent infringement. Prior to the GM/Cherry suit, Dongfeng Honda and Toyota Auto sued Hebei Shuanghuan Auto and Geely Auto for similar reasons.

Truly remarkable is the perspective of the deputy engineer from within the China Automotive Technology & Research Center, Zhang Zhenzhi, who noted in the *Shanghai Daily News*, "It's inevitable for domestic automakers to imitate other advanced technologies, no matter from other domestic companies or foreign firms. But in the future, we would be able to better our designs after getting more experience on developing our own autos." To the untrained eye, it would appear that loss of IP is expected and will continue to be accepted within the nascent Chinese auto industry.

In both of these examples, the company whose technology has been illegally used did all of the right steps to protect their intellectual property—for example, filing patents, and so on. But in the end, they found themselves caught up in an embryonic legal system, oftentimes described as a litigation quagmire of quicksand where it is all but impossible to effectively litigate patent violations. In SigmaTel's instance, they took appropriate measures to protect themselves within one of their prime markets—the United States. The fact that they prevailed in the ITC trail speaks volumes, especially given that the overt threat to SigmaTel's market share in the U.S. was successfully mitigated. That said, the injunction, levied against Actions Semi, affects only business within the U.S. and has no effect on the China or European market. While in Citroen's instance, it boils down to what they would call in prohibition-era Chicago—*gettin' the business*—where the deputy engineer from within the official Chinese Automotive Technology & Research Center viewed the apparent "borrowing" of IP as the norm—something to be expected of young companies, and something to be tolerated by the more established new-to-China foreign firms.

3dGEO – China

In 2004, Chinese citizen Yan Ming Shan, 34, of Daqing, China, pled guilty in federal court to a one-count indictment that charged him with the unauthorized access to the computer programs of 3dGEO, where he fraudulently obtained proprietary source code and other software. Shan was sentenced to two years imprisonment.

According to the DOJ press release concerning this case, from April to September 2002 Shan worked for 3dGEO Development, Inc., a Mountain View, California company that develops software used in the survey of land for sources of natural gas and oil. 3dGEO employed Shan under an agreement with one of its customers, PetroChina, a Chinese company with a division named DaQing Oil, which arranged for its employee to travel to California for training on 3dGEO's software. FBI agents arrested Mr. Shan in September 2002 as he attempted to board a flight to China. Ever since, he has been held in custody as a flight risk, pending trial.

Interestingly, in an interview with 3dGEO's president, Dimitri Bevc, which occurred shortly after the arrest of Shan, Bevc said the episode highlighted a dilemma for the company, which was seeking to secure its intellectual property but also expand its business in Asia. "There's incredible demand from Chinese firms that are hungry for technology," said Mr. Bevc. "But we are built on our own intellectual property."

Bevc continued, saying he was afraid his company was being punished in the Chinese marketplace. In addition, with the pending payments from PetroChina for work already completed, Mr. Bevc said his company's Chinese sales prospects had been drying up. "What we heard back was… that 3dGEO did something wrong" by taking action against Mr. Shan, who served most of his sentence while awaiting trial, and has since returned to China, Mr. Bevc related.

Chapter 3

When State Entities Target a Business's Intellectual Property

Introduction

Unfortunately, the threat does not stop with competitors and individuals. Indeed, it gets worse. Nations, even friendly nations, have differing issues and perspectives on how to handle international relations and international economic interaction. Therefore, it should come as no surprise when state entities, be they a foreign or domestic intelligence service, national research institute or laboratory, or a state-owned enterprise engage in activities that would fall outside the norms of normal business practices and engage in what is known as "Economic Espionage." The state-sponsored threat is a global issue, and is not unique to U.S. businesses or research centers.

Why do nations engage in economic espionage? Primarily to acquire technology to either advance a military program, to advance the economic competitiveness of the nation's industrial base, or to simply ensure that the major companies and contributors to the nation's GDP continue to make that contribution. How do these nation states affect the acquisition of the IP? In some instances, it engages the services of the nation's law enforcement or intelligence services to surreptitiously acquire the IP. While in other circumstances, the nation publicly engages the owner of the IP, demanding something the nation believes is in the best interest of their citizens.

A nation's lack of enforcement and/or engagement in the protection of intellectual property within their jurisdictional areas of responsibility leads one to conclude that this silent collusion is as damaging as the blatant or covert activities. Each year the Office of the U.S. Trade Representative produces a "Special 301 Report" that highlights those countries the U.S. has placed on their Special Watchlist. In the 2007 report, 43 countries were included in the list with China and Russia ranked number one and two respectively (see Appendix E for a complete list). The 52-page report can be found at the Office of the United States Trade Representative's Web site (www.ustr.gov).

The United States has no program or policy to provide economic or industrial competitive intelligence to U.S. businesses. Many nations do have such programs and policies. Indeed, U.S. economic policy precludes such. Governmental efforts are focused on the protection of IP owned by U.S. persons or corporate entities and keeping the economic pitch level as U.S. corporations compete within the global marketplace. Discussion points can and have been made both for and against the U.S. governmental agencies and departments, such as the Department of State, Department of Commerce, the National Intelligence Director, and the various agencies making up the U.S. intelligence community that devotes resources and provides economic intelligence to

U.S. persons and corporations. The stronger point is to maintain the status quo with respect to governmental provisions regarding information to U.S. corporations, except when corporate America is specifically the target of a foreign government sponsored activity or when the economic playing field must be leveled.

Airbus and Saudi Arabian Airlines

The international market place is an active milieu, oftentimes filled with intrigue.

One well-documented historical case is the egregious attempt by Airbus to bribe its way into the 1994 Saudi Arabian Airlines fleet modernization effort by offering bribes to individuals from both the Saudi airlines and government. During a 1994 visit to the late King Fahd, then French Prime Minister, Edouard Balladur, followed through on the Airbus effort, and had hoped to secure the US$6 billion order for Airbus. He was derailed when the U.S. government provided to the Saudi government the content of the U.S. National Security Agency's intercepts, which fully documented the nefarious French activity. It is possible that without the U.S. government's intercession, the U.S. aviation industry would have been found "noncompetitive." But how does this translate into a threat to the intellectual property of a competitor? Simply put, if a nation is willing to support their industries in the global marketplace in this manner, the distance to supporting their industries by targeting the IP via the employees or physical assets of a foreign competitor is not great. In fact, two former directors of the French foreign intelligence service, the DGSE (Direction Generale de la Securite Exterieure), Pierre Marion and Charles Silberzahn, have stated publicly how one of the DGSE's collection priorities is to collect economic intelligence. Silberzahn noted how France had been successful in this regard, and the theft of classified and proprietary information was a long-term government policy (see *Cryptography's Role in Securing the Information Society*. The National Academies Press. Kenneth W. Dam and Herbert S. Lin, editors).

Russian Intelligence and Japanese Trade Secrets

The state-sponsored activity doesn't always occur in the United State nor is the target or victim always a U.S. firm. Ironically, sometimes the target is a company who themselves were found guilty by the legal system as having instigated instances of industrial espionage and to have stolen a competitor's IP. Let's start with a recently publicized case involving Russia's foreign intelligence service, the SVR (Sluzhba Vneshny Razvedki) and an employee of the Toshiba Corporation of Japan.

It should be noted that in late-January 2005, Russia's Prime Minister Fradkov requested the leadership of Russia's internal security service, the FSB (Federal'naya Sluzhba Bezopasnosti) to increase their efforts to assist Russian commercial enterprises. Fradkov was specific in his request: "We continue to require up-to-date information from the FSB that allows us to form a quality legal foundation and to make decisions on leveling the playing field for competition, developing businesses, and creating an attractive investment climate."

This statement is tantamount to a public declaration by the Prime Minister that the intelligence and security services of Russia should engage in intelligence collection and reporting activities in support of Russian commercial enterprises. While no surprise, since this is an activity that many believe the Russian intelligence and security services have been covertly engaged in long before the Cold War, it is a confirmation of intent nonetheless.

Evidence of the SVR's attempt to fulfill this mission statement was provided when an SVR operation apparently went awry in Japan. In late October 2005, the Public Safety Department of the Tokyo Police charged Vladimir Saveliev, an SVR officer, serving undercover as a diplomat assigned to the Russian trade mission in Tokyo, Japan as having recruited an employee of Toshiba Discrete Semiconductor Technology Corporation. Saveliev is alleged to have paid this unidentified employee a million yen (approximately US$9,000) for what the Russian believed to be confidential Toshiba proprietary information. The Japanese law enforcement investigators believe Saveliev learned confidential information that had military applicability, including information that referenced semiconductor systems of electric flux control, missile guidance systems, and jet fighter radars.

When queried about these charges on October 20, 2005, a spokesman for the SVR told the press, "In line with the practice generally accepted by all special services in the world, the SVR will not comment on the affiliation of this or that individual with the intelligence community."

How did the SVR engage in this case of Economic Espionage against a Japanese corporate entity? The activity apparently was initiated in the spring of 2004 when Saveliev introduced himself to the unidentified Japanese citizen under the cover of an "Italian consultant." The police noted in their declaration that between September 2004 and May 2005, the two met nine times in Tokyo's cheap beer shops and bistros during which Saveliev, utilizing his cover as a consultant, paid the Japanese citizen for the provision of confidential Toshiba data. The Japanese citizen provided the information to Saveliev via "smart memory cards." Apparently the Japanese citizen had natural access to the information Saveliev desired and copied this information to a temporary memory device—the "smart memory card." In June 2005, Saveliev quietly departed Japan.

Why did the SVR target Toshiba? As the SVR's press officer noted, the SVR does not comment on such. One could speculate that perhaps the technology would be used to augment Russian military knowledge of technology used in an adversary's weapon systems? Perhaps the technology was to be provided to a Russian commercial or state-owned entity to jumpstart research and development activities and garner greater market share in the global economic milieu. Regardless, the effect of the loss of the data doesn't end at Toshiba's door or that of the Japanese law enforcement and counterintelligence entities. Toshiba claims their loss is minimal, if at all, since the information taken is now freely available. However, certain long-term issues must be addressed.

Future users of the technologies stolen by Saveliev must take into consideration the fact that this technology was of sufficient importance to the government of the Russian Federation to use their most valuable intelligence resource—an undercover intelligence officer—to acquire the technology. Remember, Saveliev was posted abroad serving under diplomatic cover within the Russian commercial office in Tokyo. He opted to undertake a high-risk operation—operating in an alias persona as an Italian consultant in Tokyo, a city where he is well known in his true persona. Is this a case of incompetence? Why was the information of such import as to warrant the risk of discovery, when it would appear that the information could have been obtained by Saveliev, the commercial officer, via direct overt contact? The SVR Resident in Tokyo (Resident is the head of the SVR field entity) weighed the risks, or blowback, of his activities in Tokyo to the SVR and to the Russian Federation against the potential gain. One must conclude that the technical requirement levied by SVR Headquarters was extraordinarily important. Interestingly, there has been no public protest by the government of Italy on Saveliev's choice of nationality as a cover for his covert activities. While no public statement has been made, one may be assured that the SVR Resident in Rome received a tongue-lashing from the leadership of the Italian special services.

Then in August 2006, a separate Russian intelligence officer, this time from Russia's military intelligence organization (the GRU, or *Glavnoe Razvedyvatel'noe Upravlenie*), but also serving undercover as a diplomat assigned to the Russian trade mission in Tokyo was charged with having recruited an employee of Nikon Corporation.

The technology of interest in this instance is Nikon's variable optical attenuator (VOA), for which the recruited employee was the lead researcher. The R&D for this device was conducted at Nikon's facility at Chiyoda Ward, Tokyo. According to the open source material available about this device, the VOA is used to control and intensify light as it passes through fiber optics, something that Nikon considered a key piece of intellectual property.

The manner in which the GRU intelligence officer identified, courted, and recruited the Nikon researcher parallels that of the SVR's officer's activities. The researcher was met during a business exhibition, and then over the course of two years the two are believed to have had at least ten meetings at bars and other Tokyo locations. In exchange for the information provided, the researcher was paid tens of thousands of yen. Upon discovery, the Nikon researcher resigned from Nikon, noting his unhappiness with his employment contract.

Japan and the Cleveland Clinic Foundation

The preceding two examples of Russian intelligence targeting commercial enterprises are straightforward and relatively easy to understand. The discovery of the SVR activity being conducted out of the same physical establishment within Tokyo, and the "diplomat" being sent back to Russia, were clearly not an effective deterrent. The GRU had its own operation in full swing and was producing key documents of interest. Since there was no incentive to stop, it continued. In these examples, the government has a need and the special services move forward to fulfill that need using their human intelligence tools—such as recruiting an individual who has access to information of interest of them: a player known as an insider.

That isn't the only covert methodology used by a nation state. Let's look at the well-documented and publicized case involving the world-renown Cleveland Clinic Foundation (CCF), located in Cleveland, Ohio. In May 2001, the U.S. attorney in the Northern District of Ohio indicted two individuals for the theft of intellectual property belonging to the CCF.

According to the DOJ, Takashi Okamoto and Hiroaki Serizawa were charged and convicted of stealing the intellectual property created by the Lerner Research Institute of the CCF. From January 1998 through September 1999, Serizawa and Okamoto conspired to misappropriate from the CCF genetic research materials—specifically, "the deoxyribonucleic acid (DNA) and cell line reagents and constructs which were developed by researchers employed by CCF, with funding provided by the CCF and the National Institutes of Health, to study the genetic cause of, and possible treatment for, Alzheimer's Disease."

The indictments charged Okamoto and Serizawa with having provided the stolen research (DNA and cell line reagents and constructs) to the Japanese Institute of Physical and Chemical Research (RIKEN), a research facility owned by the government of Japan. The indictment continues—RIKEN, at the direction of the Japanese Ministry of Science and Technology, formed a Brain Science Institute to conduct research in the area of neuroscience (which includes the genetic cause and possible treatments for Alzheimer's disease).

According to the indictment, not only was it Okamoto's intent to purloin the research and results from CCF, but also to destroy and sabotage the DNA and cell line reagents and constructs that were left behind at CCF and not removed. The boxes of materials stolen by Okamoto were shipped from Cleveland to Kansas (where Serizawa resided) within days of the theft and were subsequently hand-carried to Japan about a month later by Okamoto.

The ensuing investigation showed that Okamoto had been an unwitting accomplice of Serizawa and thus had been duped into storing the stolen research at his Kansas residence. Serizawa was nonetheless convicted of making false statements to the FBI, statements that the prosecution conceded he corrected on the same day he made them. For his involvement, Serizawa was fined US$500 and placed on probation for three years. In addition, his movements were restricted, and he was ordered to perform 150 hours of community service.

The government of Japan claimed no knowledge of the activity. However, the DOJ continues to seek the extradition of Serizawa from Japan.

The theft by Okamoto set back the CCF's research efforts into Alzheimer's disease. One can only speculate on whether or not the IP stolen by Okamoto offered any advantage to the nascent RIKEN. It should be noted that both the Lerner Research Institute and RIKEN are leading research facilities in the field of Alzheimer's disease.

Though the preceding occurred many years ago, two primary questions still remain unanswered. Was Okamoto sent to the CCF's Lerner Research Institute for the purpose of obtaining a trusted position and then absconding with the IP, thus providing RIKEN a baseline from which to begin their efforts on Alzheimer's disease, or was Okamoto simply a conniving individual who saw an opportunity to propel himself to the front of the Japanese research community? Why wouldn't the government of Japan avail Okamoto for prosecution by the DOJ? The U.S. Department of Justice continues to attempt to extradite Okamoto from Japan to the United States and is continually rebuffed by the government of Japan.

China and Russia: TsNIIMASH-Export

This brings us to a most interesting case that is currently unfolding: the unlawful provision of IP involving a state-owned Russian technological concern providing information to a Chinese commercial entity. The Russian FSB has charged three senior executives of the state-owned-and-run space technology company, TsNIIMASH-Export, with embezzlement and the selling of secret Russian space technology to China. TsNIIMASH-Export is owned by the state-controlled Central Scientific Research Institute for Machine Building, and is located in Korolyov, the center of the Russian space community and the home to the "Mission Control" for all Russian space flights. According to information available from the firm's Web site, the company has participated in over 120 contracts with foreign entities.

On October 25, 2005, TsNIIMASH-Export director, Igor Reshetin, along with his deputy, Sergei Tverdokhklebov, and Tverdokhklebov's aide, Alexander Rozhkin, were all arrested by the FSB. The three were alleged to have illegally provided Russian space technology that had dual-use applicability to a Chinese precision engineering import/export firm. The dual-use technology apparently had applicability to Russian weapon systems, and could potentially provide the Chinese military with valuable secret information. The trio was also charged with having created multiple front companies through which approximately US$1 million of TsNIIMASH-Export's funds were embezzled.

The connection between the front companies and the export of sensitive information to the Chinese firm was not articulated. There has been no comment from the government of the People's Republic of China, nor has the identity of the Chinese firm or the firm's employees been revealed.

The trial began May 25, 2007 and is being closely watched by both industry and international governments to determine if this is a case of Chinese military manipulation, simple greed, or a bungled investigation.

Clearly, one can ask: Is this economic espionage, greed, opportunism, or all of the above? Regardless, it is viewed by the FSB as state-sponsored and of sufficient importance to publicize the arrest of the head of one of Russia's most respected technological concerns and link his arrest to a Chinese firm. The timing, in the midst of the successful Chinese manned space flight begs the question: Is there a message being sent to the PRC by the Russian Federation? Only time will tell.

Overt Nation State Attempts:
India, Venezuela, Brazil, and Others

With those examples under our belt, let's move on to the overt nation-state attempts to garner IP from corporate entities for a variety of reasons. Whenever discussion on this topic is initiated, Coca-Cola and their formula always spring to mind, not withstanding the 2007 conviction of two Coca-Cola employees who offered up to rival Pepsi the "secret formulas." Today, the estimated value of Coca-Cola's trademark is US$70,450 million. Would this be the current value had Coca-Cola acquiesced to the government of India in 1977? Maybe, maybe not; but Coca-Cola didn't take any chances and protected their IP. In 1977, Coca-Cola controlled the Indian cola soft drink market, and Indira Gandhi's Congress party lost control of the legislature to the Janata Party. One of the prime financial backers of Ghandi was the Coca-Cola bottler/distributor. In an apparent act of political revenge, the Industry Minister, George Fernandes, applied the Foreign Exchange Regulation Act, which in 1977 strictly limited foreign investment in domestic firms to 40 percent. Coca-Cola's equity investment exceeded the 40-percent threshold. As the legend goes, Coca-Cola officials were summoned by Fernandes, asked to divest and to transfer their intellectual property, the syrup formula, to their Indian partners or leave the Indian market. Coca-Cola opted to leave the Indian market. It would be another 12 years (in 1989) before Coca-Cola returned to the Indian market. Interestingly, Fernandes continues to advocate removal of Coca-Cola from the Indian domestic market. Would or could this happen today? Countries can and do nationalize commercial concerns regularly—one only has to look at the current activities being undertaken by Cesar Chavez in Venezuela.

Venezuela's regional neighbor, Brazil, has opted to take an interesting tact in addressing the value and intrinsic ownership of intellectual property. In mid-2005, the Brazilian Ministry of Health presented Abbot Laboratories of Chicago with an ultimatum: Reduce the price of Abbot's drug, *Kaletra* (an effective AIDS drug), or Brazil will break the patent and produce the drug itself. After a month of negotiation, Abbott opted to reduce its price for Kaletra from $1.17/pill to $.63/pill, effectively reducing the cost to the government of Brazil by approximately $339 million over six years. Interestingly, Health Minister Jose Saraiva Felipe noted, "With the agreement, the need for breaking the patent is suspended. The price we reached is what the national AIDS program could pay." This was not the first time Brazil had engaged the pharmaceutical companies, nor will it likely be the last.

Merck Laboratories and Gilead Laboratories have both been engaged subsequent to the Abbot Laboratory settlement by Brazil in discussions aimed at reducing the price of the antiretroviral drugs they each produce. The Health Minister noted that the government of Brazil is attempting to induce Merck to allow it to produce a generic version of the drug, called *efavirenz*, and is also seeking a discount from Gilead on its drug, *tenofoyir*, which costs Brazil about $7/capsule, but is available in generic form from India at less than $1/capsule.

Then two years later, Brazil did what they said they would do, Brazilian President Luiz Inácio Lula da Silva signed a decree authorizing his country's Ministry of Health to issue a "compulsory license" for efavirenz. Merck had offered to reduce the cost to Brazil for the efavirenz pills from US$1.79 each to US$1.10 each. Brazil found this reduction insufficient and noted that Merck sells the same drug in Thailand at $.65 per pill. When Merck declined, as noted, Brazil followed through on their threat and has taken the path to break the patent and offer to the pharmaceutical a much smaller "royalty" stipend.

There is nothing covert about Brazil's effort—the policy decision is stated publicly. The amount of funds available in the nation's coffers to provide free AIDS/HIV antiretroviral drugs to the infected population of Brazil is defined. Brazil has opted to engage in a frontal attack on the pharmaceutical industry. Some call this tactic nothing more than industrial blackmail, while others call it socialism at its best. Whatever it's called name, the pharmaceutical industry calls it bad news.

But Brazil isn't alone in going after the pharmaceutical companies. The Avian Flu outbreak in the Far East has created a fear of a global pandemic. Roche Holdings of Switzerland is finding itself having to address governments around the globe, which are demanding product. In India, Dr. Ashwani Kumar, Drug Controller General of India, noted that Roche does not have a Tamiflu product patent in India, and therefore India does not recognize the International Patent license that Roche possesses. Kumar continued that the International Patent is not enough to protect the Tamiflu patent, according to Indian patent laws. Kumar invited Indian companies to file license applications with the government to produce a generic form of Tamiflu.

Though invited to break the patent, two separate Indian biopharmaceutical manufacturers, Cipla and Ranbaxy, are reported to be working with Roche to license Tamiflu and then develop a generic Tamiflu—Oseltamivir—without resorting to breaking the patent. In addition, Roche has approached a number of drug manufacturers to discuss licensing Tamiflu, which Roche itself obtained, via exclusive license agreements from Gilead Laboratories in 1996. Roche notes that while there is no guarantee any of these discussions will lead to a licensing agreement, it is hopeful that such will be possible, and that an equitable relationship will be sought to address the emergency need for Tamiflu.

While Roche stood to earn approximately $1 billion from Tamiflu sales in 2005 alone and had encountered requests from a number of countries to allow generic production of the drug, Roche is standing firm on its unwillingness to relinquish the patent, which is protected into 2016, and is demanding a licensing fee. Roche's spokeswoman, Martina Rupp, defends the position: "Since we have been making this drug for the last ten years, it would be best for countries to enter into discussion with us." Rupp noted that the ten-step process of manufacturing Tamiflu is complex.

What of these frontal attacks on private enterprise and the value of intellectual property owned by these firms? The for-profit firms earn tremendous amounts of revenue and provide substantial returns to their investors. Why would anyone have one iota of concern whether they earn a few less million dollars? Where will the research and development of future therapeutics occur? Public-funded programs are highly unlikely to move as quickly or adroitly to bring therapeutics to the market as the commercial firms, who answer to the free market economy.

The "public health" rubric is an easily comprehensible area for the potential of the state insinuating itself into the market equation and turning the expected return on investment into a tizzy. If the free market prohibits the provision of a return on investment through the tactic of breaking patents, the deleterious affect will be tremendous. What is to stop a nation from extending the concept that worked so well with pharmaceutical manufacturers to other sectors? The precedent has been sent. The World Intellectual Property Organization must address this issue, otherwise the basic incentive to invent, create, and innovate will be negated.

Current and Future Threats to Economic Security

We've discussed a number of cases that provide a taste of the intrigue concerning how the geo-political milieu can have a direct effect on the fortunes of private enterprises. But really, just how serious is the issue? In the United States, it is very serious. The United States is under economic attack, according to the United States National Counterintelligence Executive's report to Congress in February 2005. In March 2005, the National Counterintelligence Strategy was outlined, and in May 2005, the National Counterintelligence Executive noted that U.S. businesses must not only protect themselves against their competitors, but also the foreign intelligence services of their competitors' countries. The report goes into some depth in identifying the types of foreign entities conducting industrial and economic espionage; the kind of information targeted by these foreign entities; and which foreign entities are attempting to acquire sensitive U.S. technology (either classified or proprietary)— be they private or governmental.

It is prudent to discuss the reports findings since it is directly germane to this discussion. The report indicates that individuals from almost 100 separate countries attempted to acquire sensitive U.S. information. The role of the state-supported intelligence collection effort against U.S. technology/IP was characterized in the report's findings with the statement, "It is clear, however, that some foreign countries, including the major players, also continued to employ state actors—including their intelligence services—as well as commercial enterprises, particularly when seeking the most sensitive and difficult-to-acquire technologies."

The report identified the following dual-use areas as being targeted: information systems, military production processes and communication systems, aeronautics, electronics, and armaments and energetic materials. The report laments the difficulty in tracking foreign targeting of purely civilian technologies and highlights the reluctance of U.S. firms to share information. The report opines that such reluctance is due to U.S. firms not wishing to highlight their loss, as doing so may have a deleterious effect on "investor and consumer confidence and stock prices." That said, the identified commercial technologies stolen by foreign entities included semiconductor production processes, computer microprocessors, software, proprietary information, and chemical formulas.

It is especially noteworthy, that the U.S. Counterintelligence Community expects no decline in foreign intelligence activities, while also noting that stemming the flow of information will become more difficult. Specifically mentioned is the challenge of isolating trade secrets from foreign managers and employees, and U.S. firms increasing practice of placing their research and development centers in foreign environs. The reality of this is that the theft of intellectual property will continue to be a thorn in the side of both industry and governments.

In 2006, the Defense Security Service upped the number of countries engaged in industrial espionage in the United States The UN has only 119 member states, so it would have been easier to simply note the 17 nations not involved.

The FBI estimates that more than 3,000 Chinese "front companies" operate in the U.S. with the express purpose of gathering intelligence and technology. Much of this is "dual use," with both civil and military uses. The FBI has stated publicly that the number of Chinese counterintelligence cases in Silicon Valley alone is increasing by 20 to 30 percent each year.

Can we in good conscience advocate a change in current U.S. policy, simply because other countries engage in such practices? Maintaining the current policy would seem to be the prudent course of action at this time, since it is one thing to ask our law enforcement and intelligence personnel and entities to take extraordinary risks to protect the nation from external threats (both physical and economical) and quite another to ask these same entities to take a similar level of risk to provide information that may help a specific company's bottom line. In the global marketplace, the free market economy should be the arbiter. Those with the best product, service, execution, and so on, will achieve the greatest fiscal success and be the market victor.

According to a study published in late October 2005 by USA for Innovation, a nonprofit organization dedicated to the protection of intellectual property (IP), the United States alone carried a value of US$5–5.5 trillion, equivalent to 45 percent of the United State's GDP, far larger than the GDP of any other nation. In essence, the IP retained by companies in the United States is the heart of the economic security in the U.S. This study also indicates that there exists a direct correlation between the level of a nation state's protection of foreign-owned IP and the level of foreign investment in that same country -- Where the state increases protection of the investor's IP; investors increase their investment in the nation's economy. In sum, U.S. corporations must take appropriate steps, on their own, to incorporate security procedures to effectively protect their IP against the efforts of foreign governments eager to obtain that same IP.

Chapter 4

When Piracy, Counterfeiting, and Organized Crime Target a Business's Intellectual Property

Introduction

Previously, we discussed the vector posed by the "Insider and Competitor" and the "State Entity." The greatest and most insidious threat to one's Intellectual Property (IP), however, involves counterfeiting and piracy, and often times, these activities are sponsored by organized crime.

The threat to IP from backroom thieves who produce counterfeit and pirated products is absolutely the most pervasive threat to the global economy as a whole. The U.S. Chamber of Commerce (Chamber) estimates that counterfeiting and pirated products account for 5 to 7 percent of the global economy, costing the United States alone over 750,000 jobs, and socks U.S. industry for a loss of sales in the area of $250 billion. The Chamber has directed its efforts, via trade missions and educational programs, toward China, Brazil, South Korea, and Russia with the goal of encouraging enhanced enforcement of IP protection laws within. In addition, the Chamber on each of these countries offers an IP protection toolkit. In 2005–2007, the Chamber, working together with various law enforcement entities, not only initiated the STOP (Strategy Targeting Organized Piracy), but has continued to expand the footprint (www.uschamber.com/ncf/initiatives/counterfeiting.htm).

In most instances, the motive to pirate or counterfeit is simple: "economic greed"—to manufacture and sell goods without the overhead and costs incurred by the rightful owner of the IP. Thus, they are able to bring a product to market that is manufactured, marketed, and sold at a fraction of the cost borne by the original manufacturer. Innumerable examples exist; we offer a selection, across many industrial sectors. Additionally, given the infrastructure necessary, it is not surprising the most robust enterprises have ties to organized criminal networks.

It is not only the Chamber that recognizes the ties between piracy and counterfeiting and organized criminal elements. In the U.K., the "Alliance Against IP Theft" (Alliance) has produced a 40-page primer, "*Proving the Connection – Links Between Intellectual Property Theft and Organised Crime*," on the issue, detailing the deleterious effect on the U.K. economy and the clear and unambiguous involvement of organized criminal elements. The primer's case studies identified organizations with points of origin in Russia (mafia), South Asia (multiple countries), China (triad organizations), and Ireland. All of which served as points of origin for either the fiscal wherewithal to affect the manufacture, distribution, and sale of pirated and counterfeit goods in the U.K., or the initial point of origin of the bogus goods. The Alliance puts the value of these illegal items at over £9 billion (www.allianceagainstiptheft.co.uk).

We took the liberty of reviewing the available data on intellectual property regimes which are, in our opinion, not up to par in the area of intellectual property protection, both with respect to the existence of laws and/or the ability or willingness to enforce those laws that do exist. Figure 4.1 was derived from available data found in the 2007 BASCAP (Business Action to Stop Counterfeiting and Piracy) report, the 2007 BSA (British Software Association) Piracy data report, the U.S. Trade Representative's 2007 301 report, and our own analysis. This chart identifies the ten lowest-rated countries with respect to a regime designed and enforced to protect intellectual property.

Figure 4.1 The 10 Lowest Ranked Countries with IP Regimes

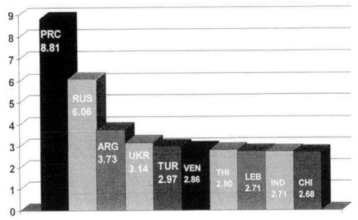

Using much of the same data found in both the 2007 BASCAP and the 2007 BSA Piracy data report, coupled with our own analysis, we have created our own read on those countries we believe have earned the honor of being the Top Five countries with an intellectual property protection and enforcement regime in place and in use (see Figure 4.2).

Figure 4.2 The Top Five Countries with IP Regimes

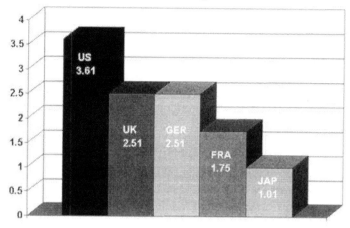

According to the United Kingdom's National Criminal Intelligence Service (NCIS), organized crime is defined as:

- Collaboration of a minimum of three people

- Criminal activity which has, or is intended to be, continued over a prolonged period

- The commission of serious criminal offenses which, taken as a whole, are of considerable importance

- Being motivated by the pursuit of power or profit

- Operations that are international, national, or regional

- Crime using violence or intimidation

- Criminal activity using commercial or business-like structures

- Crime that engages in money laundering

- Criminal activity that exerts an influence upon politics, the media, public administration, judicial authorities, or the economy (www.allianceagainstiptheft. co.uk/Proving-the-Connection.pdf; pages 12-23 of hard copy)

- Software piracy

While software piracy costs the global economy financially, it also costs countries jobs, according to a study commissioned by the Business Software Alliance (BSA).

The 2007 global study notes that in 2006, piracy rates in 13 countries had increase over the prior year. Leading the list are Armenia, Azerbaijan, Moldova, and the rest of the Commonwealth of Independent States (CIS), where it is estimated that between 94 to 96 percent of all software purchased is a pirated copy. While the top 20 countries with a high rate of software piracy are comprised mostly of developing nations, the list also includes China with a rate of 82 percent, and Russia, which tails close behind at 80 percent. By comparison, the United States has the lowest rate at 21 percent. The 2006 study opines that a 10-point drop in piracy in the Asia-Pacific region alone would generate $135 billion worth of additional economic growth and create approximately 2 million new jobs. The 2007 study of the 2006 piracy situation notes that losses from piracy rose by more than $5 billion, a 15 percent increase over 2005.

But enforcement remains an issue. Let's look at a typical case of enforcement, in the Philippines where the manufacture and sale of pirated software is not uncommon. In October 2005 in Cebu City, two persons were arrested for IP rights violations— the two were charged with attempting to sell pirated software, valued at approximately nine million Filipino pesos (US$160,000+). One of the individuals was identified as a U.S. citizen and the other a Filipino citizen. The pair is facing fines of between 50,000 and 1.5 million Filipino pesos (approximately $900 to $25,000) and incarceration of one to nine years, if convicted. It should be noted that, according to the Filipino press, no individual has ever been convicted of software piracy in the Philippines. The fiscal deterrent is minimal, though the incarceration may be sufficient to catch the attention of an individual contemplating entry into the criminal milieu; the track record of the legal process tends to negate these deterrents. It would appear that these are token arrests and enforcement efforts, and not directed at the large wholesale piracy efforts.

As the aforementioned study indicated, piracy of IP is a problem within Brazil and not a priority of the Brazilian government. To punctuate this fact, on the October 18, 2005 flight from Moscow to Brasilia, President Lula's presidential aircraft showed a pirated DVD-version of *Filhos de Francisco*, a film released in Brazil in August 2005 and not yet available on DVD. This, coupled with Brazil's declaration in mid-2005 to the pharmaceutical world, "cut your drug price or we'll take your IP," makes Brazil an interesting conundrum for companies contemplating doing business in this market.

The incongruous perspective presented to the international community needs addressing. Perhaps to adjust this perception, the Brazilian National Council to Combat Piracy and Intellectual Property Violations announced that between November 2004 and November 2005, Brazil has seized counterfeit and pirated goods valued at approximately

US$87 million—a 130 percent increase over the amount seized in 2004. The Brazilian's claim, "*the main entryway for contraband is the Brazilian borders with Paraguay, in Foz do Iguaçu, in the state of Paraná.*" Brazilian government officials claim that "barriers" set up in the region have reduced importation of counterfeit goods by approximately 60 percent. This would suggest that tightening a country's borders may reduce the inflow of illicit goods and thus reduce the opportunity for the sale/purchase of pirated/counterfeit items.

Technology Counterfeiting

Counterfeiting isn't limited to software. Take the example of the network gear manufacturer, D-Link. D-Link's intellectual property was being successfully pirated/counterfeited within the Indian market. In late August 2005, a number of D-Link products were found in New Delhi's Nehru Place market area by Indian law enforcement officials from the Criminal Bureau of Investigation (CBI) (some of the seized products included Ethernet switches [model DS1016D and DES 1024D]). Interestingly, D-Link's distributors in India have a remarkable degree of understanding as to why customers would willingly purchase fake products, as customer support is unimportant. According to Pankaj Surekha, proprietor of Surekha Compunet, a D-link distributor, "D-link has a very tiring and time-consuming replacement process, which at times distracts customers from the brand. Hence, the company should revise and minimize the replacement cycle to help customers retain long-lasting faith in the brand."

Perspective oftentimes is determined by where you stand, and in this case, it would appear that the distributor is advocating a more streamlined process on the part of the manufacturer that may lead potential customers to make their buy-choice based on robust product support—something that is lacking when a pirated product is purchased.

Korea technology manufacturer Samsung has been victimized repeatedly. The crimes range from outright theft of their IP to the counterfeiting of their cutting-edge product lines. In November 2005, four current and former Samsung employees pilfered the blueprints and documents for a new mobile phone design and were caught by Korea's National Intelligence Service (Korea's Counterespionage organization), who discovered the group attempting to spirit the files to China mobile phone manufacturers. Samsung notes that its investment in the design project was 25 billion RMB (approximately $25 million). Had the quartet been successful, Samsung may have taken a market hit of approximately 500 million RMB (US$500,000) in the handset market, and it stood to lose almost 8.8 trillion RMB (approximately $8.8 billion) worth of intellectual property on their entire line of technology products which were included in the data trove. What company can withstand a fiscal loss valued at over $8 billion due to their blueprints and documents being stolen?

Samsung has a "policy" in place that prohibits employees from sharing data outside the company or retaining or copying such data for personal retention. That said, one of the individuals arrested was discovered sharing approximately four gigabytes of computer files. These files included documents, blueprints, program source code, and circuit diagrams of mobile phones. This individual used multiple technological avenues to affect the transfer of data to his co-conspirators by using DVDs, e-mail, and wireless connectivity between laptops to successfully transfer the data outside of Samsung.

It begs the question, especially in this day and age of Sarbanes-Oxley (SOX) enforcement, if this were a U.S. firm, what liability would the corporate hierarchy hold for lax protection of their intellectual property? And which corporate officer would the shareholders hold liable?

Perhaps as interesting is the lamentable fact that in the United States the likelihood of this type of event being serendipitously discovered by U.S. governmental agencies is slim. This country's own privacy laws prohibit random and pervasive monitoring of private communications.

It is just as interesting to note that the Korean NIS has the capability and exercises their counterespionage capability within the Economic Espionage milieu in support of Korea's industrial base. A separate report from the Samsung Economic Research Institute on the topic of stolen Korean technologies indicates that 39 percent of all technology stolen from Korea is destined for China.

Korean manufacturers of mobile phones and other electronic devices such as MP3 players have noted that approximately 70 percent of the products manufactured by LG and Samsung available in the Chinese marketplace were counterfeit products. In their effort to thwart counterfeit activity, a Hong Kong–based company, Marksman Consultants Ltd., has conducted surveys and investigations, working closely with the Chinese law enforcement entities. According to Joseph Tsang, Chairman of Marksman, "One big problem: Too many scammers have ties to local officials, who see counterfeit operations as a major source of employment, and pillars of the local economy. Two or three of our raids have failed because of local protection."

The Apparel Industry

But piracy isn't limited to the technology or software industries. The apparel industry is also victimized. Counterfeit shoes are commonplace in the open markets of Southeast Asia. Adidas, the German sports clothing conglomerate, recently filed a lawsuit against three separate Chinese companies for IP violations.

- **Aile Clothing and Shoe Company** Adidas alleges that Aile is using the three-stripe design on shoes manufactured by Aile, which violates Adidas' three-stripe trademarked logo.

- **Beijng Jianlijia Aile Sports Good Shop** Adidas alleges that this firm is selling goods that violate the Adidas trademark.

- **Beijing Ruiguan Sports Goods Company** Adidas alleges that this firm is selling goods that violate the Adidas trademark.

Adidas requested three million RMB (approximately USD 370,000 in compensation) from the three companies for violating Adidas' logo and trademarks.

The apparel and fashion goods industries are a ripe target as well. In early November 2005, the Assistant U.S. attorney for the District of Massachusetts and the U.S. Immigration and Customs Enforcement in New England, along with the U.S. Internal Revenue Service, announced the arrest and indictment of four individuals charged with trafficking in more than USD 1.4 million worth of counterfeit goods. The ten-count indictment details how the four used 13 separate self-storage units within a storage facility located in Revere, MA as their base of operations (ten of the units were for storage, two were show rooms and one was the manufacturing facility). When raided, the units contained 12,231 counterfeit handbags; 7,651 counterfeit wallets; 17,000+ generic handbags and wallets; and counterfeit labels and medallions in sufficient quantity to turn more than 50,000 generic handbags and wallets into copies of the originals. The following trademarked brands were copied: Louis Vuitton, Kate Spade, Prada, Gucci, Fendi, Burberry, Coach, and additional bags and wallets of other manufacturers. In addition, numerous other items were also contained in the storage units, including scarves, belts, umbrellas, sunglasses, duffle bags, hats, visors, garment bags, coats, shoes, necklaces, bracelets, rings, and earrings bearing counterfeit marks owned by these and other victim companies. The indictment places the value of the "counterfeit" goods at approximately USD 1.4 million, and USD 6.0 million had the goods been authentic.

The sales methodology used by this group of counterfeiters, according to the indictment, was to sell their items at flea markets or "purse parties" in the Revere,

MA area. Indeed, it is alleged that they held more than 230 purse parties throughout Massachusetts. The goods they acquired were purchased from both legitimate generic goods manufacturers and illegal suppliers of goods in New York. According to ICE, "The public needs to know that when they buy a counterfeit purse at a house party or on the street, their dollars are ultimately helping to finance large-scale counterfeiting organizations. And every time they buy a knock-off purse, they are contributing to legitimate companies losing billions of dollars in revenue to counterfeiting every year."

In 2007, the government of Italy's domestic intelligence service, SISDE (Servizio per le Informazioni e la Sicurezza Democratica, Italian for *Service for Information and Democratic Security*) accused Chinese hackers, apparently operating with the acquiescence of the government of China, of the wholesale theft of industrial methodologies associated with the apparel and fashion goods industry. While the Chinese government denied all allegations, the Italian government was adamant that the Chinese were purloining the intellectual property of the Italian firms so as to enhance the production and bring the Chinese knock-offs closer to the quality of the real Italian merchandise. A news piece notes, how SISDE's alarm has been echoed by reports from the China desk of Italy's special anti-Mafia investigative directorate.

The Entertainment Industry

Now we'll discuss the pervasiveness of IP theft that occurs with artistic products produced by the entertainment industry. In late 2005, a judge in Hong Kong sentenced a Hong Kong resident, Chan Nai-ming, to three months in jail for the copy and distribution of three motion pictures via the Internet. Chan operated under the Internet alias "Big Crook" and apparently did not charge for the films that he availed to the internet community. Chan utilized the BitTorrent software program to conduct his Internet file sharing. This case is the first that resulted in a jail sentence for the online piracy of motion pictures in Hong Kong. Hong Kong customs investigators determined that between 30 and 40 individuals had accessed Chan's computer to obtain illicit copies of the copyrighted materials. The fact that Chan did not charge for the films was not found to be material.

While in Sweden in mid-2005, it became illegal to share music and films over the Internet, the Swedish anti-piracy group Antipiratbyrån (APB) found itself being disciplined by the country's Data Inspection Board for breaking privacy data rules in its hunt for illegal file-sharers.

In their exuberance to locate and identify individuals who were sharing, illegally, music and film files over the Internet, they hired a paid informant within the Swedish ISP Bahnof to provide the Internet protocol addresses of "file shares" from within the Swedish ISP's network. The Data Inspection Board noted that an individual's Internet protocol address is considered private; the manner in which the information was collected illegal. Subsequent to the discovery of a paid informant within Bahnof, the ISP fired two employees, including the paid informant for the APB.

In late-2005, again in Sweden, a judge sentenced Andreas Bawer, a Swedish citizen, to approximately USD 2,000 in civil penalties but no jail time for the illegal online distribution of a pirated motion picture. The court found that Bawer had violated Swedish copyright laws by making a Swedish movie available via the Internet for others to download. The software used by Bawer was not identified, and it is believed that Bawer had only copied one film and was not a large-scale provider of films via the Internet.

In mid-summer 2005, the Motion Picture Association of America (MPAA) declared losses to the motion picture industry to be approximately US$1.9 billion, due to Internet-driven film piracy. The MPAA continued, detailing how the overall piracy of films in other formats was identified as being valued at approximately USD 3.5 billion. One would expect that the MPAA would be in search of large wholesale pirates, but then the MPAA, on behalf of the major studios, filed 286 lawsuits against individuals whose names were provided by the 30 bit-torrent site operators that were shut down earlier in 2005.

These prosecutions, while totally appropriate, are truly small potatoes. Put differently, the prosecutions against "individuals" aren't difficult, because the individual doesn't have the fiscal capabilities to compete with the MPAA or industry proper. It can be argued that it would be more appropriate for the MPAA to invest its investigative funds to identify those organizations with robust infrastructures that produce thousands of copies.

In closing, and as noted in the press release from the Business Action to Stop Piracy issued on the heels of the May 2007 Group of Eight (G8) conference, counterfeiting and piracy costs businesses to lose a total of over USD 600 billion to counterfeiters each year.

Juxtapose this against the October 2005 DOPIP Security Counterfeit Intelligence Report that noted more than 341 separate incidents involving goods valued at more than USD 1 billion, and involving more than 54 separate countries. Not surprisingly, the top ten brands counterfeited were Adidas, Nike, Louis Vuitton, Microsoft, Chanel, Gucci, Prada, Fendi, Manchester United, and Puma. The report also noted that there appears to be evidence of a link between copyright and trademark infringements and more serious crimes. The report, continued that in 37 percent of the cases, counterfeiters were found to be involved in drug trafficking and use, 20 percent carry weapons, 11 percent commit other frauds, and 26 percent carry out other crimes such as assault, extortion, murder, theft, immigration violations, money laundering, identity theft, and robbery. Increasingly, a more violent type of criminal is being attracted to this activity as profit margins become larger, and penalties and chances of being arrested are relatively low (http://i-newswire.com/pr50468.html).

This vector is on a near vertical growth path, and until governments and industries unite in both reactive and proactive steps, the criminal elements will always have the upper hand and the loss of intellectual property will continue.

Chapter 5

Virtual Roundtable on Intellectual Property and Economic Espionage

Introduction

In the first four chapters, using real-world examples, we explored the diverse vectors, motivations, and modus operandi of those engaged in intellectual property theft and economic espionage.

In this chapter, we conduct a virtual roundtable to take a look at some of the twenty-first century challenges and opportunities that confront those who seek to thwart such activity. We believe their seemingly unique perspectives, focused on an identical mission, will be of great assistance to you, as you yourself wrestle with the situation wherein you are faced with a conundrum and think that perhaps you are the first to have had this experience. The perspective of the several subject matter experts in various aspects of law, security, risk, investigations, and intelligence participated in this virtual roundtable, they are:

- **Naomi Fine, Pro-Tec Data** Naomi Fine, Esq., President and CEO of Pro-Tec Data (www.pro-tecdata.com). Naomi is an internationally recognized expert on intellectual property theft and economic espionage. She incorporates legal, computer security, corporate security, human resource, and audit disciplines in her approach. Her depth of knowledge comes from working with hundreds of world-class companies to identify sensitive information, assess needs for protecting it, develop tailored strategies, establish policies and procedures, and provide training and tools that secure competitive advantage. Her clients have included many Fortune 500 companies, such as 3Com, Apple Computer, Caterpillar, Charles Schwab, Eastman Kodak, International Paper, Intel, Johnson & Johnson, Levi Strauss, MCI, McDonald's, Michelin, Mobil Oil, National Semiconductor, Nortel Networks, PECO Energy, Procter & Gamble, Ralston Purina, Rockwell International, SC Johnson Wax, Seagate, Sun Microsystems, Visa and Xerox.

- **Keith Rhodes, US General Accountability Office** Keith Rhodes serves as the Chief Technologist for the Government Accountability Office, the investigative arm of the Congress. He also serves as the Director of GAO's Center for Technology & Engineering. In these roles, he is the senior advisor to Congress on investigations requiring significant technical and scientific analysis. He has covered issues such as information security, privacy, non-proliferation, e-government, technical intelligence, and unconventional weapons systems.

- **Ed Stroz, Stroz Associates** Ed Stroz served for 16 distinguished years in the US Federal Bureau of Investigation (FBI), during which he established the New York City FBI computer crime squad, one of the first two in the country, and directed several significant FBI investigations, including the high-profile international case of Vladimir Levin, a Russian hacker who broke into Citibank. In 2000, Stroz founded a private investigation (PI) firm in 2000, and has assisted his corporate clients in responding to Internet-extortions, denial-of-service (DoS) attacks, hacks and unauthorized access, and theft of trade secrets. He has also pioneered the concept of incorporating behavioral science into the methodology for addressing computer crime and abuse. Stroz, an expert in addressing the threat of computer crime and abuse posed by insiders, has supervised numerous forensic assignments for federal prosecutors, defense attorneys, and civil litigants, and conducted network security audits for major public and private entities.

- **James Christy, US Department of Defense:** In 2006, Christy retired after more than 20 years as a special agent specializing in cyber crime investigations and digital evidence and 35 total years of federal service. Jim is currently the Director of Futures Exploration for the Defense Cyber Crime Center (DC3) For three years prior to retirement, Supervisory Special Agent Jim Christy, was the Director of the Defense Cyber Crime Institute (DCCI), DC3. The DCCI is responsible for the research and development and test and evaluation of forensic and investigative tools for the department of Defense (DoD) Law Enforcement and Counterintelligence organizations. The Institute is also charged with intelligence analysis, outreach, and policy for DC3.

- **Rebecca Herold, Rebecca Herold, LLC:** Rebecca Herold, CISM, CISSP, CISA, CIPP, FLMI, is currently an information privacy, security, and compliance consultant, author, and instructor with her own company. Herold is also an adjunct professor for the Norwich University Master of Science in Information Assurance program. She has provided information security, privacy, and regulatory services to organizations from a wide range of industries throughout the world. Herold has over 15 years of information privacy, security, and compliance experience. She was instrumental in building the information security and privacy program while at Principal Financial Group, which was awarded the 1998 CSI Information Security Program of the Year award. Rebecca assists organizations of all sizes within all industries with their information privacy, security, and regulatory compliance programs, content development, and strategy development and implementation.

The Legal Perspective: Naomi Fine

Burgess and Power: From your perspective, as a legal expert on intellectual property theft and economic espionage, how has the theft of trade secrets and other forms of intellectual property changed over the last few decades? Is the means of attack less dependent on the insider than previously? Is it more oriented toward technological means of acquiring secrets than previously? Certainly, the impact of both globalization and the WWW has been significant. Have the players changed? Have the likely targets increased? What are the challenges of protecting intellectual property and trade secrets in the Global Economy and the Information Age? There is the need for executives to understand what information is at risk, and what information they should invest extra care in protecting. Our sense is that many more kinds of organizations and intellectual property are at risk than "conventional wisdom" would assume. There is a great deal of focus on the risk to corporate treasures like the formula for Coca-Cola, the programming code for Windows, and the designs for microprocessor and weapons systems. But little attention is paid to other forms of intellectual property in other industry segments. Could you talk a bit about how an organization should evaluate its exposure, i.e., what it has to lose and how it is vulnerable?

Naomi Fine: I was hired by McDonald's a decade or so ago, and I thought, "Well, what have they got beside 'Secret Sauce' that would be considered confidential?" It was only after working with them that I learned how much of their information—e.g., their business strategy, their relationships with franchisees, how they developed their menu, how they decided which were going to be corporate stores and which were going to be franchise stores, their whole IT group and the kinds of technology they developed to enable the kinds of operations they have in their stores, even the delivery—was vital to the enterprise and therefore should be protected.

At the time that I worked with them, beanie baby doll products were very popular, and they were going to be giving some of them out at some of their stores. Which stores were going to have the giveaways and how many was a major secret. People would literally line up outside all night long. There were thefts in the area when they were giving them out. Those are some of the issues that companies in the low-tech environment might not be aware of. But even as I am telling you this, one of the things I am saying is that one of the aspects of their work that was confidential was the IT aspect, and there is not a single company in any industry that isn't using information technology in one way or another to facilitate the operations if not the evolution of their products, so for that reason alone, what they are using and how they are using it to improve their competitive advantage is clearly confidential information for these companies.

After MacDonald's came Levi-Strauss and Safeway. All of those low-tech companies basically said, 'Hey, we recognize that how we recruit our employees, the materials we use in our products, the way that we hold our inventory, our yield results, our manufacturing processes, etc., all of those things, are highly confidential.

So I have found that most companies are fairly aware that they have confidential information (to protect).

The first level of awareness is "Do we have something that is confidential?" and most executives are aware that they have something that is worth protecting.

The next level of awareness is how widespread is the application of that principle within the company? In other words, "OK, we're Coca-Cola, we know that Coca-Cola's secret formula is confidential, but do we recognize that our recruiting process for employees or the way that we strategize about giving to communities around the world as a P.R. function are also confidential?"

The third level is recognizing the bits and pieces that go into understanding what is confidential? So, let's take the example of strategy for using community service within the corporation to enhance P.R. What is the information that provides pieces to the puzzle that would allow an outsider to know what that strategy is? It is not just the document that says this is our P.R. strategy and in it is the sub-strategy on specifically how we are going to use community service to improve our image, it is also a meeting between Coca-Cola and the Trust for Public Land, or the Nature Conservancy and the Sierra Club. An executive's plan to go to Washington, D.C., to meet with a representative of the Sierra Club would be one of the pieces of information that could provide a piece of the puzzle that when put together would reveal the mosaic.

What's interesting is that while company executives may not be aware of that layer of granularity, clearly the folks in the IT department have to grapple with the question, "Where should we be applying our IT security dollars?" They need to know at a granular level whether it is only the P.R. strategy, or is it also the Outlook calendars of the executives who are going to meet the people in the conservation movement.

Now there is another layer, which is the leading edge technology (e.g., content monitoring and filtering technology), is only useful if you can identify words and phrases. So the question is not just, "Is the Outlook calendar a piece of the P.R. strategy, which is part of the overall information asset management inventory of the company?" but also, "What are the key words and phrases that we might find not only in an Outlook calendar but in an Excel spreadsheet, a Power Point document, or a database?" We need to identify those key words and phrases so that we can apply security technologies.

Most companies in most industries recognize that they have got something that is confidential that they must protect. But how far have they taken it? To what level of granularity? Do they recognize both because of the competitive intelligence threat, i.e., there are some very smart people out there who are adept at taking little bits and pieces of information and putting them together to understand a company's strategies? But has someone in the organization broken it down further: "There are all these technologies to stop our employees and contractors from sharing information that they shouldn't share, what are we doing to apply them?" The response may come back as, "Well, we are looking at them, but in order to apply them, we have got to not only understand what our confidential information is, we have got to be able to break it down to keywords and phrases."

Burgess and Power: *What kind of legal strategy should an organization develop to deal with the threat of intellectual property theft and economic espionage? What are the key elements? How should this strategy be developed and implemented? What should the working relationship be between in-house legal counsels and/or outside expert counsels?*

Naomi Fine: Intellectual property has been an issue, literally, for millennia. And there have been challenges to the protection of intellectual property, particularly in the form of the globalization of the workforce, and the advancements in technology, and the mobilization of both people and technology, which make that information more vulnerable. And although that has been evolving over the last decade, there isn't anything that radically new, but one thing that has changed radically is the perception that private information is something that we need to protect. Suddenly, there is attention to our personal, private information.

There has been this wave of regulation that obligates companies to protect personal and private information. One of the fallouts of this change, which is also a benefit, is that now you have folks in the General Counsel's office who are saying, "We better understand the technical aspects of protecting intellectual property. We can no longer rely on a piece of paper that says Non-Disclosure Agreement at the top of it. We can no longer rely on those Power Point presentations that we are perfectly capable of giving. We need to marry these things with technologies that help to protect our information." And conversely, the folks in the IT department who had previously said, "Bah humbug, those legal folks don't know what the hell they are talking about. They do not know what a bit or a byte is. They don't know the difference between source code and object code. We're the ones that have got to secure the system, and let the legal people go ahead with their non-disclosure agreements and whatever else they do. We are here in the trenches doing the work of protecting this electronic information," have changed their tune, because suddenly there are these privacy regulations, we had better know what they are. They are using words like encryption. We're the ones that have to implement it.

So there is camaraderie between the IT folks and the legal counsel folks that never existed before. The lawyers have a keen desire to understand the technology, and the technologists have a keen desire to understand the legal underpinnings to their implementation of the technical solutions.

However, one of the things that has not changed in terms of legal strategy when you look at the most recent legislation, e.g., CA 1386, which says if you have had any private data on any individual stolen, you have to report it, and there is another section that says you have to take reasonable measures to protect that information.

Burgess and Power: *Yes, this is the crux. It is an absolute requirement if you expect to garner any protection with respect to stolen data. If you do not try and protect the data then you have no recourse when you lose the data. The California Uniform Trade Secrets Act provides protection for a broad category of sensitive business information. The Act provides both injunctive relief and damages for misappropriation of a trade secret. The Act defines a "trade secret" as information—including a formula, pattern, compilation, program, device, method, technique, or process—that derives value from not being generally known and about which some effort has been made to keep the information secret. It is important for businesses to realize that the definition requires them to take steps to keep the information secret; an employer may not claim misappropriation of a trade secret if there was no effort to treat the information as secret (http://w3.uchastings.edu/patent_01/Handouts/California%20Uniform%20Trade%20 Secrets%20Act.pdf).*

Naomi Fine: But just as with the trade secret laws, we still don't define what those reasonable measures are, and I hope we never get to a place where we do. I say I hope we never do because there is an evolving standard, and what was "reasonable" yesterday may no longer be "reasonable" tomorrow when, e.g., we get a new encryption standard or digital rights management becomes commonplace, or when content monitoring and filtering technologies cannot only monitor and filter for structured data, but can easily search out and capture the unstructured data.

There are some technologies that claim they can do that. Maybe they can, but when it becomes more of a standard instead of bleeding edge technology, then it also should become part of the standard for "reasonable measure to protect information."

So, one of the things that is different is there needs to be this collaboration between the legal department and the IT department, but that being said, information, while most of it is developed at some point and stored at some point in electronic form, that is not the only form. Here we are having a conversation. Conversations can also divulge confidential information and open up a real risk. I am talking to you on my cell phone. My cell phone is also a PDA. It has lots of confidential information in it, so, it is not just the information systems at some corporate office that need to be protected, but also all of these mobile endpoints.

And so the legal strategy has to take into account the people, the processes, the technologies, and the environment, so that you can really enable the people and all of the tools they use to transfer or exchange information and still protect it.

Law is basically a driver of obligation and redress. In terms of obligation, most of the laws effecting the protection of information still leave it up to taking reasonable precautions, and those reasonable precautions evolve. For example, in the Economic Espionage Act (EEA), the gold standard set for compliance, is drawn from guidelines that used to give us just five steps for compliance, but now the guidelines say very clearly we have to establish a culture of compliance, which means really making sure users who have the mind-set, as well as the skills, to protect information.

The human factor is always going to be the center piece of any legal strategy for protecting information, making sure that people who have access to information know which information is confidential, know what their responsibilities are to protect it, and have the tools and resources for doing that.

Burgess and Power: *If the enterprise does not invest in an awareness program to make their employees knowledgeable of what data must be protected, then they are placing themselves in needless jeopardy. Next question, where are we now, a decade after the signing of the EEA in the US? How effective has it been? How has it evolved or devolved over the years? What do you recommend to your clients in regard to the EEA? Is compliance still an issue and an advantage? Has its overall influence been positive? Has it been used for the best and to the best?*

Naomi Fine: It is difficult to give you a clear answer to that question, because you first have to ask, "What is the expectation from a law like that?" My expectation is that it is a law that should be on the books. We have been prosecuting clear criminals as a result of it. It has had some impact. I remember, though, in 1997, delivering speeches called "The Grey Zone," and asking, "With the EEA, are we going to have people who overhear a conversation on an airplane being criminally indicted?" The truth is it probably could lead to such an indictment. But we as a society and government do not have the money or resources to do that, so you know I think it has been effective. But only because my expectations were not higher than what has been achieved.

Other people may have had higher or lower expectations. But look at other laws and how they have been implemented, and I would say it is doing its job.

The OpSec Perspective: Keith Rhodes

Burgess and Power: What impact do economic espionage and intellectual property theft have on the economic and national security of the USA? What is at risk? How high are the stakes? What are some of the indicators that we can see around us? Are whole sectors being gutted? Is our leadership in technology and scientific research slipping away? How bad is it? And what direction is it all going? What is government's role? What is it doing? What does it need to do? And is it just the USA that is targeted, or is the threat as dire for other developed economies, e.g., Japan and the EU?

Keith Rhodes: The thrust of your questions is very clear to me: What is the state of the world today relative to industrial espionage? Are there new threats and adversaries, and are there new vulnerabilities? What's at risk? Who's the "bad guy," and how good is s/he? While it may seem that the world has changed due to technology, and, therefore, the threat has changed due to technology, I would argue that the threat is what it has always been, with the exception that it is broader and faster, more subtle and insidious, more non-linear.

As background, I want to explain that I use the classic operations security (OPSEC) risk model as the basis for all my risk analyses. In this model:

- **Risk = Threat * Vulnerability * Impact.**
- **The Threat = Adversary + Capability + Intent;**
- **The Vulnerability = Opportunity, and the Impact = Asset Value.**

In this model, the threat is always human, as the technology itself does not attack; there is always an operator.

Burgess and Power: Technology does not equal security.

Keith Rhodes: The vulnerability is both human and technological, as all processes utilize both people and technology. Finally, the impact is also both human and technological, in that humans define the losses even though the loss may be a physical asset. The problem with threat response is that I see organizations trying to factor human beings out of the risk equation, as though they were some kind of variable that can be replaced. This is folly. Human beings are absolutely necessary to all processes and operations, and are the first and last line of security. Technology certainly can enhance the ability of human beings to secure their environment, but it cannot do it alone.

Every nation is at risk from every other nation. Every nation is being intellectually gutted. Some nations, like China, may seem to be on top now, but they, too, have a soft underbelly: rampant corruption and an absolute requirement for a blazing economy. China has to have a >10 percent economic growth, so they can support the old manufacturing sectors in the western provinces. This will be impossible to maintain. No nation is immune. Nations try to maintain some control over their interests, but it is becoming almost impossible, even for totalitarian regimes, to manage economies. Currencies and exports can be controlled to some degree, but the moment it impairs a domestic industrial sector, that sector will leave. Thus, governments both have and do not have power in the global economy; the governments are allowed to come along, so long as they do not interfere.

The old saying that there are friendly nations but no friendly intelligence services is still true. Their role has not changed; they collect everything they can, as the immediate value of the collection is not always understood. Collecting an opponent's military capability requires collecting an opponent's industrial capability. Figuring out the stability of an unfriendly regime requires understanding the regime's economy. This also applies to allies, as on one day we may be partners and on the next day we may be competitors. In reality, we may be partners and competitors on the same day at the same time. This may seem to be a new world, but if one takes the time to read about world history, one quickly sees that alliances have always been fluid and that even during times of war, nations preserved their assets on neutral ground. Thus, the threat is now as it has been: internal and external. There is no guarantee that either threat will be clearly manifest, although the internal threat is usually the more complicated one to define and interdict. Clearly defined lines of demarcation make an external threat intuitively obvious to the casual observer, but those opponents who stand right before us may be nearly invisible.

I think this is where the threat may have changed in degree but not in form. The insider has always been with us, but now it seems that the insider is much more pervasive and capricious a threat than before. Loyalty is not something I see much of anymore. I am no psychologist, but one does not have to think very hard about the causes for this loss of loyalty: Organizations buy and sell themselves without any care for employees; national interests no longer take care of the citizens; the rich get richer and the poor get poorer, and the general populace becomes more and more detached and cynical. Expectations center on what one can do for him or her alone.

Guru Puja said that, "To cherish oneself only brings downfall." It would seem that he was correct at least insofar as loyalty is concerned. It is hard to secure an environment in which there is no loyalty to a common cause. The word "loyalty" may sound rather anachronistic, but it is a stabilizing concept, and it does have to flow in both directions. Without some sense of loyalty, all insiders can "turn" at any moment, but not necessarily in a malicious way. One may just quit one day, and walk out with the intellectual capital of a firm rolling around in her/his head. Some will argue that this has always been the case, which we have always had to operate with the assumption that anyone can "turn" at any time. I would argue that today we have to assume that everyone can "turn" at any moment, and that is a more complicated threat scenario.

This does not just apply to the employees; rather, it extends to the boardroom. There have always been chief executives who have made foolish decisions that brought down their firms. There is an old Tibetan story about a group of monkeys trying to get the moon out of a well, because their leader says that they must get the moon out of the well. The other monkeys see the moon, and link themselves together in order to reach it. The branch they are holding breaks, of course, and they all fall into the well. This is an example of the usual folly of the boardroom; they go headlong into disaster at the bidding of the "boss." Today, however, someone from the inner circle is as likely to "turn" as is the lowest employee. The loyalty is not to the firm, but to accretion of personal wealth and power. This also is true of the firm's loyalty to its country of origin. Firms are global, more global than nations, and they do not see themselves as beholding to any set of GPS coordinates. The adage, "Having drunk the country's water, one should obey the country's laws," means nothing anymore. In reality, the adage would read today, "Drink as much as you can, as fast as you can, from as many sources as you can, and don't get caught." When the driver is money, free trade, microchips, and toaster ovens, then there is no room for compliance and loyalty.

Burgess and Power: *The business life style of the twenty-first century road warrior, e.g., laptops, PDAs, wireless, VOIP, working on planes, etc. How has it changed the nature of attacks and countermeasures related to economic espionage and intellectual property theft? What opportunities has it opened up for the attacker? What specific countermeasures and controls should be implemented?*

Similarly, the paperless office, telecommuting, corporate intranets, have all changed the information environment in profound ways. Secrets that were once on a mainframe or in a safe are now held on networked servers and accessed via remote workstations and even home computers. How has it changed the nature of attacks and countermeasures related to economic espionage and intellectual property theft? What opportunities has it opened up for the attacker? What specific countermeasures and controls should be implemented?

Keith Rhodes: Now we get to see this pervasive threat in an interconnected world. The phrase you use, "[t]he business life style of the twenty-first century road warrior," is quite telling. Once upon a time, monarchs established guilds to maintain standards and to keep power centralized. This can be seen in the guilds for longbow archers in Europe or the Samurai in Japan. The "road warrior" is a very powerful individual and a very easy target. I was sitting on an airplane a while ago trying out a new laptop I had on loan from a computer company. They had, of course, given me a machine with everything on it. All I wanted to determine was the ergonomics of it, but the company had thought they could impress me with myriad gadgets. I booted up, and immediately the computer had every kind of wireless connection searching for a signal. I immediately started turning the functions off, when I noticed that the infrared connection was acquiring the computer next to me, and my computer was asking me if I wanted to mount their drive to my system. I turned off the device, but thought that it was very interesting that the person next to me hadn't noticed that my machine was trying to ultimately hijack his computer. I wondered what he did for a living, so I could judge his risk, and found out that he was the European Marketing Director for a large industrial firm. I also saw that he had drafts of the 5- and 10-year strategic plans for the company on his computer. I thought to myself, can security knowledge really be that bad? The answer, of course, was (and still is), "Yes."

Burgess and Power: Yes, we challenge the reader at their next conference to turn on the *blue tooth* and see how many shares are available. One of us did this at an INFOSEC conference and of the 100+ individuals, there were over 40 shares available to me! These are the "watchers," the lack of general education on how data can be transferred from your laptop, PDA, etc., to any other device. Most people focus on getting data in, hardly any focus on how data is exfiltrated.

Keith Rhodes: Thus, if I were to attack an opponent from an industrial espionage/ intellectual property perspective, I would use all the tools available to me, both logical and physical. I would "case the joint," as it were, both wired and wireless, by sweeping the airwaves and by walking around. I will seek the path of least resistance. Why should I spend time trying to break in through a fortified Web site if I can lie my way into a building by dressing up as a HVAC worker? Likewise, why should I expose myself to physical harm, if the Web site if easily captured?

Burgess and Power: What are the elements of a comprehensive protection program focused on the issues of intellectual property theft and economic espionage?

Keith Rhodes: The next logical question is to ask, "How do we establish counter this?" I go back to my OPSEC training. There are five steps:

1. Identification of critical information
2. Analysis of threats
3. Analysis of vulnerabilities
4. Assessment of risks
5. Application of appropriate countermeasures

The first step is always the hardest, because the organization has to decide what is and what is not important. This cannot be outsourced to a contractor. This is an internal discussion that begins with the question, "What do we do for a living?"

It may seem a silly question to ask, but in my experience, it is the most difficult one for any organization to answer. It is easy to regurgitate a corporate vision statement or organizational charter, but to put those usually vague words into concrete examples and actions is very hard.

The second step is also difficult, as it is asking, "Who is our adversary?" To answer honestly, the organization has to see itself as its worst enemy, as it may leak more information to an opponent than the opponent could ever hope to steal. Think of the earlier scenario on the plane. What is the value of a 5- or 10-year strategic plan? I can't say for certain, but I would think it is very important.

Then one moves to steps three and four, where discussions of giving workers constant access has to be balanced against security. In my experience, these discussions do not take place, as the "always on" requirement overrides security concerns every time, as "always on" is synonymous with "always making money." It should be synonymous with "always transmitting," but that is an opaque idea to a boardroom. A chief executive may have bodyguards and armored cars, but the "always on" PDA does not. Thus, in that scenario, I would just drive behind the car stealing the ideas directly off the wireless device. When last I checked, corporate security vehicles usually included blast resistance, but not signal insulation.

Notice in the above five steps that the application of countermeasures is the last item, that there is a lot of thinking that needs to occur before a solution is chosen. I would argue that the solution is mostly in education. People have to be educated that they are assets to be acquired, that they are targets, that there is a threat, and that they are the key to the solution.

There is, of course, technology, but there is also common sense. Many young new employees do not even realize that they live in ubiquity. They are, indeed, power users, but they do not necessarily understand how their technology works.

That is part of the education. They need to be shown the opponent's ability.

Technologically savvy users are usually surprised to see what can be done remotely to their computers. Also, employees need to understand the corporate policies regarding their role in securing the corporate assets.

"Appropriate use" is a phrase that is heard often these days, but is not clearly understood by employees. When I ask employees at organizations what "appropriate use" means, they usually reply, "No porn." That's part of the answer, but not the whole answer. Going to disapproved sites is an important rule, but how and when and to whom one can send corporate information is also important. I am less worried about people reading the on-line newspapers than about them text-messaging colleagues about password changes or corporate acquisition decisions. Likewise, I am less worried about what stays in the building than about what leaves the building with the employees every night. A briefcase full of documents is very important, but I need to actually physically steal them. A leaking PDA is no problem at all for an adversary.

Burgess and Power: In addition, how many companies ask their employees, "Do you cohabitate with a competitor's employee?" If so, does your enterprise give these employees additional awareness and sensitivity training to better protect their inadvertent loss of the enterprise's data? Does the enterprise have a work-from-home policy and does this policy include how you may leave your computer at home when you are not present? Perhaps you must have the computer locked, encrypted, etc. Do you use firewalls? VPN into enterprise? If you have a roommate or spouse employed by a competitor, what is the expectation? Most will say none. There is a general Code of Business Conduct that addresses the need to protect corporate data, but no examples of what might be innocent, inadvertent damaging disclosure.

The Professional Investigator's Perspective: Ed Stroz

Burgess and Power: From your perspective, as a professional investigator, how has the theft of trade secrets changed over the last few decades? Is the means of attack less dependent on the insider than previously? Is it more oriented toward technological means of acquiring secrets than previously? Certainly, the impact of both globalization and the WWW has been significant. Have the players changed? Have the likely targets increased? What are the challenges of conducting such an investigation in the Global Economy and the Information Age?

Ed Stroz: Decades are relatively long periods of time. In the 1980s and earlier, trade secrets were much more likely to be stolen or passed on a paper medium. Today, virtually all trade secret information is digital, and handled in the form of a computer file, even if that file is capable of being printed. Because digital files can be accessed remotely, and copied rather than being "taken" in a way that shows them missing from where they had been, a thief doesn't have to have an insider with physical access. This is a big difference from trying to steal a paper document that is inside a person's desk. Clearly, using technological means is the more prevalent and likely method of accessing and stealing trade secrets. This also takes us to the point that the players have changed. Companies in the US have more ways of protecting trade secrets, based on federal laws passed in the 1990s and later. So companies operating in the US are "players" in the sense that they are likely to be targets and victims, but they also have protections available to them that allow them to hit back under the law, if they have their act together technically and legally.

Burgess and Power: Bank robbers rob banks as that is where the money is. IP thieves operate around the globe, but operate in the US largely due to the fact that this is where there is an abundance of *new* IP.

Ed Stroz: As for the "players" who are bad guys, yes, I would say that has changed too. It is much more likely now for employees who jump to a new employer to be tempted to take computerized files with them from their old employer. Often, their former employer considers these files trade secrets. So, many domestic players who don't fit the profile of a "spy" can wind up stealing trade secrets. In addition, you have computer networks being massively compromised by computers with connections originating overseas, often undetected for long periods of time. It is often difficult or impossible to know whether the apparent overseas origination point is a pass-through location, or the true point of origin. Whatever the answer to that question is, this type of activity is growing. The challenge to our global economy is how do we resolve such indications of an overseas penetration when there is no worldwide body of law or law enforcement either in place at all, or that can work quickly enough to be effective? While there certainly has been progress in this area, it is patchy and often slow in its effectiveness.

Burgess and Power: There is the need for executives to understand what information is at risk, and what information they should invest extra care in protecting. There is also a vital mix of cyber security, physical security, and personnel security issues. Could you talk about some of the proactive and preventative controls and countermeasures that organizations can take to mitigate the risk of intellectual property theft and economic espionage that strike you as the most important or effective?

Ed Stroz: Some of this is quite simple. For example, intellectual property (IP) that constitutes a "trade secret" has to be recognized, and treated as such, by the company that owns it. It's not enough for an executive to think that anything he doesn't want someone else to know about his business is a trade secret and will be honored as being one in court. It must be protected in a way that will stand up in court. This is why it is vital to involve legal counsel early and regularly, to determine whether to claim resolutions and protections if a trade secret has been compromised. Besides knowing which IP is a trade secret, as a matter of law, it will have to be treated and protected as a secret. This means protecting the information and the media on which it is stored. Protection includes physical security, information security, and through proper policies and procedures. This has caused companies to make increasing use of background checks with regular updates, including some contractor personnel. It also means more companies are focusing on the data inside their computer networks, and where it is going, rather than on looking for intruders coming in through the perimeter of their network. While intrusion detection is still important, extrusion protection gets much more attention now than in the past.

Burgess and Power: *One could argue that today it is as important to monitor what is leaving the company as what is trying to get into the company. Perhaps more so.*

Ed Stroz: There is also more awareness of the need to monitor e-mail and other forms of electronic communication in order to detect disgruntlement or other precursors to trade secret compromise. The most important part of managing this risk, in my opinion, is to utilize a threat matrix that categorizes those people who are in the position to do the most harm due to their access levels and technological prowess. The higher a person is on that scale, the more monitoring that should be considered. I believe that insights from behavioral science are not used enough in screening for problem situations in advance so that you have a chance to intervene and defuse before an actual compromise happens. It's good to keep in mind that all criminal activity is about human behavior, not the behavior of computers.

Burgess and Power: *Technology does not equal Security and behind every piece of technology designed to compromise your data is an individual with motivation. What are some of the mistakes and oversights in terms of personnel security, e.g., background checks, etc., that expose organizations to insider initiated intellectual property theft and economic espionage?*

Ed Stroz: The first mistake is not doing a background investigation of adequate depth on the person to be hired. This means doing a little more than just a credit and arrest check. It means checking employment references and looking for on-line data by people experienced with background checks. For some serious positions, including staff positions with significant access to critical information, more work is necessary than for someone who is filling a less critical role. Secondly, I think it's a mistake not to monitor to some degree the e-mail and network activity of critical insiders while they are at work. It should be part of a policy that is disclosed to employees as they are hired. Some companies are concerned that this could be prying into people's private communications, but it needn't be that at all if the employee is notified properly. Also, in some instances such monitoring finds that employees are spying on other employees! It's not helping anyone's privacy to be blind to that kind of activity. Today, it is possible to monitor employee behavior using charts and graphs without going all the way down into actually reading employee e-mail unless that is justified and necessary. This kind of "controllable drill-down" strikes a nice balance between the equally problematic extremes of "willful blindness" on the one hand to "big brother" on the other.

Burgess and Power: Just as the overall space has changed over the last few decades, i.e., the WWW, globalization, etc., so has the nature of the insider. Determining who is an insider and who is an outsider is problematic in this era of outsourcing, contracting, etc. Talk about the problems that arise in this environment?

Ed Stroz: That's a good point. They used to consider insiders as those functioning inside the "perimeter" of a computer network, but that definition was not always adequate. Today I would say companies have to keep clear records about who is "authorized" to access certain data and for what purpose(s). Those records include written and signed employment agreements, contractor agreements, and contracts with outsourced entities that might have possession of trade secrets. An insider might best be defined as anyone who is authorized to have access, even if it is only the access to possess your intellectual property. By defining terms clearly, you are more likely to think about your IP correctly and manage it by asking better questions. For example, shouldn't the attorneys at your law firm be considered an insider?

Burgess and Power: What are some of the mistakes that insiders engaged in intellectual property theft and economic espionage typically make that lead to their detection?

Ed Stroz: The mistake is to believe that tracks can be completely wiped away. This is rarely true. In my experience at the FBI, the more sophisticated white collar criminals understood that evidence may be left behind anywhere they operated. Amateurs tend to think they know it all. Today, there is an enormous amount of computer data generated by our business activities, innocent or otherwise. Computers store information that the users don't see about the actions they take. For example, if an employee plugs in a thumb drive into their work computer and then copies trade secret information onto it, there will be information within that computer about those actions. However, the employee may not know that, but mistakenly believe that such evidence doesn't exist.

Burgess and Power: *What are some of the mistakes and oversights in terms of cyber security that expose organizations to outsider-initiated intellectual property theft and economic espionage?*

Ed Stroz: The failure to document that "insiders" (as defined above) have been informed what they are authorized, and not authorized, to do with their access privileges to intellectual property. Without clear knowledge of what the employer forbids, it will be difficult to establish requisite "intent" to violate company policy, and that would make it difficult or impossible to address in a court of law later. We also see that many organizations do not adequately log and monitor the access to intellectual property. Then, if an incident arises in which intellectual property is suspected of having been compromised, it becomes difficult or impossible to prove who did, or did not, have access to it. Such failure to keep adequate records can also cause innocent parties to be cast into suspicion if the records do not prove they did not access critical information.

Burgess and Power: *What are some of the mistakes and oversights in terms of physical security that expose organizations to outsider-initiated intellectual property theft and economic espionage?*

Ed Stroz: Physical security requires that people be held accountable for their actions, movements, and access to property. This includes all people who enter buildings or log onto networks. It also means that hardware capable of storing intellectual property has to be controlled. Today, cell phones and cameras can take pictures of documents, and can be activated to record conversations. A conscious decision has to be made where these devices may and may not be carried into the workplace. Also, some companies outsource their IT to such an extent that they even lease their laptops. If a computer breaks, or for some reason needs to be returned to the vendor, it's important to know what is happening to the data on the hard drive of the device before it leaves the building. It's often a good idea to have it wiped before it leaves. I'd also like to point out that having a good topography of a company's computer system is often important in mapping out the devices and connections that make up a computer network. Topographies, both logical and physical, are often neglected in companies that are then in the position of having to show how careful they were with their trade secrets.

Burgess and Power: *What are some of the mistakes that outsiders engaged in intellectual property theft and economic espionage typically make that lead to their detection?*

Ed Stroz: There are parallels to the points made above about insiders. However, outsiders are less worried about getting caught if they take steps to "launder" their access through overseas territories. That is, an outsider isn't worried about being fired if caught.

Burgess and Power: *Could you give us an overview of what you do when you are brought in by an organization concerned over incidents or suspicion of intellectual property theft or economic espionage? Where do you begin? What are the stages of an investigation? What are the biggest obstacles? How much does the success of an investigation of this sort depend on how well organized and implemented the organization's security is up front?*

Ed Stroz: We start by listening carefully to our client and the facts behind what caused them to contact us. The first phase is concerned with gaining a complete understanding of the facts and circumstances relevant to the client's problem. We establish what role outside legal counsel is, or may, play in the problem. I like to have an organization chart of the company and a topology of its computer network for reference. As part of the first phase, we are also trying to think of what law(s) might have been violated, so that we can identify the elements of that statute and use those elements to guide our investigation. Phase two is usually one in which we preserve the evidence that needs to be gathered. This may involve mirror-imaging computers in a forensically sound way, storing backup tapes and computer media, deciding whether routine practices like de-fragmentation routines and overwriting of backup tapes needs to be suspended, and interviews of key personnel. Speed is often important. The success and efficiency of our efforts is heavily dependent on how well organized our client's operations are.

Burgess and Power: *What are some of the issues involved in forensic evidence, both cyber and physical? How could an organization better prepare itself for the gathering and preservation of such evidence? What are some of the technological and legal challenges involved?*

Ed Stroz: It may be helpful to think of the handling of forensic evidence in these categories: identifying it; preserving it; and analyzing it. Issues can arise at all three levels. With digital intellectual property, it is easy to miss all the locations where it may be stored, that is to make errors in identifying the presence of this forensic evidence. For example, are you thinking of e-mail correspondence as existing only on the mail server? If so, you haven't identified the forensic evidence from browser-based e-mails, like Yahoo, that may only show themselves on the hard drive of the user, not in the mail server data. Preserving that evidence is also tricky. It requires start-to-finish care with a forensically sound chain-of-custody procedure. Sometime we face situations in which a client has already rummaged around in a computer suspected of being used in an intellectual property breach. The action of looking through the computer destroys valuable evidence and contaminates what otherwise could have been preserved. The last category, analysis, is the most sophisticated and is the hardest to discuss in general terms. This is where we actually examine, using forensic software, the actions taken by people with the intellectual property. The analysis steps are affected by many factors, including the age and size of the computer, the operating system, file system, and the way it was set up by the IT staff. But the analysis is very dependent on having a forensically preserved mirror-image of the data. As for advice, I would recommend that companies use someone with expertise in forensics when conducting an investigation. Whether they have expertise in-house or use an outside firm, it is not for amateurs.

Burgess and Power: We concur 100 percent. And make this forensic expertise in-house completely. You don't want an NDA as your only line of defense should your most sensitive data be revealed by the contract forensic investigator – you fire him, you seek damages – but what about the other damages – investigation revealed, investigation compromised, chaos at every level? You have directed investigations both for government and in the private sector. From your wealth of experience, what do you advise organizations to do? What are the pros and cons? Should they turn to law enforcement? Under what circumstances should they? And at what point in an internal investigation should they?

Ed Stroz: Listen to the advice provided in answers to the earlier questions. In a nutshell, it is intellectual property (IP) that will drive the value of most companies, and that IP has to be handled properly if you are to realize its value. That means it has to be treated properly if you ever have to investigate whether it has been stolen or compromised in some way, and then to pursue your rights under the law. The law enforcement card is a very important part of the solution. Even if a company thinks that it does not want or need law enforcement help, those decisions often change. Law enforcement authorities have powers to take actions, such as executing search warrants that cannot be done under civil law procedures. However, a company seeking law enforcement assistance needs to have its facts together and to have handled their matter properly.

Burgess and Power: Law enforcement entities will gladly share the level of detail required to engage them effectively, i.e., how to prepare for the engagement. The enterprise must keep in mind, once you bring law enforcement into the equation, you may not be pleased with the direction the investigation now takes, as YOU no longer control the investigation. Law enforcement will drive the investigation as their goal is prosecution, not necessarily reputation preservation.

Ed Stroz: Sometimes there aren't good reasons to go law enforcement; sometimes there are good reasons for doing so. As to when that decision needs to be made, it varies. However, you do not want to contact them half-cocked or without having done a reasonable amount of homework.

Burgess and Power: There are insiders and outsiders. There are professionals and amateurs. There are governments and corporate competitors. What would you say about the array of bad actors in the space of intellectual property theft and economic espionage? Do you have any thoughts on regions of the world or particular types of criminal enterprises? Are there an increasing number of third parties involved, i.e., information brokers? People who will steal secrets and then sell them to competitors, or be covertly contracted to do this work on spec? What is your analysis of the latest intelligence?

Ed Stroz: I don't have a good answer on this, beyond what I've already said. It's a very big question. Most of the intellectual property violations that we have seen, and that are actionable, involve insider activity.

Burgess and Power: How do theft of proprietary information and economic espionage investigations differ from other types of corporate investigations? How would you characterize the differences? Are there more sophisticated technologies utilized in these attacks? Are the adversaries more professionals? Is it more difficult to detect, identify, and track down? Are investigations typically longer and more extensive? The stakes are certainly higher? Your answer of course probably varies for disloyal insider versus professional outsider attacks. Give us a sense of how these types of investigations distinguish themselves?

Ed Stroz: These are a subset of white-collar crime. They tend to be motivated by financial greed, involve deception or hidden actions, and are non-violent. This means that the investigation cannot count on a confession from the guilty party, if there is one. However, a confession is much more likely to be elicited from a guilty person if they are confronted with documentary evidence of the actions they took that are at the heart of the problem. Often, it is only after showing the person these documents that they confess. These investigations tend to require more time, resources, and cunning than the investigation of physical property crimes or crimes of violence.

The DoD Cyber Sleuth's Perspective: James Christy

Burgess and Power: What impact do economic espionage and intellectual property theft have on the economic and national security of the USA? What is at risk? How high are the stakes? What are some of the indicators that we can see around us? Are whole sectors being gutted? Is our leadership in technology and scientific research slipping away? How bad is it? And what direction is it all going? What is government's role? What is it doing? What does it need to do? And is it just the USA that is targeted, or is the threat as dire for other developed economies, e.g., Japan and the EU?

James Christy: There is absolutely no measure of the loss for many reasons. Economic espionage and intellectual property theft is usually covered up for many good and cogent reasons by the private sector victims. I have seen entire corporate networks of over 100,000 systems completely compromised and hundreds of thousands of files ex-filtrated. The only reason the government knows about it is because much of the information compromised and exfiltrated was government data and the companies couldn't stop the hemorrhaging on their own. Evidence today is only antidotal because the private sector doesn't report losses or compromises if in fact they even know about them.

Burgess and Power: *The business life style of the twenty-first century road warrior, e.g., laptops, PDAs, wireless, VOIP, working on planes, etc. How has it changed the nature of attacks and countermeasures related to economic espionage and intellectual property theft? What opportunities has it opened up for the attacker? What specific countermeasures and controls should be implemented?*

James Christy: Due to the power and the capacities of portable and wireless devices today, when there is a loss or compromise, you could lose everything. So the possibility of a catastrophic loss is far greater since these devices are being employed by more and more employees and the capacities are far greater. Couple in with non-secure wireless communication between these devices and the mother ship, the potential is more devastating.

Burgess and Power: *Similarly, the paperless office, telecommuting, corporate intranets, have all changed the information environment in profound ways. Secrets that were once on a mainframe or in a safe are now held on networked servers and accessed via remote workstations and even home computers, etc. How has it changed the nature of attacks and countermeasures related to economic espionage and intellectual property theft? What opportunities has it opened up for the attacker? What specific countermeasures and controls should be implemented?*

James Christy: In the old days, information deemed not to be too sensitive was stored in file cabinets in an office, in a locked building. Today, all of this information is now stored online and accessible. If a single document in one file cabinet, in one particular office was compromised, it didn't have an impact. Today, thieves can now access all of the file cabinets in multiple offices, in multiple buildings, in multiple physical localities, and aggregate the information, compromising entire projects. Each individual piece of information, if compromised, wouldn't have an impact, but putting all of the disparate pieces together can.

Burgess and Power: *Yes, you need to defend 360 degrees and 24×7, but your adversary only needs to be right once. If you were to conduct a penetration test that emphasized attacks* *related to economic espionage and intellectual property theft in this twenty-first century information environment, what would be some of the ways you would go after the client's secrets? What would be some of the traditional ways, related to physical security, etc. (e.g., dumpster diving) which are still relevant? What would be some of the more cutting edge ways, related to recent technological advances (e.g., war-driving)?*

James Christy: All of the old techniques still work as well as they ever have. Social engineering is the easiest and least risky. Employees are generally unwilling to challenge strangers and are usually eager to brag about what they do. Most are naïve that they would even be a target and most are very trusting. I went to the building manager of a very well-known DoD facility and gave them a business card and said that I was performing a vulnerability study for a requesting DoD agency that processed highly classified information. I told the building manager that we ran the assessment in two phases: a covert phase for a week, and an overt phase for two weeks. All of that was true, but the building manager didn't ask for credentials and didn't call anyone to check out my claim. I told the building manger that I wanted to observe the employees of this organization in their day-to-day operations. I asked if there was a way to get into the facility as a janitor. He wanted to help so bad that he offered me two building maintenance uniforms, equipment to measure air flow from the HVAC, a light meter, and an industrial thermometer. He then wrote a backstopping letter that said we were doing an environmental study and that we didn't have any clearances. He then put a closing paragraph that told the reader that if they had any questions to call him directly. All based on a business card.

My partner and I donned the maintenance uniforms and showed up at the facility during lunch. I told my partner that once we entered the facility, he should go in one direction and I would go in the opposite direction and steal top secret material out of the burn bags, because those documents wouldn't be missed. The escort should make us stay together. We hit the buzzer and the loan person left in this 10-person facility let us in. We explained what we were doing and gave him a copy of the backstopping letter from the building manager. We told him we would be there for a couple of hours. He suggested we work out of a vacant cube they had that was behind a partition. My partner then went one way and I went the other. The escort didn't want to challenge us so he walked down the hall and spent 2 to 3 minutes with my partner and then walked down and spent a couple of minutes with me. Whichever one of us who wasn't being watched was pilfering the top secret trash from the burn bags, putting it in our clipboards until we had a chance to go back to our cube and unload in it in our toolbox.

When the rest of the crew came back from lunch, they fired up their classified computers. One put on a set of headphones and started working on a secret document, while I stood behind him writing down the classified information while my partner distracted his office mate.

It all goes back to human nature. People don't want to be jerks and challenge others.

Burgess and Power: What are some of the issues involved in forensic evidence, both cyber and physical? How could an organization better prepare itself for the gathering and preservation of such evidence? What are some of the technological and legal challenges involved?

James Christy: We all know digital media and devices are becoming increasing prevalent in our world. Beyond personal computers, laptops, cell phones, PDA's, digital music players, flash media, game consoles, CDs, and DVDs are a part of everyday life.

I don't have to tell you that such items are commonly being found to have direct relevance in criminal cases. And, it is clear that the rising trend in the amount and importance of digital evidence in counterintelligence and law enforcement operations will not abate soon.

I believe it is vitally important that we increase the dialogue between law enforcement personnel confronted with digital evidence issues and digital forensic examiners skilled in the art of extracting information from digital media and devices.

Digital media is extremely susceptible to environmental conditions. Data modification or loss can result from exposure to such elements as heat, humidity, dust, or electromagnetic waves.

This potential change in or loss of information is a vitally important issue that can have a direct impact on the outcome of a case.

Digital evidence deterioration will have a significant effect on the ability of the forensic examiner to extract information and obtain matching hash values that verify the accuracy of a copied image.

Federal and military rules of evidence require that evidence introduced at trial be in the same condition as when it was seized. Although there are legal ways to admit damaged evidence at trial, the perceptions of the judge and jury could complicate the prosecutor's case. Additionally, the defense may be prompted to claim incompetence, negligence, tampering, or assert that the lost evidence proved the defendant's innocence.

Following correct handling procedures and maintaining proper evidence room conditions are the most effective means to protect digital evidence from adverse environmental factors. Some best practices include:

- Preserve digital evidence in anti-static bags.

- Protect digital devices from extreme environmental conditions during transport to storage facilities.

- Inspect evidence room conditions for heat, humidity, and cleanliness.

- When poor evidence room conditions cannot be corrected, consult with superiors and the legal office on a separate storage location for digital media and devices.

- Best practices related to digital forensics tools and techniques, investigative procedures, and evidence acquisition, handling, and preservation.

The Security and Privacy Consultant's Perspective: Rebecca Herold

Burgess and Power: The business life style of the twenty-first century road warrior, e.g., laptops, PDAs, wireless, VOIP, working on planes, etc. How has it changed the nature of attacks and countermeasures related to economic espionage and intellectual property theft? What opportunities has it opened up for the attacker? What specific countermeasures and controls should be implemented?

Herold: New methods of social engineering can now occur via P2P methods, such as instant messaging, and now that personally identifiable information (PII) is more portable there are more ways in which cyber crime can occur.

Burgess and Power: Similarly, the paperless office, telecommuting, corporate intranets, have all changed the information environment in profound ways. Secrets that were once on a mainframe or in a safe are now held on networked servers and accessed via remote workstations and even home computers, etc. How has it changed the nature of attacks and countermeasures related to economic espionage and intellectual property theft? What opportunities has it opened up for the attacker? What specific countermeasures and controls should be implemented?

Herold: Opportunities now exist via multiple social engineering vectors, such as phishing attacks, bogus Web sites, and similar methods, along with opportunities arising from the carelessness of businesses when they retire computers and do not remove the information from the hard drives. There has also been an increased move to regain money on computer investments by selling old computers, which again has resulted in some significant and embarrassing privacy incidents and cyber crime.

Burgess and Power: What is the role of awareness and education in a protection program focused on the issues of intellectual property theft and economic espionage?

Herold: Without awareness and training, basically a comprehensive education program, theft and espionage can occur right under people's noses without them knowing it…without them recognizing it. Humans are both the weakest link information protection, but they can also be the strongest. When people know how to recognize the signs of potential theft and espionage they can report it early and help to lessen the impact, or even prevent the theft or espionage.

Organizations must educate all personnel and business partners about how to prevent property theft in order to make the property theft prevention program effective. Organizations must educate all personnel about how to recognize economic espionage to make the anti-espionage program effective.

Education must occur from the highest position all the way down through the positions that you may mistakenly assume do not need to know about preventing the theft of intellectual property and preventing economic espionage. The unaware personnel will become the path of choice for the criminal.

Burgess and Power: *What are some vital and/or sensitive aspects of an awareness and education in a protection program focused on the issues of intellectual property theft and economic espionage? What are the unique challenges?*

Herold: Personnel must understand and learn how to recognize the signs of attempts to commit intellectual property theft and to whom they should report these attempts.

Personnel must understand and learn how to recognize the signs of economic espionage and know to whom they need to report suspicious behavior.

Personnel need to understand the methods used to commit intellectual property theft and economic espionage. Too many managers are afraid that this will tell people how to commit crimes. However, the majority of employees want to keep their jobs and help make their companies successful.

Keep in mind that if you have personnel who are planning to steal, they will already know how to do it. Providing training to alert your honest employees to how to recognize crime will give you more eyes and ears within your organization to spot the criminals; it will not create new criminals.

It is important that you provide GOOD training and awareness communications. Too many organizations slap a copy of an excerpt from the text of a law onto a PowerPoint and call it training; that is NOT training!

Just because so-called training products are expensive also does not mean it is GOOD training. Document the characteristics and features that you want to have within your training content, and the different methods you want to use to deliver awareness communications, and then choose your products based upon the quality of the vendor products, not based upon who has the most razzle dazzle in their sales pitch.

Probably the biggest challenge is getting the resources and time commitments for the training. Awareness, because it is more passive than training, is often easier to sell to management and to deliver. The active aspect of training requires the dedicated attention of personnel. Getting management to commit to sending their personnel to a 1-hour, or even 30-minute, session is often a challenge. This is just one of the many reasons when training and awareness efforts must be clearly and strongly supported by executive management.

Burgess and Power: *How has the theft of trade secrets and other forms of intellectual property changed over the last few decades? Is the means of attack less dependent on the insider than previously? Is it more oriented toward technological means of acquiring secrets than previously? Certainly, the impact of both globalization and the WWW has been significant. Have the players changed? Have the likely targets increased? What are the challenges of protecting intellectual property and trade secrets in the Global Economy and the Information Age?*

Herold: The insider threat is still as significant as it ever was, perhaps even more. More news is reported about people getting jobs within an organization with the specific intent of stealing intellectual property, or providing information to customers.

There are many more ways to do these crimes, but the old, tried and true methods are still as effective as ever. Most organizations are dumping all their money into technology controls and defenses, but then completely ignoring such things as disposal of information, paper document controls, and other safeguards that should be common sense now.

The players have not necessarily changed; now there are just MORE players. That is the challenge; trying to identify all the threats. There are so many; several that are still unknown. It is hard to defend against the unknown.

Burgess and Power: *What are some of the mistakes and oversights in terms of personnel security, e.g., background checks, etc., that expose organizations to insider-initiated intellectual property theft and economic espionage?*

Herold: Too few organizations perform background checks on potential employees. And even fewer perform regular background checks on existing employees. Employees change over time; they encounter hardships and situations in which they may get involved with criminal activities. It is important to regularly check so that such activities can be caught as early as possible.

It is also important to perform due diligence on the organizations contracted and entrusted to process, store, or otherwise handle and access sensitive data; those to whom activities have been outsourced. Organizations need to check to ensure THEY perform background checks, including criminal checks, on their employees. Many crimes have occurred as a result of employees within outsourced organizations doing bad things.

Burgess and Power: Just as the overall space has changed over the last few decades, i.e., the WWW, globalization, etc., so has the nature of the insider. Determining who is an insider and who is an outsider is problematic in this era of outsourcing, contracting, etc. Talk about the problems that arise in this environment?

Herold: Now basically anyone who has access to your information and systems should be considered an insider. This includes not only your employees, but also your contractors, consultants, folks hired to clean the offices, folks hired to be security guards, companies providing managed security services, ISPs, and the list can go on and on.

Burgess and Power: What are some of the mistakes that insiders engaged in intellectual property theft and economic espionage typically make that lead to their detection?

Herold: They leave trails. Electronic trails are very hard to remove; especially when the criminal does not know of all the trails he or she is leaving. They also assume that no one is smart enough to figure out what they did because doing bad things electronically seems like such an anonymous activity. They assume if they cannot see evidence of what they did that there is no evidence. They don't realize the bits and bytes of their actions have been accumulating as they've been performing their illicit acts. Most criminals are also proud of what they did and start bragging about how they outsmarted the system. Egos are the downfall of a large portion of criminals.

Burgess and Power: What are some of the mistakes and oversights in terms of cyber security that expose organizations to outsider-initiated intellectual property theft and economic espionage?

Herold: Most organizations underestimate the power and value of awareness communications and providing training. Organizations need to deliver ongoing awareness messages to let personnel know the risks the organization faces regarding IP theft and espionage. They must make personnel understand the threats and associated IP theft methods. They must let them know how to keep from being vulnerable to these threats while they are performing their job responsibilities.

Burgess and Power: What are some of the mistakes and oversights in terms of physical security that expose organizations to outsider-initiated intellectual property theft and economic espionage?

Herold: Mobile computing devices and storage devices are not protected within most organizations. Data on these devices need to be encrypted so that if and when the devices fall into criminals' hands they will not be able to use the data.

Burgess and Power: Generally speaking, what is the level of executive comprehension and awareness about the threats and the issues involved in the space of intellectual property theft and economic espionage? What kind of mind-set do you encounter in the boardroom? What are the major psychological blocks and pre-conceived notions that have to be overcome?

Herold: Most executives under-estimate the threats their organization faces. They often have the opinion that if nothing bad has happened yet, then nothing bad will happen. Many organizations are also of the opinion that they have nothing valuable that other organizations would find valuable; that they have no reason to be a target. And still many more executives say, "We trust our employees. We do not want to send the signal that we don't by implementing controls that are not really necessary."

The Strategy

In Part 1, we gave you a look at the nature of the challenge and the shadowy forces (inner and outer) that make it into such a formidable one.

In Part 2, we will offer you our ideas on how to develop a winning strategy to overcome this formidable challenge.

In Chapter six, "Elements of a Holistic Program," we outline the key ingredients of the winning strategy.

In Chapters seven, eight, and nine, we share three powerful case studies that underscore the vital role of awareness and education (if done right).

In Chapters 10, 11, and 12, we drill down into what it takes to make the three strong gears of personnel security, physical security, and information security lock in to each other and turn the great wheel together. In each of these three chapters, you will find an assessment tool in Q-and-A format. If you answer (or delegate the answering) of the questions in these three assessment tools, you have a far better understanding of the current intellectual property protection posture of your enterprise, as well as a clear vision of what needs to be done.

In Chapters 13 and 14, we explore two often ignored aspects of intellectual property protection: Chapter 13, "The Intelligent Approach," explores the ways in which an intelligence program can enlighten you strategically and embolden you tactically. Chapter 14, "Protecting Intellectual Property in a Crisis Situation," sheds light on the ways in which your business continuity and crisis management plans need to factor in IP-related issues so that you do not go ahead and rescue everyone—and recover everything—only to find that in the process you lost the business itself.

Chapter 15, "How to Sell Your Intellectual Property Protection Program," presents five figures on why and how (i.e., makes the business case) your enterprise needs to confront the twenty-first century challenge of IP theft and economic espionage with a twenty-first century IP protection strategy. The presentation is calibrated for board-of-directors level leadership, and presenter's notes are included with each figure.

Elements of a Holistic Program

Introduction

In many environments, security as an element of business culture has been hit with the double-whammy—that is, it suffers from both an image problem and an identity crisis. Many people think of corporate security as the "guards, guns, and gates" guys and cyber security as those "snoops who read employees' e-mail."

Security often is seen as a controlling or constricting force within an enterprise. It is frequently thought of as something that gets in the way of business. And lacking either a real mandate or a bold vision, many people within security slip into a reactive mode and resort to playing whack-a-mole, thus contributing to the bad image and deepening the identity crisis.

Security also is harried from a pack of false memes, which hound it, as well as some structural impairment, which hobbles it.

False Memes Lead People the Wrong Way

For example, a false meme tells you that teenage hackers with purple Mohawks and skateboards are responsible for most network break-ins; they don't really mean any real harm or do much damage. That might have been true fifteen years ago, but it hasn't been true for quite some time.

Another false meme assures you that 80 percent of all serious cyber-crime is perpetrated by insiders, for example, by dishonest or disgruntled employees. Again, looking in the rear-view mirror, at a great distance, that might have been true years ago, but it is a dangerous assumption in today's world. It is not that the insider threat has been diminished; it is that the threat from outside has increased dramatically. Furthermore, the lines between insider and outsider have been blurred both by technology and business practice.

A third false meme (there are several others) states that "most industrial espionage is done by the turning of insiders." Like the notion about "insiders" being the cause of most problems, this meme about the turning of insiders is particularly dangerous because it is a half-truth. The turning of insiders was the principle method, and it still is a major factor, but the business environment has changed radically, and methods of collection, and those eager to collect, have changed along with it.

From the Industrial Age to the Information Age

Of course, just as the Agricultural Age did not drop away when we entered into the Industrial Age, the Industrial Age is still with us, but an added dimension, the Information Age, is laid over the top of the two earlier paradigms. We are up to our necks in what Toffler called the Third Wave, and it has brought with it tremendous opportunity and profound challenge.

Unfortunately, this Third Wave has yet to sweep away a lot of Second Wave thinking about the nature of security.

To understand what security should look and feel like in the twenty-first century, pull out a piece of black paper. First, draw a big circle on it, and write along the curve of the circle, "Global Economy." Next, draw a second big circle of the same circumference on top of the first circle, and then write along side of the curve of this second, superimposed circle, "Cyberspace."

Within these two dimensions, which share the same space, you cannot draw a perimeter for your enterprise. And certainly, if you cannot draw a perimeter, you cannot protect it. Of course, you could draw a smaller circle, or a square, within the shared circle of the global economy and cyberspace, and you could imagine that the lines of the smaller shape delineated your enterprise's perimeter, but you would be deluding yourself. The reality is that the smaller shape is permeated by both the global economy and cyberspace, both are inside of your enterprise, you cannot keep them outside, and they are integral to how we do business today.

This new world demands a new security paradigm. We think of it as a holistic vision of security.

We have described the bad image, the identity crisis, and the false memes, but what about the structural impairment? Just as intelligence suffers from stove-piping (i.e., unless intelligence can be cross-referenced and aggregated in many ways, and analyzed afresh from different angles, something very important will probably slip by), so does security; if personnel security, physical security, and information security are all stove-piped within an enterprise, each is less than it could be, and all could well be working at cross-purposes. Figure 6.1 shows how awareness and intelligence can help mitigate risk and threats within an organization.

Figure 6.1 Personnel, Physical, and Information Security Mitigate the Scope of Risks and Threats

In life, in nature, in business, and in security, everything is interconnected, one way or another, just as the size of the glacier pack impacts the flow of the river, which, in turn, impacts the irrigation and reservoirs upon which human habitation has come to rely. In security, all the various elements interconnect for good or bad. If your most sensitive information is stored on an insecure server, your investment in physical and personnel security will be wasted. Conversely, if inadequate attention is paid to your physical security, then all your diligence in implementing personnel and information security controls could be for naught. Figure 6.2 shows how integration of physical, personnel, and cyber security helps narrow the scope of risks and threats within an organization.

Figure 6.2 Integrating Physical, Personnel, and Cyber Security

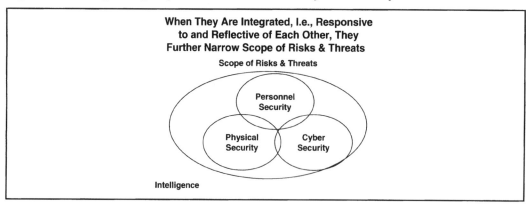

Each has to strengthen the other; each has to resonate with the whole (see Figure 6.3).

Figure 6.3 Serious Commitment to Awareness/Education and Intelligence Optimize Mitigating Factors

Here are some recommendations for a comprehensive program:

- **Organization:** Where security reports within an organization is perhaps the most vital issue of all. Consider appointing a Chief Security Officer (CSO), who reports to either the Chief Executive Office (CEO) or the Chief Financial Officer (CFO). This person should hold the reins of personnel security, physical security, and information security, and should not be a stranger to the boardroom.

- **Awareness and Education:** Educate your work force on an ongoing basis about the threats of economic espionage, intellectual property theft, counterfeiting, and piracy. Help them understand your expectation that they will protect the enterprise's intellectual property, and by extension, their own livelihood. Provide general education for the entire workforce, and specialized education for executives, managers, technical personnel, among others.

- **Personnel Security:** Implement a "Personnel Security" program that includes both background investigations and termination procedures. You need policies that establish checks and balances, and you need to enforce them. Know the people you are going to hire. Don't lose touch with them while they work for you. Consciously manage the termination process if and when they leave the enterprise.

- **Information Security:** Recruit certified information security professionals (e.g., CISSP, CISM, etc.) Adopt best practices, and establish a baseline. Utilize appropriate information security technologies, such as firewalls, intrusion detection, encryption, strong authentication devices, and the like. Pay attention to data retention and data destruction as well as data access.

- **Physical Security:** Do not overlook the "duh" factor. It is pointless to invest in information security, or commit to background investigations, if agents of an unscrupulous competitor or a foreign government can simply walk away with what they covet.

- **Intelligence:** You need both business and security intelligence. Know your competition, your partners, and your customers. Research the market environment. Keep abreast of the latest trends in hacking, organized crime, financial fraud, and state-sponsored economic espionage. You can outsource this expertise. But someone must be looking at both streams of intelligence, with the particulars of your enterprise in mind.

- **Industry Outreach:** Actively participate in industry working groups appropriate to your sector and environment. Talk with your peers about the types of attacks or threats they are encountering.

- **Government Liaison:** Leverage your tax dollars. Avail yourself of threat information from law enforcement, foreign ministries, elected officials, regulatory and trade organizations in your enterprise's country, and in those countries where you conduct business.

- **Legal Strategies:** Realize that even when right is on your side, a market may be lost to you, and protecting a portion of the global market is sometimes a viable survival strategy. Litigation is not the solution; it is confirmation that intellectual property theft has occurred. Work to protect your intellectual property and avoid the costs associated with litigation. Don't let a small legal mind make decisions about big legal issues. Get expert legal advice on intellectual property issues.

In sum, your security is in your hands. Employees tend to apply effort and intellect to the issue in portions commensurate with management attention to the topic of intellectual property protection. Employees line up smartly behind the leader providing direction, guidance, and support. Providing that leadership is essential to your firm's own continued economic viability in the global economy of the twenty-first century.

In *Part 2: The Strategy*, we will explore how such a holistic program would work, with particular emphasis on practical implementation. We present three case studies. One case study discusses the creation of an award-winning security awareness effort; the second case study discusses a less successful endeavor. A third case study discusses social engineering attacks. It is our goal to provide to you both the "how to" as well as the "how not to" so that you may see both the road to success and the road that may be filled with potholes.

Chapter 7

Case Study: Cisco's Award-Winning Awareness Program

Introduction

A man dressed in an orange prisoner jumpsuit, sitting in an interrogation room (see Figure 7.1), says: "Usually they make it so easy."

A detective asks, "The victims?"

"I am in and out with their stuff before they get a clue."

"What was different about this? Look, you got nothing to lose by being straight with us. You take pride in your work. High-tech thieves always do."

"You got a cigarette?"

The detective hands him one from across the table.

"How about a light?"

"No smoking allowed."

The prisoner says "Thanks," with an edge of sarcasm, and then resumes his narrative: "Those execs were open targets at the conference, which was the perfect set-up."

Figure 7.1 We Are the Targets—A High-Tech Thief Being Interrogated by Law Enforcement (*Photo Courtesy of Cisco*)

Cut to the outside of a conference center.

A camera shutter clicks, capturing a photo of three conference attendees greeting each other and shaking hands.

The lens zooms in on the conference and the employee ID badge hanging from one of the attendees' jackets.

Cut to the lobby of the conference center.

"The first exec was easy to find—near the restaurant, with all his gear. He looked worn-out. Perfect. I asked him a few questions about his PDA, and then I saw the confidential information on his laptop. He asked to see my badge and I showed him one I snagged."

The thief engages the executive in small talk.

"Then I just had to wait for the window of opportunity."

He follows the executive into the washroom. The executive puts down his laptop case, and turns his back on it, to wash his face at the sink. The thief steals the laptop case.

The executive goes to a security guard in the lobby and reports his bag missing.

"After I put the laptop in my van, I had to move fast. But I sensed my luck was turning."

His eyes follow another one of the executives riding the up escalator.

"The other guy had already dropped his bags in his room."

Cut to the other executive warning the woman that a laptop may have been stolen and that she should keep an eye on hers.

His cell phone rings.

"Since the word was getting out I had to be quick and grab what I could."

The thief bumps into the executive talking on the cell phone, as he turns and walks away. He snags his hotel key card, which was hanging out of the back pocket of his trousers.

"I used his key card and his laptop was right out in the open, just as I had suspected. I didn't have the cable cutters on me."

So the thief inserts a flash stick into the laptop.

"Couldn't access the system because it was password protected. I snagged some paperwork to see if there was anything in it. Found a calendar printout about a meeting in the mezzanine with the woman, about future acquisitions (see Figure 7.2).

"I figured a little inside information wouldn't hurt. I thought I would give it a last shot. The mezzanine meeting was a perfect opportunity."

Figure 7.2 We Are the Targets—Having Failed to Steal the Laptop, He Steals Documents from the Executive's Hotel Room (*Photo Courtesy of Cisco*)

The detective interjects, "You underestimated them."

"I didn't think they'd become so aware so quick."

Cut to the mezzanine.

"I showed her my cell, told her it was out of juice and I had to call my kid at school. Figured I try to get some acquisition contacts from her PDA. When I got her PDA there was some kind of pin number lock on it. When she asked for a photo ID, I knew it was time to bail."

The detective boasts, "And we caught you on your way out?"

"Lucky for you."

"As soon as the first laptop was stolen, all the executives knew they were targets."

"Lucky for them. There will always be exceptions."

The detective leans over him, puts his hand on the thief's shoulder and remarks, "And your targets are getting wiser."

What Is This Scenario?

Is this scenario the opening of a Hollywood thriller about high-tech espionage? No. It is the script for "We Are the Targets" (available online at www.cisco.com/go/cspo), an award-winning security awareness video developed by Cisco's Corporate Security Programs Organization (CSPO).

The four-minute film offers compelling evidence that a twenty-first century security awareness program can be sophisticated, entertaining, and provocative.

The era of raising awareness with little more than coffee mugs and key-chains has been eclipsed (if, indeed, such *tchotchkes* were ever more than marginally effective). If your organization is a world-class entity, and you are trying to communicate the importance of security, then you need a world-class vehicle to deliver that message. If your sales and marketing content is of a high quality, if it has some sizzle and style, how can you gain the respect or even the attention of your workforce unless you create awareness content that also has an edge?

"We Are the Targets" concludes with a montage of practical recommendations juxtaposed with critical moments from the film:

- Use a notebook privacy filter.

- Lock away Cisco equipment (laptop) and confidential documents.

- Travel with a cable lockdown device.

- Enable a password screensaver on your laptop after ten minutes.

- Be aware of your surroundings.

- Never leave your laptop or other sensitive information unattended.

- Activate verification features on all wireless devices.

- It's a tough world in the competitive trenches.

- Know that you are a potential target.

The video is a rich media component of Cisco's larger internal security awareness campaign. This campaign's rich media content is based on global real-life scenarios showing actual incidents, for example, thieves who blend into the environment of the workplace to steal information effortlessly to gain competitive advantage.

The concept of the CSPO video was to deliver a short, dramatic, five-minute video (sans talking heads) that was fresh and current, but portrayed Cisco employees as smart, aware, responsible, and security-savvy citizens.

The script was written by an internal video resource from IT Flex Services and based on the collective input of the CSPO team. Security experts from a cross-section of Cisco security groups—including Global Risk Management, Global Protective Services, Safety & Security, and Information Security—were selected to work with Mia Bradway Winter, CSPO's Security Awareness Program Manager, and video director, Paul Wood, the internal expert from IT Flex Services.

The video was produced on a remarkably modest budget of $30,000 and took eight weeks to complete. There were weekly team meetings and script reviews in development and preproduction. The filming was done over a two-day period. Services provided by the internal video unit included writing the Statement of Work, cross-charging the CSPO Awareness budget at the end of the quarter, contracting and coordinating the use of external professional services like professional actors, professional film crew, sound crew, location scouting, video direction, and script writing in close collaboration with CSPO.

The Cisco team competed against worldwide ad agencies producing safety and training videos at four different international video events. Typically, ad agencies create the videos or ads for their client (global Fortune 500 companies), and charge the client over $100,000.

"We Are the Targets" received three industry awards in the Safety & Security Training category from the following video competitions:

- The 2007 New York Festivals: International Film and Video Awards (Silver World Medal)

- The 2006 Digital Video International Competition (Crystal Award) for outstanding achievement in digital video

- The 2006 Cine International Awards

The film has more than tripled its return on investment.

The Message Is the Medium: Be a Security Champion

"In yesterday's age, a security 'team' was frequently relied upon to defend against attack. Not so in today's threat environment; security is everyone's responsibility," John N. Stewart, Cisco's Chief Security Officer, stresses, "whether you are designing a new protocol, working on our buildings, or talking to our customers, security is integral to our corporate culture."

Working with Stewart's vision, the CSPO awareness team decided on some very simple messaging to reach across all cultures within the Cisco environment: "Keeping Cisco Secure," a message that serves as an overarching theme, and "Be a Security Champion," a message that is intended to empower the workforce.

With those two messages, you can do a lot of things. Neither message says "Infosec" or "Safety and Security." It can be used by any security organization, because it is generic.

CSPO built its annual, company-wide, Web-based e-learning course—a twenty-minute flash presentation—around the "Be a Security Champion" theme. This theme proved to be a champion—the internal campaign was recognized with two MarCom Creative Awards in 2006:

- Platinum Award for the "Cisco Systems, Inc., Internal Security Awareness Campaign (Category: Marketing/Promotion/Campaign/Promotion Materials)

- Platinum Award for the Cisco Systems, Inc. video: Cisco Security Champion

The "Cisco Security Champion" video was designed as a sequel to the first video, with the use of the same actor portraying the same perpetrator. In this scenario, a few basic security lessons were identified and emphasized, and an effort was made to "internationalize" the message.

The Message

- Allow only appropriately badged personnel into Cisco facilities.

- Protect Cisco information.

- Don't leave paper lying about at the printer (print and pick up).

- Be mindful of elicitation by both known and unknown persons.

- Do not use non-Cisco computers for Cisco work.

- Use laptop encryption.

The scenario shows the international aspect of organized criminal elements, which realize that stealing a company's information assets and selling them to a willing buyer may give the buyer "competitive advantage."

In this video, the perpetrator has fled the country, after having met bail from his previous arrest following an attempt at stealing Cisco's intellectual property. He pulls together an international team to target Cisco's newest technology.

Figure 7.3 Be a Security Champion—Sizing Up an Employee for Elicitation and Tailgating (*Photo Courtesy of Cisco*)

The video's touch points include:

- Stealing a laptop (only to find that it is encrypted and thus has the value of an expensive paperweight)

- Expectation that an employee would use a public kiosk and personal e-mail to conduct business (only to find that the employee, in accordance with information security policy, was using the personal e-mail for personal items and took steps to protect his personal identifying information)

- Elicitation (see Figure 7.3)—an attempt to elicit from employees outside of the Cisco buildings information on projects and technologies (thwarted by Cisco employees mindful of the need to know and to know with whom you are speaking about your work)

- Tailgating (see Figure 7.4)—an attempt to ingratiate oneself and pass oneself off as a Cisco colleague and tailgate into the building feigning that he had forgotten his badge, only to be told in a polite, yet firm manner that corporate policy required the nonbadged individual to go to the main building entrance and sign-in.

- Badge theft—as a means to garner access to a Cisco facility and conduct a "snatch and grab" of paper near printers and nonsecured devices (PDAs, laptops, etc.)

Figure 7.4 Be a Security Champion—Employee Thwarting an Attempt at Tailgating in a Cisco Facility (*Photo Courtesy of Cisco*)

Again, as with the first video, the video demonstrated the desired behavior, and projected the image of Cisco employees exercising the behavior encouraged in the Cisco training, as opposed to what unfortunately has been the industry norm in videos, showing employees engaged in incorrect behavior. This perspective projects the positive aspect of the behavior, and thus allows for the employee audience to relate to the characters being projected; that is to say, Cisco employees engaged in making the right security decisions in a clear and unambiguous manner.

The comprehensive, multiple touch point marketing campaign that enveloped the video featured coordinated posters, lens clothes, highlighters (highlighting security), pads, pens, key fobs, and more, which all amplified the key message on a continuum: Be a Security Champion and Keep Cisco Secure.

This was an effective use of *tchotchkes*, or trinkets, because they were tied into the films, larger and more sophisticated vehicles for the messages. Because the films were hip and highly successful, the trinkets associated with them become a hot commodity and a personal statement. Without this kind of linkage, the use of *tchotchkes* trivializes the issues involved and the messages you are trying to convey.

When Your Message Reaches the Employees They Become Your Messengers

Taking the vision of personal responsibility and empowerment to the next level, the management team wanted to be able to reward people within Cisco (excluding CSPO team members, of course) who make some significant change in the way the business views security or its implementation.

CSPO put together an awards and recognition program, the "Cisco Security Champion Awards" to empower and recognize security ambassadors across Cisco who have demonstrated measurable security leadership behaviors that have changed the way his or her business unit views security. The fact that awards are given out twice a year is strategic. In December, during the holiday season, it taps into the spirit of giving. The other ceremony is in June, just before Cisco employees' annual review. That means a lot to people. It is a real feather in your cap to have that in your annual review.

CSPO team members (approximately 200 people) are invited to identify and nominate potential security champions whom they think have made a difference in the security of Cisco. The award competition is competitive. The more nominations made, the more the CSPO is provided documented evidence that the message is spreading and adhering.

The winners get recognition. At the CSPO global all-hands meeting, John Stewart awards them with a beautiful marble plaque. They get a cash award. Money is important. The company makes a big deal out of it, and their management has to commit to acknowledge this win at their next staff meeting, so that this award does not go unnoticed. Then at the end of the calendar year, all 10 winners' names are perpetualized on a team plaque displayed in one of the campus lobbies.

One of Cisco's first Security Champion honorees worked in China. He created an initiative to modularize the code that people work on, which is working very well. When you are given a source code project to work on, you are given only that component to work with; you do not get access to every single thing. There are many challenges to rolling out a security awareness program in a far-flung, fast-paced global corporation. You must seize every opportunity available to you.

At a global sales conference, CSPO partnered with Global Protective Services, for booth space. Their goal was introduce the sales force to the use of privacy filters on their laptops while traveling. That is one call to action that anyone can answer to protect the information they control. They came away with 153 leads on people who wanted to know more about privacy filters.

Although new hires received them with their company laptops, there is an existing base of many thousands who got their laptops before the privacy filters became standard-issue, and there are also many people in emerging markets where procurement has not been established yet.

CSPOs also were encouraging people to take the training. And once they took the training, if they were in an emerging market, or somewhere else they could not get a privacy filter, we would take their names down and we would give away privacy filters (a $40 value). One of the people with whom we made contact was a Russian gentleman who was a development director for the Middle East and Africa. He encouraged all his team members to take the training and contact me for a privacy filter. To this day, CSPO team members are still getting requests from Saudi Arabia, Kenya, and other locations. It is the "Tell a Friend" mentality, and even though it is comprised of baby steps, it will eventually become pervasive.

Staying on Message

The CISCO security awareness program is still evolving. Its creators don't claim it is the best. They point out that there are plenty of organizations out there that have been developing their programs for years.

Nevertheless, taking a look at the security awareness program developed by Cisco's CSPO offers some invaluable insights, whether you have been tasked to launch a new effort or to reenergize an existing one.

On day one, the awareness component within CSPO had a zero budget; within three years it had $150,000 in annual funding.

It started off as a one-person operation. In year two, a project manager tasked to devote 50 percent of his workload to the program was added. In year three, a Web developer and a coordinator were allocated to the virtual team.

To develop the awareness program, Stewart brought in an "outsider" with strong communications skills yet no background in security. The choice reveals an understanding of the serious obstacles that confront any such awareness program in a sprawling, global technology company.

Winter offers some further elucidation:

"Before I began I had no idea what information security might mean. However, I did have 20 years experience in external communications, public relations, media relations, and analyst relations. While I had never done internal communications or internal awareness before, I said, 'OK, it is a different animal, but if we use those same principles from external communications and PR and move them into internal communications, we can make something happen.'"

However, it is important to note that just as having world-class information security expertise and no communications and marketing skills is weakness for many programs, the opposite imbalance is just as self-defeating—having world-class communications and marketing skills with insufficient attention to the relevance, authenticity, and credibility of the content also results in failure. The substantive input and review of subject matter experts is essential to developing powerful content. In assessing awareness and education programs throughout the world, we have seen both sorts of imbalance.

The Cisco CSPO videos proved successful because they had both vital elements—sophisticated creative components (e.g., a strong script, professional actors, crisp editing, etc.) reflect the contribution of communications and marketing professionals, and the credible and compelling content reflects the input of information security subject matter experts.

Reputation and credibility are key ingredients—without them, people won't listen.

The first six months of the effort to build a CSPO security awareness program focused on researching and understanding Cisco from the inside. There are many challenging complexities in a large-scale corporate environment. As in all corporations its size, there are different cultures within Cisco. There are different functional organizations with different agendas and different styles (e.g., Sales is completely different than Engineering). In most corporations, Sales and Engineering don't necessarily communicate in the same manner. They have different mind-sets and, thus, have different touch points. And, of course, there are the corporate executives. They operate at a very different level. For them, everything is fast-paced. They need the facts distilled to the nitty-gritty. They need the facts immediately. They need the facts before you even talk to them.

Another challenge is that within a large corporation like Cisco, your audience is both static and dynamic: static in the sense that the bulk of the audience, engineers, and such have been around for some time; and dynamic in the sense that a large corporation like Cisco acquires new companies and people are going into divergent markets. Both the landscape and the headcount are constantly changing.

Researching Cisco from the inside meant a lot of engagement, and a lot of one-on-ones at all levels.

During this research, various functional groups and the key people inside those groups were identified. Those individuals who are influencers inside the group, the ones who could leverage CSPO's communications message beyond or internally within their functional organization, also were identified.

During the first year, 50 different contacts throughout Cisco were established, including several on the Cisco Employee Connection team, an internal news portal for all Cisco employees formerly run by HR. These portals are theater specific: US/Canada, Asia-Pacific, Japan, Europe, Emerging Markets.

If you get a story or a video or some kind of communication piece placed there, it cascades to the other geographies, so your reach is greater.

By year three, the CSPO security awareness team had 160 contacts that could be called on within Cisco.

Taking advantage of internal corporate events is vital. What better way to reach all the executives? What better way to reach the global population? What better common denominator can you tap into? There were nine different, internal Cisco events CSPO could tap into. One of them was the Strategic Leadership Off-Site, which is a gathering of all the directors and higher positions within the company—about 2,000 executives of Cisco globally—and they attend the annual meeting. That's where the CEO actually talks about the strategy, the vision, and the initiatives for the next full year, and unveils them.

Of course, CSPO is not the only group trying to impart vital training to the workforce. Unless these efforts are coordinated and complimentary, inefficiencies abound and cross-purposes arise.

There are other groups within Cisco that have compliance training that is required, so Winters sits on the compliance training working group, along with representatives from Legal, Safety and Security, and so on. This effort is managed by the Ethics group. Its goal is to get a compliance training suite that actually is required for all employees to take, and to be a part of that offering. Otherwise, it is very hard to get your training program socialized. You are all targeting the same audience, the same people, and you are hitting them at various times of the year, and it is not fair to the employee. The hope is that one functional group (e.g., HR or Legal) could take the training suite and deliver it to the employees, and then the awareness group could focus on creating rich content.

It Takes More Than Compelling Content and Hard Work

Despite the compelling nature of the content, and the hard work invested in establishing relationships throughout a huge organization, there is a third factor; it is the secret ingredient of success. Without this secret ingredient, the compelling content would be wasted, and all the hard work would be for naught.

That secret ingredient is a real mandate from on high.

There is no executive in the world that would say, for attribution, that he or she doesn't take security seriously. And there is no executive in the world that would deny that his or her security team has a mandate to heighten awareness and harden security within the enterprise.

But just as the devil is in the details, the proof is in the pushback.

No matter how strong your message, no matter how persuasive your presentation, no matter how much sweat-equity you have invested in networking and leveraging, no matter how honed your marketing and PR skills—if your CSO does not really have the authority he or she projects, if those to whom he or she reports within the executive suite do not really understand what is demanded of them to make security an enterprise-wide imperative—your awareness and education campaign will soon run out of organizational momentum, or get lost in the cacophony of competing initiatives, or be suppressed by those who feel that the style of work will be inhibited.

When the pushback comes, it has to be clear that this is the will of the executive. That is easier said than done, and more often promised than delivered.

Only a strong, credible CSO with the unequivocal and perceptible backing of the CEO and the Board of Directors can bring about a paradigm shift in your corporate culture.

(For insights into what can happen to a great program in the absence of such a mandate, refer to Chapter 8, *Case Study: A Bold New Approach to Awareness and Education, and How It Met an Ignoble Fate.*)

Lessons Learned

Based on the ongoing experience of its award-winning awareness efforts, Cisco has distilled "10 Steps Toward Pervasive Security Awareness" (*CSO Magazine*, August 2006 advertising supplement):

1. **Get buy-in from upper management.** Indeed, John Chambers' name and rank carry the necessary clout to open doors at Cisco. When the CEO says security is important and practices what he preaches, those in the trenches take notice. The same goes for all executives and managers down the line.

2. **Appoint the right person(s) to lead the charge.** It's critical to dedicate at least one resource to the job—someone who is excited about security awareness and can focus 110 percent on the task at hand. It's absolutely essential to appoint an individual with exemplary communications skills; someone who knows how to sell, market, and build relationships—in Cisco's case, a PR veteran.

3. **Conduct extensive research.** Stewart's team conducted over six months of research before launching Cisco's Internal Security Awareness Program. One must understand the target audiences and the culture of their respective organizations. "You may identify many, many target audiences," Winter says. "But with a complete understanding of each, you can customize your message [for greater retention]."

4. **Build relationships.** A successful security awareness program requires that the security message infiltrate the enterprise. Winter is part of a small team, so she needs all the additional voices she can muster. She gets her support by building strong relationships—engaging influencers and nurturing those connections. She encourages relentless pursuit, but warns that respect for an influencer's time and effort is paramount.

5. **Create security ambassadors.** What Winter cultivates from many of these relationships are security ambassadors; that is, individuals who evangelize security awareness messaging and directly influence behavior change. One such ambassador for Cisco is an employee in the Voice Technology Group who persuaded 800 individuals to take online security awareness training—resulting in a staggering 98 percent completion rate.

6. **Identify the right communications vehicles.** Look for opportunities to tell the security story to the masses. Piggyback on special events (like management summits and global sales meetings) and newsletters that are already in circulation. Don't be afraid to reuse initiatives that have worked in the past. Winter adopted streaming video to get her message across. She "copied" the concept and creative process from an existing program, tailoring it with her own message.

7. **Use credible sources.** When creating messaging for large audiences, it's important to feature people who are recognized and trusted by the audience. Winter targets her influencers and security ambassadors very carefully, relying on individuals who are more likely to be "heard" by the target audience. It's equally important to use communications vehicles that garner respect, such as a widely read newsletter. Plaques in a meeting room may say more than posters in the cafeteria.

8. **Keep your messages short and simple.** Like any great marketing campaign, it's better to keep things simple. Short messages are easier to retain. Cisco uses pithy lines like "Keeping Cisco Secure" or "Be a Security Champion." Remember, Winter warns, message retention comes from a continuous, sustaining program, so repetition is a must.

9. **Use rewards and recognition.** The best way to motivate change is by rewarding those who take the challenge to heart. Cisco uses a semi-annual Security Champion Awards system, whereby individuals who have gone above and beyond to effect change are rewarded. In addition to a marble plaque and monetary incentives, these individuals are recognized by the CSO at an "all-hands" meeting. And their managers personally acknowledge them among their peers. Cisco also gives away Security Champion t-shirts and privacy filters.

10. **Make training companywide.** Security awareness training is successful only if individuals participate and internalize the course work. It's essential to make training available at all levels and encourage participation. There may never be an ideal time to put "real" work aside to take the training, but if the message is strong enough, it happens anyway. And the results can be impressive.

Chapter 8

Case Study: A Bold New Approach in Awareness and Education Meets an Ignoble Fate

Introduction

Here is a case study on the launch of a powerful, unique, and comprehensive awareness and education program for a global entity, which we will refer to as "Entity X." In the course of the case study, we will articulate the essential components of an effective and economical program, and explore some of the critical issues involved in developing it, rolling it out, and institutionalizing it.

Of course, this story is both a case study and a cautionary tale. Indeed, if you follow this recipe you will soon find out if your executive team is really serious about changing the corporate culture and making security an integral workforce value, or is making noise to satisfy their customers and critics. Their reaction may pleasantly surprise you or disappoint or disturb you.

The Mission, the Medium, the Message

The mission, as described to the security professional recruited to undertake it, was to "change the corporate security culture." The existing corporate security culture was one that allowed laxness in all aspects of security (i.e., physical, personnel, and cyber).

The medium chosen was the establishment of a global security team to provide a range of services (policies and standards, security assessments, operational support, awareness and education, implementation, audits, inspections, and so forth) for a confederation of organizations operating in over 100 countries, with a collective workforce of over 100,000 people. In many ways, this environment was even more challenging than that of a multi-national corporation, as each entity was truly an independent organization. On one hand, the confederation shared a global brand, a global client base, and a global body of methodologies and traditions. On the other hand, they were determined not to share liability, and had a varying understanding that what was good for the confederation as a whole was good for their independent entity.

The message that this global entity wanted to convey to clients and government regulators throughout the world who were subjecting their industry to ever-increasing inspections/audits, and to its own workforce, was that it took all facets of security seriously.

Meaningful Content and Persuasive Delivery

Just as the best military professionals understand that Psychological Operations (PSYOP) (i.e., winning hearts and minds) is an essential element of Information Operations (IO) in any successful endeavor, whether a war or a peace-keeping mission, the developer of the program examined in this case study understood that awareness and education needed to be incorporated into a comprehensive internal public relations effort in order to change the global entity's deeply entrenched corporate culture, which was both hostile to security and lacking in command structure with respect to security.

Within the global security team, the intelligence function, the communications function, and the awareness and education function were aggregated together.

The concept was revolutionary at that time. The intention was to escalate awareness and education into something much more than emblazoning reminders about password security, software piracy, e-mail etiquettes, computer viruses, and so forth on coffee mugs, key chains, coasters, and wall posters. The intention was to infuse awareness and education efforts with real-world, real-time intelligence, and produce a comprehensive security campaign that was timely, engaging, and compelling to the workforce.

The new unit's objectives reflected this bold and sweeping vision:

- To analyze intelligence and conduct research relevant to cyber security in general and the cyber security of the Entity X in particular, so as to better protect both Entity X's intellectual property, but also those of Entity X's customers, partners, and vendors.

- To heighten the level of security awareness, inculcate core security values, and increase security competency at all levels throughout Entity X, so as to ensure that all level of employees understood how a good security regime was a market differentiator.

- To enable and enhance global security team communications on strategic initiatives and activities, and ensure that they are of the highest caliber, so to provide to the employees, customers, partners, and vendors of Entity X with communications truly worth reading versus a communication that is greeted with "another one for the dust-bin."

- To enrich the cyber security culture of Entity X through participating in and contributing to industry and government initiatives and activities, so as to truly be a leader both in and outside of the Entity X corporate footprint. This recognition would serve to bolster the internal credentials of those active with theses organization, but also is a demonstrable means by which Entity X as a whole derives great positive benefit via the interaction.

The new unit's structure was unique. The Intelligence Officer (in this instance, someone with extensive writing and speaking skills) reported directly to the Chief Security Officer (CSO). The team's Communications Officer reported to the

Intelligence Officer. The Intelligence Officer and the Communications Officer shared responsibility for the awareness and education function. The Intelligence Officer designed the program based on concepts of 21st century influence warfare, generated its content based on open source intelligence, best practices, and so forth, and provided the strategic vision and championed the program at the executive level. The Communications Officer took the program to market (i.e., rolled it out, socialized it, spread its reach, and administered it) on an ongoing basis, within global entity on a managerial level.

Investment and Empowerment

Just as the Intelligence Officer of Entity X's global security program started with a bold, innovative organizational approach (i.e., integrating intelligence, communications, and awareness/education into an integrated unit), the team also started out with a bold, innovative motivational approach:

- Instead of talking down to the workforce, show them how they are invested in security for better or worse, both in their personal and professional lives.

- Instead of playing to their fears (of either the bogey man or getting fired), engage, initiate, and empower the employees to be a part of the process and solution.

- Instead of just citing dry policies and standards in the workplace, provide them with common sense advice on best practices for security in aspects of personal lives (i.e., child safety online, identity theft, personal firewalls, emergency preparedness in the home, travel security for vacations, and so forth).

Following these principles, the team believed Entity X could demonstrate how many security controls required in the work place (e.g., strong passwords, secure laptops, regular backups) carry through to the home environment, and thereby heightened attentiveness and strengthen adherence to them in both realms. Following these principles, the team believed Entity X could establish trust with its workforce, and get them to view security as an integral value essential to living and working well in the 21st century.

Three-Phase Approach

To achieve the stated GSI objectives (e.g., "to heighten the level of security awareness, inculcate core security values, and increase security competency at all levels") in a labyrinthine and large-scale global environment with a corporate culture, which was both many decades old and passively hostile to security, demanded a phased approach to introduction and implementation.

The programmatic approach taken by the team was to design a three-phase plan to be implemented over a three-year timeline.

Phase I: Engage Everyone Economically and Effectively

Phase I focused on the roll out of a five-point initiative to reach the entire workforce with cyber security fundamentals:

- Create a task force composed of participants from Information Technology, Human Resources, Risk Management, Physical Security, Legal, and other stakeholders representing both global and local organizations within Entity X.

- Launch a bi-monthly electronic newsletter to be delivered in every user's inbox and posted on the innumerable intranet portals.

- Incorporate a 45-minute PowerPoint presentation on the security responsibilities of Entity X's workforce into the two-day new hire orientation process.

- Establish a globally and annually observed Security Day within Entity X to bring the workforce together for edification and entertainment with security as the focus.

- Deliver a 45-minute e-learning module on the fundamentals of security to be used both for all new hires and for incentive and refresher training of those already assimilated into the workforce.

By the end of Phase I implementation, Entity X's global security team could reach the entire workforce in four distinct ways:

- As they come into Entity X via new hire orientation

- On a bi-monthly basis via e-mail and the intranet

- Annually through on-site and virtual Security Day events

- Additionally, at least once more, through the use of the e-learning module as an orientation or refresher training resource

The theme of the electronic newsletter was "practical tips for computing both at work and at home," and delivered via e-mail and the intranet. It cost practically nothing to produce or distribute.

The newsletter's editorial calendar included:

- Password security

- Child safety on-line

- Laptop security

- Identity theft

- E-mail security

- Home PC security

- Social engineering

- Virus/worm defenses

- Internet usage

- Telecom security

- Back-up and recovery

- Economic espionage

- Physical security (office and home)

- Business travel security

- Emergency preparedness (office and home)

The e-learning module covered the fundamentals of cyber security for the end-user, and was organized into seven subject areas:

- Creating strong passwords

- User-oriented anti-virus measures

- Physical security (including laptop security)

- Appropriate Internet and e-mail usage

- Software piracy

- Backing up your files

- Counterespionage: How to thwart social engineering

Each subject area included two important security controls for the user to exercise, and three test questions (both multiple choice and true or false).

The electronic newsletter and the e-learning modules were also translated into over 20 languages.

The 45-minute PowerPoint presentation for new hire orientation was an electronic file, provided as a template, so that local organizations within Entity X could adapt it and expand it as needed. It included suggested comments on the Notes pages for each slide to help those whose primary task was not Information Technology (IT) security in delivering the presentation effectively. Its theme was "Your Role in Entity X's Security." The presentation referenced excerpts from relevant policies and standards, included a simple but powerful checklist, and provided hyperlinks to the global security team's online awareness and education resources.

Delivered by the intelligence officer, the length of the on-site Security Day briefing could be tailored for one- or two-hour sessions, and its content could be calibrated for different audiences (e.g., technical or non-technical, executive, or administrative). It was global, not US-centric, and provided an overview of major security concerns in work and life, a summary of Entity X's "Global Security Strategy," and a practical checklist for security in both the audience's personal and professional lives.

Phase II: A Rising Tide Lifts All the Boats

Phase II featured regional, two-day technical security training seminars for IT professionals. The model devised made it possible for organizations within Entity X to provide their IT professionals with expert-level instruction that would otherwise be cost-prohibitive. World-class instructors were contracted, using the global security team's GSI budget dollars, and participating local organizations in each country had only to cover travel and lodging expenses of the small number of IT professionals within their own groups designated to receive the technical training.

Because the two-day seminars were organized on a regional basis, even the travel and lodging expenses were somewhat more modest than they might otherwise have been for the organizations or the individuals themselves.

The curriculum of the technical IT security training centered on a range of knowledge areas selected to provide an immediate boost in core competencies throughout the pool of Entity X's IT professionals, including:

- Windows, Internet attacks, and countermeasures

- How to do security assessments

- Global intrusion detection framework

- Global incident response

- Preparation for both Certified Information Systems Security Professional (CISSP) and Certified Information Security Manager (CISM) tests

There was another benefit to Entity X as a whole, an invaluable although intangible one. At each of the seminars, participants from different countries, with different backgrounds and different areas of expertise studied, broke bread and clinked glasses together for three days, talking shop, sharing frustrations, trading scuttle-butt and bonding deeply in ways that cannot be measured, but that prove priceless at moments of crisis, or when truly tough collaborative efforts are required. The trust and bond developed in these engagements made the seemingly impossible now not only possible, but with a higher probability of success, as all involved were working together from a basis of collaborative trust. Such training also sends a very important message to each of the participants; you are valuable to us, and we, Entity X, are investing in you to ensure the security of Entity X and Entity X's leadership role.

Another element of Phase II was to expand the program, and leverage the resources created in Phase I, to incorporate general security awareness and education (i.e., Physical Security, Personnel Security, and Crisis Management)

Leverage existing awareness and education resources to deliver general security awareness and education to all Entity X's people globally.

So, for example, the electronic newsletter and the PowerPoint presentation for new hire orientation began to provide information on emergency preparedness and security guidelines for travel to high-risk destinations, as well as on cyber security. On-site Security Day briefings included updates on terrorism, global warming and bird flu, as well as on hacking, financial fraud, and laptop theft. And a complimentary e-learning module, dealing with physical and personnel security issues, was developed.

Phase III: Deliver Vital Intelligence and Early Warning to the Executive

Phase III brought the capstone to the pyramidal program: bi-weekly security briefings for the top echelons of Entity X executives.

The team lead in this regard was the intelligence officer, who designed a briefing format based on a few simple rules:

- No executive wants to read a lengthy report, or even one of only a few pages. No executive wants to hear about a problem without being told what is being done about it.

- Every briefing must include five sections: one on each Entity X's three geographical regions (i.e., Europe, Middle East and Africa, Asia Pacific, and Latin America), plus one on an overriding global issue, and one on an issue from cyberspace.

- Each briefing must be contained on a single 8-1/2-inch by 11-inch page, with no more than one or two paragraphs for risks and threats in each section, including at least one or two bulleted items outlining mitigation efforts being undertaken to address them.

- The Corporate Security Officer must tightly control distribution of the briefings, and limit such distribution to only the handful of executives designated to receive them, and those on the global security team required to prepare them.

Other elements of Phase III were intended to roll out methods for measuring the effectiveness of the awareness and education program, and for incorporating security knowledge and compliance into performance criteria.

But something happened along the way…

Don't Be Surprised If…

In an internal survey of IT directors and managers in both the global and local entities taken a year after the establishment of the global security team, over 80 percent reported that the global security team had strengthened Entity X's overall security posture. The results also indicated increased reliance on the global security team in general (more than 60 percent wanted its help in conducting annual security reviews), and on the awareness and education program in particular (70 percent of those who had not already adopted it planned to within the next year).

Attendee evaluations for regional technical cyber security training held in Europe and Asia also highlighted the effectiveness of the program:

- Over 65 percent of Asian attendees and over 70 percent of European attendees reported that class objectives were relevant to their needs

- Over 70 percent of both Asian and European attendees reported gaining new knowledge and skills

- Over 60 percent of Asian attendees and almost 60 percent of European attendees reported that the training would help them do their job better and more effectively

Local entities participating in on-site Security Day briefings on "Security Challenges in Your Person and Professional Life" grew from three international cities in the first year, to eight international cities the next year, to a projected 20 international cities in the third year.

Grateful readers of the electronic newsletter, from all over the world, e-mailed the global security team with personal queries, concerns, and suggestions.

The program outlined in this case study is a model that can be applied effectively and economically in many environments. If you have a workforce of over 100,000, you can provide it for less than two US dollars per person per year.

So how does the case study end? Well, sadly, in ignominy. There are many security professionals who will see a bit of their own story in this cautionary tale.

Even as the security team tasked to change this old and intractable corporate culture had actually gained traction, and was succeeding in raising the level of awareness and deepening core competencies throughout Entity X's global environment, its mandate shriveled up and blew away.

What's the moral of the story? When they bring you in and tell you they want you to "change corporate culture," ensure that you have executive backing to accomplish the task; discuss the measurable and milestone events that will define success or failure. The buzzwords are a dime-a-dozen and bantered about willy-nilly. Be specific. Do not take them at their word. Define their words. As you progress, do so incrementally. Do not get too far ahead of your executive sponsors. If they don't get it, they can't support it. Ensure the General Counsel is included in the circle of sponsors and has bought in at the outset. If he or she isn't included, or if he or she is small-minded or risk-averse, he may convince the executive sponsors that the greatest liability is in knowing, rather than in not knowing.

In this case, the individuals brought in to change the culture moved along to new jobs where executive leadership was serious about the need for a culture of security to be developed within their organizations.

The good news is that there are many engagements available. The bad news is that there are many corporations without leadership backing for a strong and fully integrated security regime and culture within their organizations. Table 8.1 is an example of an IP protection program assessment tool.

Table 8.1 IP Protection Program Assessment Tool–Awareness and Education

IP Protection Program Assessment Tool: Security Awareness and Education	Current Posture				
	100%	50%	0%	N/A	Remarks
Does your enterprise have a formal security awareness and education program?					
Does your enterprise's security awareness and education program provide content with messaging calibrated for different audiences within the enterprise, e.g., the workforce as a whole, executive leadership, sales and marketing, engineering, new hires, etc.?					
Does your enterprise's awareness and education program include a substantive briefing on security procedures, requirements and personal responsibilities in its new hire orientation process?					
Does your enterprise include copies of relevant security policies as part of their orientation package for new hire employees?					
Does your enterprise require new hire employees to sign a statement indicating that they have read the documentation, understand their security responsibilities, and will adhere to established policies and procedures?					

Continued

Table 8.1 Continued. IP Protection Program Assessment Tool–Awareness and Education

IP Protection Program Assessment Tool: Security Awareness and Education	Current Posture				
	100%	50%	0%	N/A	Remarks
Does your enterprise's security awareness and education program include a regular electronic newsletter (e.g., monthly or quarterly), which appears in the inboxes of all employees?					
Does your enterprise's security awareness and education program include at least one annual event (e.g. "Global Security Day"), which brings the workforce together, whether on a global, regional, or local scale, to underscore the importance of and personal responsibility for security?					
Does your enterprise's security awareness and education program include an e-learning course on the fundamentals of physical, personnel, travel, and information security for all employees?					
Does your enterprise's security awareness and education program include an intranet Web site to serve as a central resource for security-related information within your corporate culture?					
Does the budget for your enterprise's security awareness and education program include sufficient resources to produce compelling audio/video content (e.g., a 5-minute narrative film) on a regular basis (e.g., annually or bi-annually)?					

Continued

Table 8.1 Continued. IP Protection Program Assessment Tool–Awareness and Education

IP Protection Program Assessment Tool: Security Awareness and Education	Current Posture				
	100%	50%	0%	N/A	Remarks
Is there a security awareness/ education working group, which includes representatives from Human Resources, Information Technology and Security for all locales and regions, and is empowered to develop the program, address relevant issues, and drive adoption throughout the enterprise?					
Does executive management actively participate in delivering the security awareness and education message to underscore its importance to the enterprise?					
Does your enterprise's security awareness and education program have some methods and metrics for measuring its permeation of the corporate culture (e.g., inclusion in agendas of corporate meetings, percent of workforce which has undergone training, etc.) and the effectiveness of its messaging (e.g., workforce surveys, aggregate date from job performance reviews, etc.)?					

Chapter 9

Case Study: The Mysterious Social Engineering Attacks on Entity Y

Introduction

Social engineering, the practice of conning people into sharing sensitive information, be it in everyday person-to-person interaction, or via cyber interconnectivity, is a real security threat that has evolved in sophistication and broadened in scope over the decade we have been both writing about it and training people how to thwart it. Unfortunately, in most organizations, countermeasures against social engineering have not kept pace, and thus the adversaries to the enterprise continue to stretch their lead and put in danger the intellectual properties of those ill-prepared corporations.

Most organizations acknowledge it as a problem, but treat it as a nuisance rather than a very serious issue. Accordingly, most organizations do not invest any, let alone, enough in the one real countermeasure—effective and empowering security awareness and education for all employees as well as extra training for those in sensitive positions or positions of extreme trust (e.g., executives, executive assistants, human resources staff, and help desk personnel). We want to stress "effective" and "empowering," because as we noted in the previous chapter (*Case Study: A Bold New Approach to Awareness and Education, And How It Met An Ignoble Fate*), just having a program is not enough. To be effective it has to be compelling and show your employees, in meaningful ways, that they have a stake in security and that the enterprise security depends upon their efforts. It also has to empower these employees instead of simply scare them or leave them with the sensation that they are being talked down to by the "security people."

And as these three news stories on a scandal that erupted at Hewlett-Packard in the fall of 2006 illustrates, it is not only hackers or competitors, but also your organization's executives and investigators in their hire that have to be considered as potential risks if not direct threats, literally originating from the inside of the organization:

Investigators hired by Hewlett-Packard to find a media leak used sensitive information to access phone-company computers and get the calling records of nine reporters without authorization.... The revelations came a day after complaints by a former member of HP's board of directors forced the company to file a statement with the U.S. Securities and Exchange Commission (SEC), acknowledging that investigators hired by the board had fraudulently accessed the private telephone records of board members and reporters. The private investigators fraudulently used the identities of the victims to get the necessary login credentials to access online telephone records without authorization, according to media reports.... (HP-funded hacking included reporters' data, Security Focus, 9-8-06).

Not only did investigators impersonate board members, employees and journalists to obtain their phone records, but according to multiple reports, they also put an HP director and a reporter for CNet

Networks Inc under surveillance. They sent monitoring spyware in an e-mail to that reporter by concocting a phony story tip. They even snooped on the phone records of former CEO and Chairwoman Carly Fiorina, who had launched the quest to identify media sources in the first place. And in a twist that might seem preposterous if it happened in a movie, The New York Times reported that HP consultants considered hiring spies to pose as clerical or custodial workers at CNet and The Wall Street Journal. (Hewlett-Packard scandal gets wider and weirder, The Age, 9-21-06).

The news has once again highlighted a growing problem plaguing the telecommunications industry called "pretexting," a scam where unauthorized individuals pretend to be someone they're not to obtain personal information. Private investigators and con artists have been using this technique for years not just to obtain phone records, but also to get access to bank records, credit card information and other sensitive information. The telecommunications industry came under fire nine months ago when news reports pointed to Web sites where customer records could be openly purchased. The news prompted several phone companies, including Cingular Wireless, Sprint, T-Mobile and Verizon Wireless, to sue brokers selling customers' phone records.... (Security breaches are wake-up calls to phone companies, CNET News.com 9-11-06).

Fundamentals of Social Engineering Attacks

There are two types of social engineering: *technology-based deception* and *human-based deception*. In both cases, the perpetrator relies on the natural human tendency to trust, as the means by which they manipulate the individual into engaging in a demonstrable activity, which may otherwise not be in the normal course of events for that individual. The perpetrators are always well prepared, and engage in preliminary data collection to support their "engagement" with the individual whom they wish to manipulate into a desired action or actions.

Let's start with a classic example of human-based deception.

Throughout the 1990s—the formative years of the Internet and information security—hackers had taken on an almost mystical aura. To satisfy the appetite composed mostly of curiosity, which could easily evolve into fear, an important community event was the "Meet The Enemy." This event was a teleconference between hackers dialing in and an assembly of information security professionals on-site. In the years before Jeff Moss's Defcon and Black Hat conferences came to dominate the space, "Meet the Enemy," moderated by the great Ray Kaplan and hosted by the Computer Security Institute, offered the only public forum for real dialogue between the black hats and the white hats (and yes, the gray hats too).

On one legendary evening, one of the hackers who had called gave a live demonstration to substantiate his boasts about his social engineering prowess:

He dialed up a phone company, got transferred around, and reached the company's Help Desk.

Hacker: "Who's the supervisor on duty tonight?"

"Oh. It's Betty."

Hacker: "Let me talk to Betty." (He's transferred to Betty's extension)

Hacker: "Hey Betty, having a bad day?"

"No, why?"

Hacker: "Your systems are down."

"My systems aren't down, we're running fine."

Hacker: "All of my monitors here are showing that you are completely offline. Something is really wrong."

"We didn't even show a blip, we show no change."

Hacker: "Sign off again."

She did.

Hacker: "Betty, I am going to have to sign-on as you here to figure out what is happening with your ID. Let me have your user ID and password."

At this point, this senior supervisor at a Help Desk for a major telecommunications company told the hacker her user ID and password.

Hacker: "I'm signed on as you now and I can't see the difference. Shoot, I know what it is. Let me sign off. Now sign yourself back on again."

She did.

Hacker: "I know what it is. You're on day-old files. You think you're on-line but your not. You're on day-old files. Do me a favor, what changes all the time? The PIN code. Pull the PIN code file, just read me off the first ten PIN codes you've got there and I will compare them."

As she started to read off the first pin code, the hacker hung up on her.

Turning back, virtually to the audience of information security professionals, which included some stunned personnel from the telecommunications company he had just attacked, he bellowed out "I told you I could…"

Of course, human-based social engineering isn't just attempted over the telephone; it can be accomplished via e-mail, online chat, or any other communications medium. In the above example, the goal was obtaining a userid/password, pin codes, and other means to access an enterprise's infrastructure. Once in the infrastructure, recognized by the information systems as a trusted-insider, the enterprise's intellectual property is put at risk.

The many ways social engineering attacks have evolved over the years has been the development of technology-based approaches (e.g., using e-mail messages or Web sites that masquerade as some communications from or sites belonging to vendors, service providers, or clients known to your users).

In one illustrative case, Yahoo users received e-mails from an individual falsely identifying himself as a Yahoo employee. The e-mail informed the Yahoo users that they had won a fast modem from Yahoo. To receive their free gift, the recipients simply had to provide their name, address, telephone number, and credit card number, in order to cover the cost of shipping. Before Yahoo detected the con and sent out a bulletin to its users, numerous people had fallen for it. This was the earliest form of what is now known as "phishing."

Social engineering, whether human-based or technology-based, is used to gain user or administrator passwords to break into networks. It is also widely used to collect personal information for identity theft (e.g., "phishing") as well as for tricking users into clicking on booby-trapped e-mail attachments with malicious payloads (e.g., the "I Love You" worm).

How much identify theft could have been thwarted if even just the largest employers had instituted effective and empowering awareness and education programs that explain what social engineering is and how to thwart it for their work forces? How many hundreds of millions of dollars in fraud losses could have been avoided? How much anguish in people's personal lives? How much intellectual property that had been properly secured, would not have been unsecured and revealed.

But social engineering isn't just used by hackers to gain network access or fraudsters to commit identity theft.

It would be folly to simply focus your defensive efforts on thwarting the conversations that happen via technological communications mediums. Person-to-person interaction can be extraordinarily damaging. When an adversary obtains the userid/passwords they are perhaps able to gain entry to your enterprise, but they are oftentimes discovered shortly thereafter due to their lack of knowledge in moving about the infrastructure and inadvertently setting off alarms and alerts, which enables the enterprise to lockdown and inspect. But what of the adversary, who successfully obtains the userid/passwords and then sits on them, invests the time to then collect the necessary data to knowledgably transit the enterprise's infrastructure in an unalarming fashion.

This theorem begs the question, how? Through painstakingly observation and interaction with your employees, much can be accomplished without suborning an employee's loyalty to the enterprise. Some examples:

- Restaurants in proximity to the enterprise building: team meetings, after-work libations, visiting employees dining, all of which provide opportunity for the skillful to listen and learn. If it was only listening, when the artful adversary engages your employees in conversation, the elicitation begins. Scientists, engineers, and developers, individuals who are more skillful in their respective technology than in social discourse, are prime targets, as like most of the populace of the world they too are pleased when listened to and heard. The innocent employee guided through the conversation by a malevolent interlocutor can and unfortunately often will provide more information than they should.

- Monitoring of "roommate wanted" advertisements. In the initial minute of conversation the adversary can determine if the population of the abode with the vacancy comprises personnel from within the enterprise of interest. If yes, they pursue; if not they move on to the next advertisement. What happens with a "yes?" The adversary's cohabitation with the employee provides unlimited opportunity to view your employee's remote work habits and interactions. When the bond of trust is established, the conversations and comparisons of respective technologies can and will occur.

- Monitoring of the Public Relations announcements detailing wins, new technologies, new hires, and so forth, may provide the adversary with leads to individuals or simply locations where the adversary may be able to engage some elementary surveillance to determine where employees can be engaged.

These are just a few of the many avenues available to observe, elicit, and listen about how the enterprise operates and put together a more expansive brief, to enable the exploitation of the illicitly obtained userid/password.

The human-to-human aspect, unfortunately, doesn't end there. What of the employee who has been suborned? A willing and collaborative employee can boost, exponentially, the success ratio of the determined adversary in as much as they are on the other side of the technological barriers; they are knowledgeable of the infrastructure and the navigation procedures. Perhaps more importantly, once armed with the adversary's needs they can utilize their access to dig and sift through the various nooks and crannies of the enterprise.

In an earlier chapter, we spoke of how the individual is one of the nexus of the entrée to your enterprise, whether or not you wish to acknowledge such. We reiterate this point and emphasize this point, and urge you to involve yourself and empower your managers to involve themselves in investing and knowing in the work-life balance of your employee base, train in the art of listening and inquiry so as to better increase the odds that your employees know how to react and act when confronted with that unscrupulous adversary, offering inducements and attractive alternatives in the hopes of inducing them to break their trust with your enterprise.

Please realize that there are no shortages of unscrupulous organizations willing to break all the rules to gain competitive advantage over their competitors in the marketplace. And that motivation constitutes the greater threat, as both the Hewlett-Packard scandal and the following case study show.

The Mysterious Social Engineering Attacks on Entity Y

Someone called an office in a major northern European city, assuming the identity of an actual employee of Entity Y, and tried to elicit employee contact list information for an office in another northern European city. But the request was turned down.

NOTE

As we wrote about Entity X, just consider "Entity Y" an appellation ascribed to an aggregate of enlightening events and insightful experiences gained in our work with some of the global giants. And remember, as in the disclaimer often stated at the beginning of novels or movies, any resemblance to any actual person or organization is purely coincidental.

Several days later, a caller, using the same false identity, obtained the coveted contact list from an Entity Y office in Eastern Europe, from an employee who believed they were speaking to the identified employee.

A month later, an unsuccessful attempt is made to elicit client lists from an Entity Y employee in the Western USA.

Three days later, impersonating an employee from the UK and claiming a laptop malfunction, someone called an Entity Y office in Canada and requested complete contact information for the same Northern European office targeted in the initial attack.

The caller claimed to be working on an engagement with an actual client of Entity Y and requested that the information he needed be e-mailed to a private e-mail account. One of the first tangible clues.

The next day, someone impersonating an Entity Y employee from the UK called an Entity Y office on the Mediterranean. He claimed his laptop was malfunctioning and requested complete contact information for same Northern European office as well as one other in the Northern European region.

Two days later, in the Balkans, a second Entity Y employee succumbs to the elicitation and provides the caller with an Excel spreadsheet with the requested information. Again, from an employee who believed they were speaking to a colleague.

The next day, the attacker calls back and requests further information. But this second solicitation is rebuffed, as the employee has reflected on the totality of the provision of the spreadsheet.

The next day, someone, again impersonating an Entity Y employee, called the Northern European office directly, saying she was on assignment in Central Europe and requested the client list. The request was refused.

The next day, an Andean office received a telephone request for information on personnel in an office in a major North American city. This elicitation was successful.

In the ensuing weeks, similar calls eliciting confidential information were received in numerous Entity Y offices in Africa, the Balkans, the Baltic, North America, and Asia Pacific. There were over 30 documented incidents, targeting dozens of offices on six continents. Several of them were successful. All of the callers impersonated Entity Y employees, all of the callers claimed their laptops were malfunctioning, and all of the callers sought specific, targeted information about various groups and individuals within Entity Y and its clients.

Who were the attackers? What were they really looking for? What was their ultimate objective?

The counterintelligence component of Entity Y's global security team launched an investigation. The investigation showed that the adversary targeting Entity Y on a global basis, had done their homework and covered their trails. The telephone numbers used to call into Entity Y were non-traceable. The e-mail addresses provided, ostensibly as a personal e-mail address of a colleague, were found to be throw-away Web-based e-mail accounts. The callers were both male and female, with South African and/or British accents.

The investigation did not identify the adversary and the leads developed were insufficient to warrant and justify bringing in law enforcement entities, as all that Entity Y really had were individuals calling into their enterprise, identifying themselves as an employee, and requesting the provision of information. What would law enforcement suggest? Perhaps, make Entity Y personnel more aware of elicitation and manipulation techniques that come at Entity Y via the telephone.

So let us focus on the countermeasures that the global security team recommended be undertaken.

Bulletins were sent out only to human resources personnel in the initial stages of the investigation but then later on, when there was no longer any reason to remain discrete, the bulletins were sent to all employees, thus ensuring 100 percent of the workforce were cognizant of the activity being experienced elsewhere in the enterprise and were thus on their guard.

The bulletins were to be disseminated to all personnel via e-mail and posted on all Entity Y intranets in a high-visibility spot.

A letter from the Global HR Director was proposed. This letter was to be issued simultaneously, providing context, pointing to the bulletins and the linked instructions. This letter was to underscore the importance of following the security team's admonishments. Like the bulletins, the letter was to be disseminated to all personnel via e-mail and also be posted on all Entity Y intranets in a high-visibility spot.

Regional conference calls with HR managers were to be held by the responsible HR leaders, in coordination with the global security team. The global security team was to provide presentation materials, brief the conference call participants on the nature of the elicitation attacks, explain the proper procedures for dealing with such encounters, answer questions, and discuss related issues.

The ongoing attacks underscored the importance of all offices adopting the available awareness and education resources (e.g., an e-learning module, an electronic newsletter, a new hire orientation presentation, annual on-site events), since these resources provided guidance, suitable for general audiences, on how to deal with such attacks.

The global security team also vowed that the next generation of awareness and education resources would include a workshop for human resources and Help desk personnel, as well as executive support staff, which would go into elicitation attacks and countermeasures in greater depth.

Guidance for the Workforce

The following instructions were developed by Entity Y's global security team:

How to Recognize Elicitation

Here are some common elements in recent incidents:

- The callers have identified themselves as Entity Y employees. The names they use are real employees. Sometimes these employees are out of the office on holiday or client work, but sometimes they are not.

- The caller usually claims to be working on a client project, and the client they name is actually an Entity Y client.

- The caller asks for a listing of Entity Y employees in either a particular office or a particular business line. The caller will make an excuse as to why they cannot get the information, usually that he or she is in an airport and is having computer problems.

- The caller will ask that someone e-mail the list to him at both a valid internal Entity Y address and an external Web-based company like operamail.com.

- The callers have all been male, with a British or South African accent.

- Any time you are faced with a caller, usually without a valid caller ID, who asks for internal information of any kind, you should be suspicious of elicitation.

How to Handle the Caller

Here are some instructions on how to handle suspicious callers:

- Do not give the caller what he asks for.

- Do not give the caller any indication that you know what is happening.

- Be evasive about how and when you can provide the information. Make an excuse for not providing the information immediately (e.g., "I have to get onto another call right now – you know how it is").

- Be friendly and open, as if nothing is amiss. Imply that the information will be forthcoming.

- Ask for return voice contact information. Ask for the caller's mobile number and his point of contact at the client. If the caller will not provide this information, it confirms that he is attempting to elicit information from you. If he provides the information, it does not mean he is not making an elicitation attempt.

How to Report the Incident

Here are some instructions on how to report suspicious callers:

- Immediately report the incident to your regional HR director and the global security team.

When reporting the incident, please provide the following information:

- The time and date of the call.

- The specific information the caller requested.

- Any background noises you may have heard.

- A description of the caller's voice.

- Any information the caller gives; employee name, client, phone numbers, and so forth.

Perhaps you find it hard to believe that your co-workers, friends, or family members could fall for such cons. But social engineering is very effective. The psychological techniques are powerful and technologies are getting increasingly sophisticated.

NOTE

See Appendix F, which contains the U.S. Department of Justice questionnaire that may be used to report a loss of intellectual property within the United States.

General User-Oriented Guidance on How to Detect and Defeat Social Engineering

Here is a more generalized checklist developed to provide personnel with some ways to detect and defeat social engineering attacks:

- Be alert for the telltale signs of a social engineering attack. Is the caller reluctant to provide contact information? Is the caller rushing you to provide the information they have requested? Is the caller name-dropping (i.e., using names of important people or even family members)? Is the caller trying to manipulate your emotions (e.g., fear, sympathy, ambition)? Has the caller made any small mistakes (e.g., misspellings, misnomers)?

- Remember, an individual using the telephone as the instrument of engagement and social engineering methodology is always going to be playing on your emotions: The attacker might play on your fear, by using intimidation; or conversely the attacker might play on your desire to help others, by appealing to your sympathy, or even on your ambition, your desire to get ahead, by impressing an important caller.

■ Verify the identity of callers. If you are suspicious and you cannot immediately identify them, insist on calling them back. If it is a legitimate call about security or some other sensitive issue, they will understand and appreciate your caution.

■ Do not answer unexpected or unusual requests for sensitive information unless you can verify the caller and the caller's legitimate need. Don't answer questions about other employees, particularly IT personnel, unless you can verify it is an authorized request. Do not provide information on your system or your own level of access (e.g., ID and password). Do not answer "questionnaires" or provide business information such as sales figures, marketing plans, and so forth, unless you can verify it is an authorized request.

■ Don't just shrug it off, sound the alarm. Report any suspicious encounters that you suspect may indeed be social engineering attacks immediately to the appropriate authorities within your office or to the security office It may be part of a pattern, but a pattern cannot be discerned without the sharing of experiences.

Chapter 10

Personnel Security

Introduction

As the Haephrati case discussed in Chapter 1 illustrates, the theft of trade secrets and other intellectual property has expanded beyond classic industrial age espionage (largely focused on the turning of insiders) to include information age espionage (e.g., hacking into networks or using targeted malware). And it is also true, as has been previously noted, that the severity of the insider threat is often disproportionately emphasized in relation to the severity of the outsider threat.

Nevertheless, much illegal activity, particularly in the arenas of economic espionage and trade secret theft, is still predicated on, or instigated by, insiders of one kind or another. Furthermore, this is true regardless of whether the criminal behavior is cyber-based or grounded in the physical world.

Four stories from the United States, Korea, and Canada (all of which broke within a period of several weeks in 2006) underscore both the threat from inside, and its diverse manifestations:

> "The U.S. attorney in Detroit…announced charges of stealing trade secrets against three former employees of an auto supplier, saying economic espionage stabs at the heart of the Michigan economy and is a growing priority among his federal prosecutors. The former employees of Metaldyne Corp., arraigned in U.S. District Court after a 64-count grand jury indictment was unsealed, are accused of stealing the Plymouth, Mich., company's trade secrets and sharing them with Chinese competitors. They each face up to 20 years in prison and fines of up to $250,000 if convicted. Metaldyne, which has 45 plants in 14 countries, makes a wide range of auto parts for engines, drive trains and chassis systems. The company has annual sales of $2 billion and about 6,500 employees." (Trade-secret theft charged in Detroit, *Baltimore Sun,* 7-6-06)

> "US authorities last night charged three people with a cloak-and-dagger scheme to sell secrets from Coca-Cola to soft drink arch-rival PepsiCo, which helped in the investigation…. The offer of 'confidential' information from Coca-Cola sparked an FBI investigation with an undercover agent offering $US1.5 million dollars in cash. The investigation was launched after PepsiCo turned over to its cola rival a letter in May from a person identifying himself as 'Dirk,' who claimed to be employed at a high level with Coca-Cola and offered 'very detailed and confidential information,' a US Justice Department statement said. According to authorities, an FBI

undercover agent met on June 16 with Dimson, who was posing as 'Dirk' at Hartsfield-Jackson International Airport in Atlanta. Dimson gave the agent 'a brown Armani Exchange bag containing one manila envelope with documents marked 'highly confidential' and one glass bottle with a white label containing a liquid product sample,' the statement said." (FBI lays charges on Coke secrets, *The Australian*, 7-6-06)

"About a half of Korea's top technology firms have suffered from leaks in industrial know-how one way or another over the past three years, although the companies have increased preventive measures, a report showed. According to the report released the Korea Industrial Technology Association on Monday, 11 of 20 Korean firms that had invested the most in research & development have suffered financial damage due to technology leaks in the past three years. When taking into account smaller firms, 20.9 percent out of 459 firms said that they suffered from industrial espionage cases during the period. The rate is 6.4 percentage points higher than three years ago, meaning that firms have become more vulnerable to technology theft.... As Roh pointed out, about 65 percent of the reported cases were found to involve employees from former companies. Only 18 percent and 16 percent of the cases involved current employees and subcontractors of the firms, respectively... The survey was done on 459 firms with in-house R&D departments." (Cho Jin-seo, Half of Top Tech Firms Suffer Leaks, *Korea Times*, 6-19-06)

"Intelligence files reportedly suggest that an estimated 1,000 Chinese agents and informants operate in Canada. Many of them are visiting students, scientists and business people, told to steal cutting-edge technology. An example being touted as copied technology is China's Redberry—an imitation of the Blackberry portable e-mail device, created by Waterloo, Ont.-based Research in Motion Ltd.... Juneau-Katsuya said the former Liberal government knew of the espionage, but were too afraid to act. 'We didn't want to piss off or annoy the Chinese,' said Juneau-Katsuya, who headed the agency's Asian desk. '(They're) too much of an important market.' However, he argued that industrial espionage affects Canada's employment levels. 'For every $1 million that we lose in intellectual property or business, we lose about 1,000 jobs in Canada,' he said." (Robert Fife, Government "concerned" about Chinese espionage, CTV.ca News, 4-14-06)

Without a robust, twenty-first century Personnel Security program, it won't matter how much or how well you invest in Information Security, or how fool-proof and high-tech your Physical Security has become, because the perpetrators that will take advantage of your weak or nonexisting Personnel Security program will already be inside both your physical and cyber perimeters.

In this chapter, we will highlight some of the most important aspects of what should be in your enterprise's Personnel Security program, including an overall checklist of the top 20 controls mapped to ISO, and guidelines for background checks (Figure 10.1 illustrates the "hit ratio"—the information discrepancies uncovered during background screening), data, termination procedures, and a travel security program.

Figure 10.1 Background Checks Reveal Vital Insights That Offer a Subtle Return on Investment—They Mitigate Risk and Limit Losses

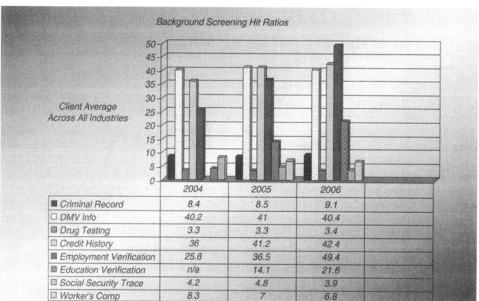

Background Screening Hit Ratios

Client Average Across All Industries

	2004	2005	2006
■ Criminal Record	8.4	8.5	9.1
□ DMV Info	40.2	41	40.4
▨ Drug Testing	3.3	3.3	3.4
□ Credit History	36	41.2	42.4
■ Employment Verification	25.8	36.5	49.4
▨ Education Verification	n/a	14.1	21.6
□ Social Security Trace	4.2	4.8	3.9
□ Worker's Comp	8.3	7	6.8

Source: Aggregate from Kroll Press Release, 2005–2007

Coming and Going: Guidelines for Background Checks and Termination Procedures

Table 10.1 assesses an enterprise's use of background checks as part of an IP Protection Program Assessment Tool for personnel security.

Table 10.1 IP Protection Program Assessment Tool: Personnel Security—Background Check

IP Protection Program Assessment Tool: Personnel Security—Background Check	Current Posture				
	100%	50%	0%	N/A	Remarks
Does your enterprise perform background checks on all potential new hires prior to making an offer, or alternately make all offers contingent upon positive results from a subsequent background check?					
Do your enterprise's background checks include of the following elements (provided they are permitted under local law)?					
■ Validate employment record for previous ten years or two most recent jobs, including dates, positions held, salary, and performance					
■ Validate education, including degrees and performance					
■ Conduct a criminal records search for any convictions or pending convictions					

Continued

Table 10.1 Continued. IP Protection Program Assessment Tool: Personnel Security—Background Check

IP Protection Program Assessment Tool: Personnel Security—Background Check	Current Posture				
	100%	50%	0%	N/A	Remarks
■ Verify identify, i.e., ID card, social security number, passport, or equivalent documentation					
■ Verify work permits (if applicable)					
■ Consult business references (minimum of three)					
■ Search any possible regulatory agency sanctions					
■ Evaluate possible conflicts of interest					
Do your enterprise's background checks for leadership positions (e.g., senior manager, director, vice president, etc.) require additional inquiries, including but not limited to the following elements?					
■ Verify any professional certifications, licenses and current status (if applicable); identify any disciplinary actions					
■ Conduct search for any relevant civil litigation, and whether or not any liens or judgments have been issued against the candidate					

Continued

Table 10.1 Continued. IP Protection Program Assessment Tool: Personnel Security—Background Check

IP Protection Program Assessment Tool: Personnel Security—Background Check	Current Posture				
	100%	50%	0%	N/A	Remarks
■ Conduct search for any negative media coverage generated					
■ Review credit history					
Does your enterprise identify sensitive positions that should also require additional background investigations, similar to those conducted for leadership positions; e.g., positions in which there is increased opportunity to commit fraud, in which the exposure to information about executives or future initiatives could be exploited in blackmail or industrial espionage, or in which mission critical systems are administered?					
Does your enterprise require third-party contracting firms to establish proof that they have conducted adequate background checks (i.e., consistent with the enterprise's own) on all potential contract workers prior to their assignment?					
Does your enterprise's body of policies and procedures declare that any false statements, misrepresentation, or omission of fact in regard to education, employment history, etc., or any other relevant information of a discrediting nature, will result in					

Continued

Table 10.1 Continued. IP Protection Program Assessment Tool: Personnel Security—Background Check

IP Protection Program Assessment Tool: Personnel Security—Background Check	Current Posture				
	100%	50%	0%	N/A	Remarks
either a retraction of the job offer if the person is a potential new hire, or termination if the person is already an employee (no matter when it is revealed)?					
Does your enterprise conduct background checks on all potential new hires regardless of any of the following considerations? ■ Permanent or temporary					
■ Full-time or part-time					
■ Student or experienced worker					
■ Professional or nonprofessional					
■ Role					
■ Grade					

Well, if you are successful in the implementation of the background investigation guidelines, perhaps you won't have much need for the termination guidelines, but we would suggest you apply them every bit as assiduously whenever you are terminating an employee (see Table 10.2).

Table 10.2 IP Protection Program Assessment Tool:
Personnel Security—Termination

IP Protection Program Assessment Tool: Personnel Security— Termination	Current Posture				
	100%	50%	0%	N/A	Remarks
Do your enterprise's personnel security policies and procedures concerning termination require that those responsible for network and systems access receive immediate notification if a potentially hostile employee has been, or preferably, is going to be terminated?					
Under such circumstances, do those responsible for network and systems access immediately take action to remove the employee's access to the enterprise's network computing environment and communi-cations resources, including e-mail, voice-mail, dial-in, etc.?					
Do your enterprise's personnel security policies and procedures require the immediate notification of any third parties who might be involved in work with the terminated employee, particularly if the terminated employee had authority to instruct					

Continued

Table 10.2 Continued. IP Protection Program Assessment Tool: Personnel Security—Termination

IP Protection Program Assessment Tool: Personnel Security—Termination	Current Posture				
	100%	50%	0%	N/A	Remarks
contractors or other third-party workers, or to sign contracts or conduct transactions?					
Do your enterprise's personnel security policies and procedures require that terminated employees who might act in a hostile manner and hold positions of responsibility for information systems controls should be immediately relieved of their job responsibilities, return all enterprise-issued equipment and information at the time of termination, and be escorted at all times until they have exited the facilities?					
Do your enterprise's personnel security policies and procedures require that terminated employees who might act in a hostile manner and hold positions of responsibility for information systems controls should be immediately relieved of their job responsibilities, return all enterprise-issued equipment and information at the					

Continued

Table 10.2 Continued. IP Protection Program Assessment Tool: Personnel Security—Termination

IP Protection Program Assessment Tool: Personnel Security— Termination	Current Posture				
	100%	50%	0%	N/A	Remarks
time of termination, and be escorted at all times until they have exited the facilities?					
Do your enterprise's personnel security policies and procedures require that terminations of employees who might react in a hostile manner should be conducted in the presence of security, human resources, or other authorized personnel, and that the terminated employees should immedi- ately pack their personal belongings in the presence of this individual and should be escorted out the door?					
Do your enterprise's personnel security policies and procedures require that terminated employees be denied access to enterprise facilities unless their entry is authorized by appropriate authority, and even then, that they should be escorted at all times while they are on the premises?					

Continued

Table 10.2 Continued. IP Protection Program Assessment Tool:
Personnel Security—Termination

IP Protection Program Assessment Tool: Personnel Security—Termination	Current Posture				
	100%	50%	0%	N/A	Remarks
Do your enterprise's personnel security policies and procedures prohibit terminated employees from retaining possession of, passing on to others, or removing from the premises, any proprietary information other than his or her own personal copies of public information and any correspondence related specifically to terms and conditions of employment?					
Do your enterprise's personnel security policies and procedures require that all other information be turned over to his or her immediate supervisor, or to security personnel, before exiting the facility?					
Do your enterprise's personnel security policies and procedures require that terminated employees return all the enterprise's property and information (e.g., laptops, handheld devices, VPN tokens, library books, documentation, files, papers, disks, tapes, building keys, access cards,					

Continued

Table 10.2 Continued. IP Protection Program Assessment Tool: Personnel Security—Termination

IP Protection Program Assessment Tool: Personnel Security— Termination	Current Posture				
	100%	**50%**	**0%**	**N/A**	**Remarks**
employee ID, etc.) in his or her possession at the time of termination?					
Do your enterprise's personnel security policies and procedures require that facilities and information technology personnel should review asset inventories and access control lists to make certain that all property assigned to the terminated employee is accounted for and all access has been revoked?					
Do your enterprise's personnel security policies and procedures require the return of all third-party (e.g., client or vendor) property or information (e.g., laptops, handheld devices, VPN tokens, library books, documentation, files, papers, disks, tapes, building keys, access cards, employee ID, etc) at the time of termination?					
Do your enterprise's personnel security policies and procedures require that all systems and					

Continued

Table 10.2 Continued. IP Protection Program Assessment Tool:
Personnel Security—Termination

IP Protection Program Assessment Tool: Personnel Security— Termination	Current Posture				
	100%	50%	0%	N/A	Remarks
network administrators change all common system passwords known to the terminated employee immediately?					
Do your enterprise's personnel security policies and procedures require that managers immediately review and document the content of the terminated employee's electronic and paper files to determine who should take on responsibility for the information and decide what should be saved and what should be erased or destroyed?					
Do your enterprise's personnel security policies and procedures require that information technology personnel erase all the terminated employees' files after a reasonable waiting period (e.g., four weeks) after termination, except for either those files that have been turned over to the next person to assume the job responsibility or					

Continued

Table 10.2 Continued. IP Protection Program Assessment Tool: Personnel Security—Termination

IP Protection Program Assessment Tool: Personnel Security—Termination	Current Posture				
	100%	**50%**	**0%**	**N/A**	**Remarks**
any other information that might be used in any future litigation?					
Do your enterprise's personnel security policies and procedures require that if the terminated employee was a system or network administrator, or otherwise could create or revoke access to compu-ting resources, then an audit should be conducted to make certain that the terminated employee did not create any hidden or disguised accounts and/or backdoors?					
Do your enterprise's personnel security policies and procedures require that if the terminated employee had reason to use system passwords or other forms of access for a third party's systems, then the third party (e.g., client, partner, vendor, consultant) should be informed immediately that those passwords, or other forms of access, are revoked?					

Two Important Caveats

- Of course, in regard to many of these recommended termination policies and procedures, there will exceptions. But they too must be subject to procedures, and require high-level authorization. Furthermore, not all employment ends in hostile termination, many separations are amicable, and there are some that are orderly, expected, and even scheduled. Nevertheless, the issues surrounding how a person leaves employment are just as important as the issues surrounding how they are brought into the enterprise's workforce.

- Whether or not to accelerate an employee's separation from the enterprise when the employee has given notice is a subject of some debate. If the employee is going to a competitor's organization, it is considered "safer" to place the employee on administrative leave for a period of two weeks when accepting the resignation rather than have the person remain inside the enterprise's perimeter. The rationale is that there is powerful temptation to pocket data points, which although obtained and garnered with the resources of the current employer, would be of great interest to the "new employer." Indeed, unscrupulous employers may intimate to the new hire that success may be dependent upon the provision of your enterprise's intellectual property. We suggest that it is always best to be mindful of whom your competition is, and make all such decisions judiciously.

And Everywhere in between: Guidelines for Travel Security and Executive Protection Programs

No aspect of a comprehensive enterprise security program offers a more compelling argument for a holistic approach than issues related to travel security and executive protection (see Table 10.3).

The threat spectrum into which the business traveler in general, and the executive business traveler in particular, encompasses all dimensions of your enterprise—cyber, physical, and psychological—and calls upon all of your security and intelligence resources.

Unless your people are adequately equipped and properly trained, the laptops, cell phones, PDAs, and flash sticks your road warriors carrying with them are brimming with both access and proprietary information; their attaché cases are stuffed with a hard copy of a confidential, and yes, sometimes even sensitive nature; the hotel rooms they leave behind when they go downstairs for dinner are like an open door into the inner sanctum of your enterprise; and every person they encounter whether in transit, social settings, or business situations could best them in the game of wits and wiles (i.e., social engineering).

Table 10.3 IP Protection Program Assessment Tool: Personnel Security—Travel

IP Protection Program Assessment Tool: Personnel Security—Travel	Current Posture				
	100%	**50%**	**0%**	**N/A**	**Remarks**
Does your enterprise have a formal travel security program?					
Does this travel security program include developing and maintaining a list of countries that may pose "high risk" or "extreme risk" to those employees or executives who travel or work outside their country of origin?					
Does your enterprise's travel security program require this list of "high risk" and "extreme risk" countries to be communicated to the executive team, as well as to any travel agencies working with your enterprise and all personnel who might be called on to travel outside their country of origin?					
Does your enterprise's travel security program identify personnel who work in					

Continued

Table 10.3 Continued. IP Protection Program Assessment Tool:
Personnel Security—Travel

IP Protection Program Assessment Tool: Personnel Security—Travel	Current Posture				
	100%	50%	0%	N/A	Remarks
"high risk" or "extreme risk" countries as "ex-patriots" (e.g., by Human Resource records)?					
Does your enterprise's travel security program identify personnel who are planning to undertake travel to "high risk" or "extreme risk" countries (e.g., by online software applications, such as Travel Locator)?					
Are there established procedures for monitoring the status of personnel who are working in or traveling to "high risk" or "extreme risk" countries?					
Are there established security protocols and procedures for travel to high risk and extreme risk destinations that articulate requirements and responsibilities concerning monitoring travel, communications during travel, exceptions, evacuations, and travel restrictions or bans?					
Does your enterprise's security awareness and education program include training and content on travel security?					

Continued

Table 10.3 Continued. IP Protection Program Assessment Tool:
Personnel Security—Travel

IP Protection Program Assessment Tool: Personnel Security—Travel	Current Posture				
	100%	50%	0%	N/A	Remarks
Does your enterprise's travel security training offer content calibrated to different levels of precaution; e.g., general business travel, travel to "high risk" destinations, and travel to "extreme risk" destinations?					
Does your enterprise have an executive protection program?					
Does your enterprise's executive protection program require threat assessments for countries or regions that executive leadership is planning to visit, including the following elements?					
■ War					
■ Terrorism					
■ Health emergencies					
■ Crime					
■ Civil unrest					
■ Natural disasters					
■ Environmental conditions					
■ Security posture of those entities to be visited					
■ Capability of local law enforcement and medical facilities					

Continued

Table 10.3 Continued. IP Protection Program Assessment Tool:
Personnel Security—Travel

IP Protection Program Assessment Tool: Personnel Security—Travel	Current Posture				
	100%	50%	0%	N/A	Remarks
Does your enterprise's executive protection program require visit security coordination, including the following elements?					
■ Gather contact information, guest lists, itineraries, and schedules					
■ Inspect areas to be visited					
■ Review logistical arrangements, including airport arrival, transportation, travel routes, hotel selection, and emergency services					
■ Consult crisis management plans for hotels, client site, or other venues be visited					
■ Establish contingency plans in the event of an emergency or other security situation					
■ Engage third-party security professionals to supplement enterprise executive protection if warranted					

Continued

Table 10.3 Continued. IP Protection Program Assessment Tool: Personnel Security—Travel

IP Protection Program Assessment Tool: Personnel Security—Travel	Current Posture				
	100%	50%	0%	N/A	Remarks
▪ Provide executive with secure locations to private telephone calls					
▪ Secure executive briefing materials throughout meetings, and destroy confidential documents following the meeting					
▪ Prohibit recording devices in executive meeting rooms					
▪ Control access to meeting areas to invited personnel only					
▪ Provide specialized electronic counter-measures to prevent electronic eaves-dropping as required					
Does your enterprise limit the numbers of executives allowed to travel on the same aircraft whenever practical?					

Chapter 11

Physical Security:
The "Duh" Factor

Introduction

If you have ever debriefed a hacker, or an industrial spy, or even a penetration tester working for the good guys, you will know that the first attempt any of them make is to simply walk through a door, whether at the front or the back of the facility. Well, perhaps they will dumpster dive prior to the direct assault. But certainly, an attacker, whether intent on breaking into your information systems, stealing your trade secrets, or demonstrating how easy it is to do either, will always probe your physical perimeter before either going cyber (e.g., gaining unauthorized network access or planting a Trojan to collect data) or even psychological (i.e., using social engineering techniques).

That's why we call physical security the "Duh" Factor. It is so easy to overlook or take for granted. And when you do, you invariably get burned. That's when people slap their foreheads and cry out, "Duh!"

Are You Owned?

How the Pros Do It

When we asked an industrial security penetration tester what his approach would be to conducting a penetration test specifically targeting intellectual property and trade secrets, one consultant responded:

"I would physically target hardware, laptops, servers, and backup media … and simply clone them en masse. I have done this countless times during "pen testing" where I simply sneak into the area, clone every computer of interest, and haul all of it off site. In other cases I simply grab the computer, and clean out everything that even remotely looked like a USB drive, external HD, CD, DVD, and ANYTHING that could even remotely contain confidential information. Sometimes the actual removal of the computer is desirable, but sometimes it is better to copy all the drives. Then consolidate all of the information onto a single drive farm, and index all of the files into a searchable data source. Yeah, I can get some of the same data by technically penetrating the computer, or owning their network, but it is much more reliable to enter the area, grab the computers, open the HDD bay and clone the drive. Extra points if you remove the HDD and leave your business card taped to the HD bay, or attached to LCD screen. I have also copied the drive (which I removed), and then hammered a steel dagger through the LCD screen or keyboard with a notice that I just cleaned them out. (I get a damage budget of maybe 50k for the gig so I can break stuff) After hours I go to the outside of every executives offices (using a ladder if required) and try to read sensitive information which they may have left out on their desk, and use a camera to read documents they have left in view.

Hit the recycling bins in the executive area, harvest documents out of shedder or recycling boxes. Visit the server closet, remove or copy the hard drives from servers. Visit alarm controller, remove it, or at least steal the computer connected to it. Ditto for the access control computers and video surveillance systems. Clean out all tapes, backups, off line storage, or other media. Locate breakers for computer room/server room and the executive areas, remove the circuit breaker for their specific areas, leave your card. Remove doors from executives' offices, unscrew from wall, and remove their chairs so that they have to stand up for a few hours. Remove all file cabinets… completely from the building…. Remove telephone headsets, leave the phone themselves. Extra points if your remove everything from the targeted offices, to include the doors, carpet, ceiling tiles, and install a milk crate and folding card table instead of their fancy desk. Leave their personal items on the desk, or place all personal items in a box in the center of the now stripped office. On top of the box leave an envelope, and in the enveloped leave them a letter that you just owned them, and that they need to get more serious about security.

I would (and have) provided the over 800 hard drives of extremely sensitive and classified information that they never knew they lost. I also try to weigh in with roughly 4,000 pounds of actual documents that I can pile up on a wall of the presentation room. I've actually rented semi-trucks to haul out the company, have grabbed entire mainframe computers, gutting complete server rooms, etc. Hit a defense contractor a couple of years ago, came across several huge caches inside the company (lots of classified documents), found that one of the executives/directors was stealing documents from one of their competitors, putting the CEO in a delicate position as he did the ethical thing and returned the stolen documents, and then offered up the head of the executive behind the thefts to the competition."

Nor is physical security merely a "Guards, Guns, and Gates" mentality that sees to the strength of the physical perimeter. In the twenty-first century, it should extend to concerns about your road warrior's mobile office, as well as conditions at the facilities of your contractors and outsourcers, and even the circumstances of any of your enterprise's storage media while in transit.

Are You Owned?

Two All-Too-Typical Tales of Woe

United Parcel Service Inc. (UPS) has confirmed that the financial data of nearly 4 million Citigroup Inc. customers has been lost…According to local media reports, Citigroup says UPS cannot account for computer tapes containing personal information—including names, Social Security numbers, account numbers and payment history—of 3.9 million of its CitiFinancial customers, including information from closed accounts. UPS was transporting the tapes to a credit bureau when they were lost, according to the report…Citigroup says it will now encrypt financial data and send it electronically. (*Secure Destruction Business On-Line*, 6-7-05)

Users of the Bank of America Corp.'s Visa Buxx prepaid debit cards are being warned that they may have had sensitive information compromised following the theft of an unencrypted laptop computer. In a letter sent to Buxx users and dated September 23, the Charlotte, North Carolina, bank warned that customers may have had their bank account numbers, routing transit numbers, names and credit card numbers compromised by the theft. Visa Buxx is a prepaid credit card for teenagers that the Bank of America (BofA) stopped selling in January. The laptop, which belonged to an unnamed Bank of America "service provider" was stolen on August 29, said Diane Wagner, a BofA spokeswoman. The bank was notified of the theft on September 9, and began sending out the letters after a two-week investigation, she said. Though the information on the laptop would not have been easily accessible to thieves, it was not encrypted, Wagner said. She would not name the service provider, say how many BofA customers had been affected or even confirm that the theft had occurred within the U.S…This is not the first time BofA has had to notify account holders of identity theft. In March, it confirmed that information on about 60,000 of its customers had been stolen by an identity-theft ring. The March disclosure came just a month after BofA revealed that it had lost digital tapes containing the credit card account records of 1.2 million U.S. federal employees. (*IDG*, 10-7-05)

Such twenty-first century physical security issues underscore the need for a holistic approach.

Mitigating the physical security vulnerabilities introduced by the road warrior's mobile office is dependent largely on awareness and education; e.g., you can supply your business travelers with laptop cable locks, but getting them to use them both consistently and cleverly is a very different challenge.

Seeing to the security posture of contractors and outsourcers demands that your enterprise has made a meaningful, organizational commitment to an intellectual property protection program and that no agreements will be signed without assurances that the security programs of contractors and outsourcers is adequate, and that processes for verification and review have been established.

The physical security of storage media, e.g., tapes and disks, in transit via third-party shipping companies, and so forth can only be adequately addressed by implementing a cyber security control, i.e., encryption. Table 11.1 is an IP protection program assessment for physical security.

Table 11.1 IP Protection Program Assessment—Physical Security

IP Protection Program Assessment Tool: Physical Security	Current Posture				
	100%	50%	0%	N/A	Remarks
Does your enterprise conduct comprehensive threat assessments, on an annual basis, for all facilities in order to identify and prioritize risks?					
Do your enterprise's local security managers, or those otherwise responsible for security at the local level, regularly interface with embassy or consulate, local law enforcement, and your enterprise's own global security team on a regular basis to review vis-à-vis threats or other developments that would impact security?					

Continued

Table 11.1 Continued. IP Protection Program Assessment—Physical Security

IP Protection Program Assessment Tool: Physical Security	Current Posture				
	100%	50%	0%	N/A	Remarks
Does your global and/or local security team liaison with other security teams of other companies with interests or facilities in the area concerning risks that confront both of your organizations?					
If you rent the space for your facilities, do you engage in regular contact with building management and as well as your fellow tenants concerning risks that confront all of you?					
Do your assessments factor in recent crimes and other security-related incidents, which have occurred either to your local facilities or its neighbors or surroundings?					
Have you conducted a security survey of all your enterprise's facilities to evaluate your overall security posture, including security physical and personnel security controls, information security controls, incident response, business continuity, and crisis management contingencies, etc.?					
Does your enterprise conduct such surveys annually?					
Does your enterprise maintain a record of all security incidents at all facilities, and review this record on an ongoing and regular basis both to monitor the progress of individual investigations and to look for emerging patterns, possible links, or developing trends?					

Continued

Table 11.1 Continued. IP Protection Program Assessment—Physical Security

IP Protection Program Assessment Tool: Physical Security	Current Posture				
	100%	50%	0%	N/A	Remarks
Have you identified which, if any, of your facilities are located in areas that are considered highly vulnerable to either natural risks (e.g., earthquakes or typhoons) or risks related to human activity (e.g., violent crime or terrorist attacks)?					
Have additional security controls and contingency plans been implemented for any or all facilities located in such high-risk areas?					
If your enterprise has facilities located in such high-risk areas, has the executive team considered relocating them in less risky environments?					
Do all your enterprise's facilities have security plans that address their unique circumstances?					
Are the security plans for these facilities updated annually?					
Do your facilities have dedicated personnel (e.g., receptionists and/ or telephone operators) who process all visitors and respond to calls coming into the enterprise's general telephone number?					

Continued

Table 11.1 Continued. IP Protection Program Assessment—Physical Security

IP Protection Program Assessment Tool: Physical Security	Current Posture				
	100%	50%	0%	N/A	Remarks
Have these receptionists and telephone operators been provided with training in regard to emergency situations (i.e., threatening or harassing telephone calls, political protest activity, bomb threats, visitors engaging in violent or otherwise inappropriate behavior, and so forth)?					
Do these receptionists and/or telephone operators have a discrete means to summon immediate assistance from security personnel (e.g., a "panic button" under their desks)?					
If there is such a means to summon immediate assistance from security personnel, are the device and the process it initiates, tested on a regular basis?					
Do your enterprise's facilities have on-site security personnel?					
Are these on-site security people employees of your enterprise, or of the building management firm, or of third-party contractors?					
If these on-site security people are not enterprise employees, are their activities controlled directly by your enterprise or by the building management firm?					
Do on-site security personnel undergo adequate background investigations, and can these background investigations be verified or reviewed to your satisfaction?					

Continued

Table 11.1 Continued. IP Protection Program Assessment—Physical Security

IP Protection Program Assessment Tool: Physical Security	Current Posture				
	100%	50%	0%	N/A	Remarks
Do on-site security personnel undergo adequate and appropriate security-related training before they are assigned, and can this training be verified and reviewed to your satisfaction?					
How many hours of such training do these on-site security people undergo, and what subject matters are addressed (e.g., criminal law, procedures for conducting searches, procedures for subduing and detaining suspects, how to handle emergency equipment, the basics of fire safety and first aid, and so forth)?					
Do on-site security personnel have a 24×7 presence in your facilities?					
Are the assigned contingents of on-site security people considered adequate to meet the needs of your facilities?					
Do the on-site security people assigned to your facilities rotate their posts regularly?					
Do the on-site security people assigned to your facilities respond to alarms?					
Do the on-site security people assigned to your facilities receive documented procedures that detail their personal duties and responsibility, and give them a clear understanding of your expectations?					

Continued

Table 11.1 Continued. IP Protection Program Assessment—Physical Security

IP Protection Program Assessment Tool: Physical Security	Current Posture				
	100%	50%	0%	N/A	Remarks
Do the on-site security personnel operate under direct, ongoing supervision?					
Do on-site security personnel conduct regular patrols both of the buildings in which your facilities are housed and their immediate areas?					
Do on-site security people have communication capabilities while they are on patrol (e.g., walkie-talkies, cell phones, and so forth)?					
Is there an on-site logbook in which all security incidents are recorded, and is this logbook adequately maintained and regularly reviewed?					
If you utilize a third-party contractor for your on-site security guards, is there adequate, current, and verifiable proof that this third-party contractor upholds appropriate recruitment criteria?					
Have you installed CCTV systems, wherever they are deemed warranted, feasible, and cost-justifiable within your facilities?					
If so, do these CCTV systems provide coverage of the whole perimeter or all points of vulnerability?					
Has the CCTV coverage for your facilities been challenged in penetration tests to determine if it has blind spots in regard to physical attempts or technical vulnerabilities to technical tampering or manipulation?					

Continued

Table 11.1 Continued. IP Protection Program Assessment—Physical Security

IP Protection Program Assessment Tool: Physical Security	Current Posture				
	100%	50%	0%	N/A	Remarks
Does someone conduct live monitoring of your CCTV system, or is it recorded, or do you do both?					
Either way, or both ways, do you have documented procedures for monitoring the CCTV system?					
Does the CCTV system record the date and time? Are the CCTV systems' recordings reviewed adequately and on a regular basis?					
Is there a program of ongoing and adequate maintenance in place for your CCTV systems, and have you received sufficient and verifiable confirmation that maintenance personnel are subject to all appropriate background checks, recruitment criteria, etc.?					
Are your CCTV systems checked on a daily basis (at minimum) to make certain that all of the cameras are functioning properly?					
Have alarm systems been installed in each of your facilities, or the buildings in which they are housed?					
Do the alarm systems only sound-off—or otherwise initiate notification—locally, or are the systems monitored at a central, off-site command center?					
Do your alarm systems link directly to appropriate law enforcement, notifying them of possible intrusions or other emergencies?					

Continued

Table 11.1 Continued. IP Protection Program Assessment—Physical Security

IP Protection Program Assessment Tool: Physical Security	Current Posture				
	100%	50%	0%	N/A	Remarks
If your alarm systems do link into appropriate law enforcement, has this law enforcement agency been provided the names and contact information of designated personnel to contact if the alarm is triggered outside of normal working hours (e.g., nights, weekends, or holidays)?					
Are the alarm systems in place throughout the whole of each building or facilities, or are they only implemented in sensitive and/or vital areas?					
What intrusion detection methods or techniques are utilized in your alarm system (e.g., disrupting an infra-red light beam, or contact with a door or window)?					
Do your alarm systems cover all your facilities' exits and entrances?					
Is a password and/or other authentication/authorization method (e.g., a key) required to activate and/or deactivate your alarm systems?					
Is the method for activating and/or deactivating the alarm systems itself adequately safeguarded? For example, if a password is required, is the password regularly changed?					

Continued

Table 11.1 Continued. IP Protection Program Assessment—Physical Security

IP Protection Program Assessment Tool: Physical Security	Current Posture				
	100%	50%	0%	N/A	Remarks
Does each person authorized to activate and/or deactivate the alarm systems have their own password or other authentication/ authorization method, or is one password or device shared among numerous people?					
Do your on-site security people conduct appropriate searches of employees, visitors, contractors, etc., as they enter or leave your facilities or the buildings in which they are housed?					
Does your enterprise have estab-lished policies and procedures that govern why, how, under what circumstances, and by whom such searches are carried out?					
Are your policies concerning searches clearly posted so that those entering and exiting the premises are made aware that your enterprise reserves the right to undertake such searches?					
Does the posted policy contain a list of those items that are not allowed into your facilities (e.g., guns, knives, illicit drugs, cameras, cell phones with cameras, audio, video recording equipment, etc.) without authorization ?					
Are searches made of bags, pack-ages and other containers being brought into or taken out of the building?					

Continued

Table 11.1 Continued. IP Protection Program Assessment—Physical Security

IP Protection Program Assessment Tool: Physical Security	Current Posture				
	100%	50%	0%	N/A	Remarks
Have your on-site security personnel been provided with instructions and proper training, on what to do if someone refuses to comply with the search, or has been revealed to be transporting your enterprise's property (whether physical or digital) or any banned item?					
Have the security officers been adequately trained in appropriate and professional (e.g., legal, efficient, courteous, etc.) search techniques?					
Is there an established system (e.g., issuance and logging of property passes) for individuals who are taking your enterprise's property out of the building or off the premises?					
Are there established procedures to directly inform all visitors of your enterprise's prohibition against the use or possession of cameras, cell phone cameras, audio and video recording devices, etc. inside your facilities?					
Are signs notifying visitors of the prohibition against cameras, etc. (unless authorized) posted at all entrances, and as appropriate, within corridors and work areas to notify visitors of the prohibition of audio and video recording?					

Continued

Table 11.1 Continued. IP Protection Program Assessment—Physical Security

IP Protection Program Assessment Tool: Physical Security	Current Posture				
	100%	50%	0%	N/A	Remarks
Are there established procedures to directly inform all those who enter (i.e., employees, contractors, visitors, and others) of your enterprise's prohibition against possession of guns, knives, illegal narcotics, etc. in your facilities?					
Are signs notifying visitors of your enterprise's prohibition against illegal narcotics, guns, knives, hazardous materials, etc. posted at all entrances, and as appropriate, within corridors and work areas to notify visitors of these prohibitions?					
Do all of your enterprise's employees have unrestricted access to facilities on a 24-hour basis, or do they have to request specific authorization and/or make special arrangements to access facilities after normal work hours or over weekend or holiday periods?					
Is there an established procedure and log book for employees to sign in if they are accessing facilities after normal working hours or over weekend or holiday periods?					
Is there a receptionist assigned to process all visitors and deal with other walk-in traffic at your facilities?					
Do you require all visitors to check in at an established reception area or security post?					

Continued

www.syngress.com

Table 11.1 Continued. IP Protection Program Assessment—Physical Security

IP Protection Program Assessment Tool: Physical Security	Current Posture				
	100%	50%	0%	N/A	Remarks
Do your facilities have clearly marked signage informing all visitors that they must report to the designated reception area or security post and showing them they way?					
Are policies and procedures in place for your employees to provide advanced notice reception and/or security to expect visitors a desig-nated day and time (including number of visitors in party and identities)?					
Are the employees notified that visitors have come to meet them by reception or security personnel?					
Do your facilities contract with an outside office cleaning service?					
Have you received assurances that the outside cleaning service's staff has been properly vetted, and is there any way to verify this assurance?					
Are your facilities cleaned during or after normal business hours?					
Are cleaning service personnel supervised when working in executive boardrooms, executive offices, and other sensitive areas?					
Do cleaning service personnel have unfettered access to your facilities, or do you control their access?					
Does your enterprise utilize access card readers at all entrances to all facilities?					

Continued

Table 11.1 Continued. IP Protection Program Assessment—Physical Security

IP Protection Program Assessment Tool: Physical Security	Current Posture				
	100%	50%	0%	N/A	Remarks
Does your enterprise utilize access card readers at all entrances to areas in which confidential information or valuable assets are stored (e.g., computer rooms or research and development laboratories)?					
Are access control reports, which list both entry and exit times for all cardholders, generated and reviewed on a regular basis?					
Do all the office and closet doors in your enterprise's facilities have locks installed on them?					
Do your facilities' cabinets have locks installed on them, so that confidential information and other valuable assets can be securely stored?					
Does your enterprise physically secure vital equipment and other valuable assets to furniture, walls, or floors as appropriate?					
Does your enterprise issue cable locks or other security devices to personnel, contractors, etc. to secure computers and other portable equipment, and are these security devices used pervasively?					
Do the buildings that house your facilities have a master key system?					
Is a registry of all master keys maintained and kept up-to-date at all times?					

Continued

Table 11.1 Continued. IP Protection Program Assessment—Physical Security

IP Protection Program Assessment Tool: Physical Security	Current Posture				
	100%	50%	0%	N/A	Remarks
Are master keys issued on a temporary or full time basis, or on one or the other depending upon the recipient?					
Are periodic inventories of the actual master keys conducted and in turn reconciled with what is listed in the registry, in order to determine whether or not all the keys are accounted for (i.e., that none are missing)?					
Does your enterprise or the building management assign a particular employee who is to bear personal responsibility for the giving out and retrieval of all master keys?					
Is there a list of those individuals who have been authorized to receive and use master keys, and is this list maintained adequately, (e.g., complete and kept up-to-date)?					
Are master keys not in use kept secured (e.g., in a locked cabinet) for which, in turn, all keys (or combinations) are tightly held?					
Are there procedures in place for reporting the loss of keys, and is a list of such reports (with their resolutions) compiled and kept available for review when called for?					
When a master key is lost are all locks impacted by the loss changed expeditiously?					

Continued

Table 11.1 Continued. IP Protection Program Assessment—Physical Security

IP Protection Program Assessment Tool: Physical Security	Current Posture				
	100%	50%	0%	N/A	Remarks
Have all your enterprise's personnel been provided with photographic identification badges?					
Does your enterprise have procedures in place for the issuance of temporary badges for both visitors and employees who have misplaced or left behind their photo identification badges?					
Are your enterprise logos and company name intentionally kept off access control badges so that they are not easily identifiable if lost?					
Are all your enterprise's employees required to wear their identification badges in such a manner that they are easily referenced in all circumstances?					
Does your enterprise issue photo identification badges to all contractors working on-site?					
Are the identification badges that your enterprise issues to contractors working on-site in extended engagements distinctly different from those issued to your enterprise's personnel?					
Do the identification badges your enterprise issues to on-site contractors working in limited engagements automatically expire at the time appointed for the conclusion of their engagement?					

Continued

Table 11.1 Continued. IP Protection Program Assessment—Physical Security

IP Protection Program Assessment Tool: Physical Security	Current Posture				
	100%	50%	0%	N/A	Remarks
Are all contractors required to wear their identification badges in such a manner that they are easily referenced in all circumstances?					
Does your enterprise have established procedures for ensuring that contractor badges are secured when not being used?					
Are all visitors required to wear their visitor identification badges in such a manner that they are easily referenced in all circumstances?					
Does your enterprise have established procedures for ensuring that contractor badges are secured when not being used?					
Are all visitors required to wear their visitor identification badges in such a manner that they are easily referenced in all circumstances?					
Do established policies and procedures require that all visitors be accompanied at all times during their stay at your enterprise's facilities?					
Does the employee responsible for escorting the visitor collect the visitor's identification badges before his or her guest leaves the facility?					
Are there established procedures to ensure that all visitor badges are adequately and appropriately secured when not signed out to visitors?					

Continued

Table 11.1 Continued. IP Protection Program Assessment—Physical Security

IP Protection Program Assessment Tool: Physical Security	Current Posture				
	100%	50%	0%	N/A	Remarks
Are all of the loading and shipping docks sufficiently separated from your facilities' internal areas?					
Is all motor vehicle access to your facilities' parking areas adequately controlled and monitored?					
Is the display of some form of sticker, tag, or other form of identification required for all authorized vehicles?					
Are all your facilities' parking areas adequately secured and monitored?					
Are all your facilities' parking areas adequately illuminated during the hours of darkness?					
Is there established procedure for maintaining a list of the license plates and owners of all motor vehicles authorized to park in your facilities' designated parking areas?					
Are all your facilities' parking areas adequately secured after normal working hours?					
Are your facilities' physical perimeters patrolled on a regular basis both during normal working hours and outside of normal working hours?					
Does the regular perimeter patrol include the inspection of doors and windows to make certain that they are adequately secured?					

Continued

Table 11.1 Continued. IP Protection Program Assessment—Physical Security

IP Protection Program Assessment Tool: Physical Security	Current Posture				
	100%	50%	0%	N/A	Remarks
Are trees, shrubs, or other growth around the facilities' perimeter trimmed on a regular basis? Are all areas surrounding your facilities properly maintained (e.g., are they kept clear of garbage to prevent an accumulation, which could create a hazard or provide cover)?					
Is all access to your facilities from building roofs safely secured?					
Is there sufficient perimeter lighting for the buildings that house your facilities?					
Are your enterprise's mailroom personnel adequately trained in the proper methods for identifying and dealing with suspicious packages and envelopes?					
Is a list of indicators for suspicious packages and envelopes posted prominently in the mailroom as a reminder to personnel handling incoming mail?					
Do all your enterprise's facilities have evacuation plans, which include the best routes out of the building and pre-determined gathering places?					
Are evacuation plans and procedures for your facilities tested annually at a minimum?					
Is there is an on-site manager (and at least one alternate) for each facility, who is responsible for making the determination that an evacuation should be initiated?					

Continued

Table 11.1 Continued. IP Protection Program Assessment—Physical Security

IP Protection Program Assessment Tool: Physical Security	Current Posture				
	100%	50%	0%	N/A	Remarks
Does your enterprise have established contingency plans for what to do in the event of a bomb threat at one of your facilities?					
Does your enterprise provide receptionists or telephone operators with training and documented procedures for dealing with bomb threats and collecting vital information concerning such threats when they are received?					
Does your enterprise provide receptionists and telephone operators with a checklist of emergency procedures, which is kept in a place immediately accessible to them at their workstations?					
Do your enterprise's emergency plans and procedures include instructions to notify appropriate law enforcement immediately?					
Does your enterprise have bomb search procedures, and are these procedures reviewed and tested as appropriate?					
Has your enterprise undertaken a threat assessment to identify areas in which most sensitive documents are produced and in which they are stored?					
Does your enterprise have established policies and procedures for the destruction of confidential information?					

Continued

www.syngress.com

Table 11.1 Continued. IP Protection Program Assessment—Physical Security

IP Protection Program Assessment Tool: Physical Security	Current Posture				
	100%	50%	0%	N/A	Remarks
Does your enterprise utilize cross-cut shredders as appropriate?					
Does your enterprise utilize secure cabinets or lockers for information that is either confidential or sensitive?					
Does your enterprise have an established "clean desk" policy for all of its facilities?					
Is your enterprise's "clean desk" policy enforced?					
Are your facilities' conference rooms properly cleaned up after meetings (e.g., any notes containing sensitive information retrieved, all white boards erased)?					
Have all of your enterprise's sensitive equipment and assets been identified and properly secured?					
Have all areas that require additional security (e.g., boardrooms, executive conference rooms, and executive offices) been identified within your enterprise's facilities?					
Are all of your enterprise's boardrooms, executive conference rooms, and executive offices kept locked when not in use?					
Does one of your enterprise's employees supervise the cleaning of boardrooms, executive conference rooms, and executive offices?					

Continued

Table 11.1 Continued. IP Protection Program Assessment—Physical Security

IP Protection Program Assessment Tool: Physical Security	Current Posture				
	100%	50%	0%	N/A	Remarks
Is special attention given to board-rooms and executive conference rooms after important meetings, to make certain that they have been cleansed of all sensitive information and other proprietary materials?					
Does your enterprise utilize electronic countermeasures, as appropriate, to thwart eavesdropping in boardrooms, executive conferences rooms, and executive offices?					

Chapter 12

Information Security

Introduction

There is a wise saying in Tibet: "As a thing is viewed, so it appears."

This is true of anything and everything. And it is an exhortation to intellectual honesty. Unless you can look beyond your own biases, they warp your perceptions. Indeed, unless you can achieve some clarity beyond your personal biases, they will defeat themselves in the pursuit of their primary purposes—your own best interests.

As information security is viewed, so it appears.

To a policy wonk, it may look like a robust body of well-crafted, well-calibrated policies and standards. To a technologist, it may look like an intricate web of sophisticated programs, schemes, and devices—trip wires, honey pots, firewalls, intrusion detection, encryption, and so on.

To some, policies and standards equal information security. To others, technology equals information security. Still others say awareness and education equal information security. Some would say budget dollars equal information security.

Of course, although these narrow, biased perceptions of what matters most, or best defines information security, reflect the predilections and preoccupations of different subcultures within the field, none of them are accurate on their own.

But what is perhaps even more important is that no combination of them in and of themselves articulates what is most important about information security, or best defines what it is. In other words, policies and standards plus technology plus awareness and education plus budget dollars does not equal information security either. If all you do is add up the sum total of these parts, they still do not constitute information security. There is an X factor still missing in the equation.

This X factor is the human factor.

There has to be an enlightened vision behind it all, imbuing it with clarity of mind. There has to be a consciousness that attends both to the big picture and the smallest details simultaneously.

Within the overall holistic vision of what your intellectual property protection program should look like and how it should all work together, information security compliments, resonates with, and amplifies personnel security, physical security, and all the other vital elements. And similarly, within information security itself, numerous vital aspects must be not only activated but also integrated into a living whole.

In short, there has to be a plan, but there also has to be a vision. There has to be a vision, but there also has to be a will. And these three have to be informed by experience and knowledge of both the facts on the ground and the direction of developing trends.

Keeping this essential caveat in mind, in this chapter, you will find some ideas on what kinds of controls should be in place across the broad spectrum of information security concerns. No list is comprehensive, because the whole is a moving, evolving target. But if the controls, processes, protocols, policies, and standards outlined here are implemented, you will no doubt significantly narrow the scope of your enterprise's exposure to the multifarious risks, threats, and vulnerabilities of cyberspace. Table 12.1 assesses an enterprise's use of information classification as part of an IP Protection Program Assessment Tool for information security.

Table 12.1 IP Protection Program Assessment: Information Security—
Information Classification

IP Protection Program Assessment Tool: Information Security— Information Classification	Current Posture					
	100%	75%	50%	25%	N/A	Remarks
Does your enterprise have established policies and procedures for information classification?						
Does your enterprise's information classification scheme draw a distinction between regulated information (i.e., information that requires controls mandated by law or contractual agreement) and unregulated information?						
Does your enterprise's information classification scheme draw further distinctions—e.g., categories such as "public," "confidential," and "special handling"—to delineate how different types of information are labeled, stored, communicated, handled, etc.?						
Does your enterprise maintain an inventory of information, in which it classifies all information in its possession?						

Continued

Table 12.1 Continued. IP Protection Program Assessment: Information Security—Information Classification

IP Protection Program Assessment Tool: Information Security—Information Classification	Current Posture					
	100%	75%	50%	25%	N/A	Remarks
Does this inventory at a minimum list all regulated information along with the format, e.g., physical and/or electronic, in which it exists?						
Does this inventory also include information of other classifications, e.g., "confidential" and "special handling"?						
Does your enterprise identify information owners responsible for all information stored, generated, or newly taken in?						
Are these information owners responsible for assigning classification categories, assigning responsibilities for information management, establishing and keeping current the information asset inventory, and determining the resolution of issues concerning the labeling, retaining, disposing, or reclassifying of all the information they "own"?						
Has your enterprise established a body of security policies, standards, procedures, and controls for the classifying, labeling, storing, accessing, distributing and communicating, copying, archiving, and destroying of regulated information?						
Has your enterprise established a body of security policies, standards, procedures, and controls for the						

Continued

Table 12.1 Continued. IP Protection Program Assessment: Information
Security—Information Classification

IP Protection Program Assessment Tool: Information Security—Information Classification	Current Posture					
	100%	75%	50%	25%	N/A	Remarks
classifying, labeling, storing, accessing, distributing and communicating, copying, archiving, and destroying for other classifications of information, e.g. "confidential" and "special handling"?						
Is all physical media that holds information (whether hard copy, e.g., envelopes, folders, papers, etc., or any other media, e.g., disks, tapes, etc.) labeled in accordance with this body of information classification policies, standards, procedures, and controls?						
Do these labels include the information's owner, the information's classification category, and the information's source, along with the date issued and the date expired?						
Does your enterprise similarly label all digital information (e.g., word processing documents, spreadsheets, database fields, etc.) classified as regulated?						
Does your enterprise similarly label all digital information (e.g., word processing documents, spreadsheets, database fields, etc.) classified as confidential, special handling, or public although unregulated?						
Does your enterprise control access to the physical media that holds regulated information?						

Continued

Table 12.1 Continued. IP Protection Program Assessment: Information
Security—Information Classification

IP Protection Program Assessment Tool: Information Security—Information Classification	Current Posture					
	100%	75%	50%	25%	N/A	Remarks
Does your enterprise control access to the physical media that holds unregulated, but otherwise classified information (e.g., confidential or special handling)?						
Does your enterprise similarly control access to digital information (e.g., word processing documents, spreadsheets, database fields, etc.), which is unregulated, but otherwise unclassified information (e.g., confidential or special handling)?						
Does your enterprise establish controls for the copying and scanning of all physical documents labeled as regulated information?						
Does your enterprise establish controls for the copying of all digital documents, which although unregulated, are otherwise classified?						
Have storing and archiving procedures and controls been established for all physical media containing regulated information?						
Have storing and archiving procedures and controls been established for all physical media containing unregulated information, but otherwise classified information?						
Have storing and archiving procedures and controls been established for all digital information that is regulated?						

Continued

Table 12.1 Continued. IP Protection Program Assessment: Information Security—Information Classification

IP Protection Program Assessment Tool: Information Security— Information Classification	Current Posture					
	100%	75%	50%	25%	N/A	Remarks
Have storing and archiving procedures and controls been established for all digital information that is unregulated, but otherwise classified?						
Has your enterprise implemented procedures and controls for disposing of all physical media (e.g., cross-shredding or incineration) that contains information that is regulated?						
Has your enterprise implemented procedures and controls for disposing of all physical media (e.g., cross-shredding or incineration) that contains information that is unregulated, but otherwise classified?						
Has your enterprise established controls for the distribution of digital information that is regulated?						
Has your enterprise established controls for the distribution of digital information that is unregulated, but otherwise classified?						

Tables 12.2 through 12.7 assess an enterprise's use of various operations procedures and policies as part of an IP Protection Program Assessment Tool for information security.

Table 12.2 IP Protection Program Assessment: Information Security—Operations: Process Control

IP Protection Program Assessment Tool: Information Security— Operations: Process Control	Current Posture					
	100%	75%	50%	25%	N/A	Remarks
Does your enterprise have a formal change control procedure that includes security testing, and is used to manage all software modifications to any software running in production on all platforms?						
Has your enterprise established "back out" procedures that would allow data processing and other vital activities to revert to earlier software versions in the event of malfunction, so that normal operations can go on with only minimum interruption?						
Has your enterprise implemented degrees of separation between the ability to manage and execute certain operational duties in order to minimize the possibility of misuse or other unauthorized activity; e.g., prohibiting IS employees from initiating original accounting transactions, receivables, payables, adjustments, corrections, check requests; and also from originating nonfinancial data entries?						
Does your enterprise separate the production environment from the development and testing environments to preserve the integrity of production data and program code?						
Does your enterprise use different people for the quality assurance testing and daily operations of systems than those it involves in the systems' development?						

Table 12.3 IP Protection Program Assessment: Information Security—Operations: Incident Management

IP Protection Program Assessment Tool: Information Security—Operations: Incident Management	Current Posture					
	100%	75%	50%	25%	N/A	Remarks
Has your enterprise established a plan for incident management?						
Does your enterprise's incident management plan address how to investigate and manage response to infections by viruses or worms?						
Does your enterprise's incident management plan address how to investigate and manage response to violations of security policy or standard?						
Does your enterprise's incident management plan address how to investigate and manage response to hacker break-in or other unauthorized access?						
Does your enterprise's incident management plan address how to investigate and manage response to denial of service or other type of abuse?						
Does your enterprise's incident management plan address how to investigate and manage response to exploitation of software or system vulnerabilities?						
Does your enterprise's incident management plan address how to investigate and manage response to confidentiality breaches?						
Does your enterprise's incident management plan address how to investigate and manage response to abuse of user or administrator privileges?						

Continued

Table 12.3 Continued. IP Protection Program Assessment: Information Security—Operations: Incident Management

IP Protection Program Assessment Tool: Information Security— Operations: Incident Management	Current Posture					
	100%	75%	50%	25%	N/A	Remarks
Does your enterprise's incident management plan include procedures for identifying incidents?						
Does your enterprise's incident management plan include procedures for initial analysis and triage?						
Does your enterprise's incident management plan include procedures for dissemination of information concerning the incident as it unfolds?						
Does your enterprise's incident management plan include procedures for the containment and resolution of the incident?						
Does your enterprise's incident management plan include procedures for follow-up reports and analysis after the incident is resolved?						
Does your enterprise have policies and procedures in place that compel employees, contractors, and other involved individuals to report any evidence of possible security breaches, violations, suspicious behavior or unauthorized activity to the appropriate internal entities and provide them with the contact information needed to do so?						

Table 12.4 IP Protection Program Assessment: Information Security—Operations: Anti-Virus Protection

IP Protection Program Assessment Tool: Information Security— Operations: Anti-Virus Protection	Current Posture				
	100%	50%	0%	N/A	Remarks
Does your enterprise install and maintain anti-virus software on all its computers, including desktops, laptops, and servers?					
Does your enterprise install and maintain anti-virus software on all hand-held devices (e.g., PDAs, smart phones, etc.) issued to its personnel?					
Is all your enterprise's anti-virus software configured to scan information downloaded from the Internet as it enters the network?					
Is all your enterprise's anti-virus software configured to update virus signature databases ASAP?					

Table 12.5 IP Protection Program Assessment: Information Security—Operations: Software Patches and Updates

IP Protection Program Assessment Tool: Information Security— Operations: Software Patches and Updates	Current Posture				
	100%	50%	0%	N/A	Remarks
Has your enterprise implemented a process for the distribution of software updates and patches that factors in prompt testing of patches and the subsequent rapid patching and updating of all vulnerable systems?					

Table 12.6 IP Protection Program Assessment: Information Security—
Operations: Backups

IP Protection Program Assessment Tool: Information Security— Operations: Backups	Current Posture				
	100%	50%	0%	N/A	Remarks
Has your enterprise implemented backup policies and procedures for critical information, applications, and systems in order to ensure successful recovery and minimal loss of work product in the event that a disaster causes disruption, dislocation, or destruction of the IT environment?					
Do your enterprise's backup policies and procedures require that these backups—along with accurate directories of what backups are available (e.g., the type of information) and when they were made (i.e., date and time) as well as the documentation necessary to restore them—are all stored in an alternate facility at a remote location?					
Do your enterprise's backup policies and procedures require that the alternate facility in which these backups are stored provides an appropriate level of security; i.e., equal or superior to that of the operating environment?					
Do your enterprise's backup policies and procedures require that backup restoration should be tested at least annually in order to validate that the process is both efficient and effective on an ongoing basis; i.e., that it will function properly in an emergency situation?					

Continued

Table 12.6 Continued. IP Protection Program Assessment: Information Security—Operations: Backups

IP Protection Program Assessment Tool: Information Security— Operations: Backups	Current Posture				
	100%	50%	0%	N/A	Remarks
Do your enterprise's backup policies and procedures also call for the incremental backup of end-user files stored on its servers after the close of each business day?					
Do your enterprise's backup policies and procedures also call for the full backup of end-user files stored on its servers after the close of day on the last day of every business week?					
Do your enterprise's backup policies and procedures require the duplication and preservation of a minimum of one generation of backup files at the place where its production computers are situated, in order to smooth the way for rapid resumption of normal operations if there is some mishap, e.g., a hard disk crash or an accidental deletion?					
Do your enterprise's backup policies and procedures require the duplication and secure storage of all applications and systems software prior to installation so that these backups can be kept in reserve for recovery from incidental problems such as virus outbreaks or damage from fire, hardware malfunction, etc.?					

Table 12.7 IP Protection Program Assessment: Information Security—Operations: Idle or Unattended Systems

IP Protection Program Assessment Tool: Information Security—Operations: Idle or Unattended Systems	Current Posture				
	100%	50%	0%	N/A	Remarks
Does your enterprise secure all its desktop systems with enterprise-standard locking devices?					
Does your enterprise require that its personnel secure all the laptops entrusted to them by utilizing enterprise-standard locking devices?					
Does your enterprise require that its personnel take appropriate enterprise-standard measures to secure all handheld devices (e.g., PDAs, cell phones, etc.) entrusted to them?					
Does your enterprise require that its personnel safeguard all removable storage media (e.g., flash-disks, CDs, etc.) by locking the media in cabinets or drawers when not in use or unattended?					
Does your enterprise require passwords to access and operate its computers and log on to its networks?					
Does your enterprise utilize password-protected screen savers for all its desktops, laptops, or other computer systems to prevent unauthorized access or use when these systems are left idle or unattended?					
Do your enterprise's password-protected screen savers activate automatically and lock systems after they have been left idle for no more than a few minutes (e.g., ten minutes)?					

Table 12.8 assesses an enterprise's use of communications and Internet usage policies as part of an IP Protection Program Assessment Tool for information security.

Table 12.8 IP Protection Program Assessment: Information Security—Users: Communications and Internet Usage Policies

IP Protection Program Assessment Tool: Information Security—Users: Communications and Internet Usage Policies	Current Posture				
	100%	50%	0%	N/A	Remarks
Does your enterprise prohibit both the installation and the use of file sharing software, streaming video, games, etc. on its systems, unless there is a valid, authorized, and documented business purpose for such activity?					
Does your enterprise allow for the occasional, reasonable personal use of its systems by employees provided that such use does not consume any significant amount of time or computing resources or impact worker productivity in any way?					
Does your enterprise have an established policy governing all electronic communications that articulates what constitutes appropriate use of the enterprise's electronic communications resources; e.g., e-mail, instant messaging, etc.?					
Is your enterprise's electronic communications policy adequately socialized; i.e., is it known to and acknowledged by all employees?					
Does your enterprise's electronic communications policy address all the following issues? ■ Passwords for e-mail and instant messaging applications should not be shared					

Continued

Table 12.8 Continued. IP Protection Program Assessment: Information Security—Users: Communications and Internet Usage Policies

IP Protection Program Assessment Tool: Information Security—Users: Communications and Internet Usage Policies	Current Posture				
	100%	50%	0%	N/A	Remarks
■ Employees must not send messages containing obscene, harassing, threatening, defamatory, discriminatory, or otherwise inappropriate content					
■ Employees must not send executable file attachments					
■ Employees must not provide contact lists or any other internal information about the enterprise or any of its employees or resources to unauthorized or unverified inquirers					
■ Employees must not violate the law or the rights of any individual or organization					
■ Employees must not lobby for, advocate, enlist for, promote, solicit, market, or endorse anything of a personal nature and is not authorized or understood as something that advances the business interests and/or reputation of the enterprise					
■ Employees must not intentionally forward chain letters, spam, viruses, or other malicious software, unauthorized files, or inappropriate content					
■ Employees must not engage in unauthorized fundraising					
■ Employees must not access or download offensive or inappropriate content (e.g., pornography or hate literature)					

Continued

Table 12.8 Continued. IP Protection Program Assessment: Information Security—Users: Communications and Internet Usage Policies

IP Protection Program Assessment Tool: Information Security—Users: Communications and Internet Usage Policies	Current Posture				
	100%	50%	0%	N/A	Remarks
■ Employees must not use enterprise computer resources to gamble online or conduct related activity (e.g., administering betting pools)					
■ Employees must not violate the intellectual property rights (e.g., copyright) of any individual or organization					
■ Employees must not disclose any of the enterprise's proprietary, classified, or confidential information					
■ Employees must not post messages to public forums using their enterprise-issued e-mail account					
■ Employees must not use e-mail or instant messaging accounts not provided by the enterprise for any official business of the enterprise					
■ Employees must not obtain access to or pry into the files or communications of other employees' for any other unauthorized or inappropriate reason					
■ Employees must not attempt to gain unauthorized access to any computer, e-mail account, voice-mail box, or other file system or equipment					
Does your enterprise have an established policy governing all Internet usage that articulates what constitutes appropriate use of the enterprise's resources for Internet access, and compliments its electronic communications policy?					

Continued

Table 12.8 Continued. IP Protection Program Assessment: Information Security—Users: Communications and Internet Usage Policies

IP Protection Program Assessment Tool: Information Security—Users: Communications and Internet Usage Policies	Current Posture				
	100%	50%	0%	N/A	Remarks
Is your enterprise's Internet usage policy adequately socialized; i.e., is it known to and acknowledged by all employees?					
Does your enterprise's Internet usage policy address all the following issues?					
■ Employees must not download software, plug-ins, freeware, etc. without prior authorization					
■ Employees must not indulge in the downloading or distribution of pirated software					
■ Employees must not upload any of the enterprise's proprietary information; e.g., information classified as confidential, regulated, or special handling					
■ Employees must not upload public information to a nonenterprise Internet site without prior authorization					
■ Employees must not post software, whether commercial or developed internally, to a nonenterprise Internet site without prior authorization					
■ Employees must not download content, e.g., video or other streaming media, or play games online					
■ Employees must not develop web sites or web pages offering enterprise products or services without prior authorization					

Continued

Table 12.8 Continued. IP Protection Program Assessment: Information Security—Users: Communications and Internet Usage Policies

IP Protection Program Assessment Tool: Information Security—Users: Communications and Internet Usage Policies	Current Posture				
	100%	50%	0%	N/A	Remarks
■ Employees must not utilize Internet file-sharing software (e.g., Kazaa, Morpheus, Napster, etc.)					
■ Employees must not access, download, print out, save to disk, or forward via e-mail any content that is illegal, or reasonably deemed immoral, unethical, pornographic, racist, or otherwise offensive or inappropriate					

Table 12.9 assesses an enterprise's use of access control policies and procedures as part of an IP Protection Program Assessment Tool for information security.

Table 12.9 IP Protection Program Assessment: Information Security— Access Control

IP Protection Program Assessment Tool: Information Security—Access Control	Current Posture				
	100%	50%	0%	N/A	Remarks
Does your enterprise have an established body of policies and procedures that articulate access control elements and measures for all systems and business processes?					
Does your enterprise's body of access control policies and procedures accomplish the following items? ■ Identify all relevant security requirements					
■ Establish policies and procedures for accessing, using, disseminating, maintaining, and authorizing information					

Continued

Table 12.9 Continued. IP Protection Program Assessment: Information Security—Access Control

IP Protection Program Assessment Tool: Information Security—Access Control	Current Posture				
	100%	50%	0%	N/A	Remarks
■ Identity all information that requires access control measures					
■ Assure that access controls are consistent throughout the enterprise					
■ Factor in all local, national, and international laws concerning access control to data, services, or other resources					
■ Factor in all contractual obligations concerning access control to data, services, or other resources					
■ Identify user and/or group profiles to define nature of access for types of positions or functions					
Does your enterprise's access control provide for a process to register and unregister users for the purpose of granting access to information, information systems, and related services?					
Does your enterprise's access control provide for a process to register and unregister users for the purpose of granting access, and include the following elements?					
■ Establish unique IDs for all users so that they can be accountable for their actions					
■ Provide confirmation that users have authorization to access specific information,information systems, and related services					
■ Provide confirmation that users have been granted levels of access consistent with business objectives, necessary for the performance of their jobs, and otherwise					

Continued

Table 12.9 Continued. IP Protection Program Assessment: Information Security—Access Control

IP Protection Program Assessment Tool: Information Security—Access Control	Current Posture				
	100%	50%	0%	N/A	Remarks
consistent with the overall body of security policies, standards, and procedures					
■ Create and keep current an inventory of registered users for the enterprise's information, information systems, and related services					
■ Allow for the adjustment of access for users who move to other jobs within the enterprise					
■ Promptly cancel the access of users who cease to be employees of the enterprise					
■ Periodically detect and delete redundant user IDs and accounts					
■ Periodically detect and delete multiple user IDs provided to the same user					
Does your enterprise's access control system establish expiration periods for user IDs, after which user IDs are disabled?					
Does your enterprise's access control system inform users of the impending expiration and allow them to submit a request for reauthorization or extension?					
Does your enterprise conduct such surveys annually?					
Does your enterprise's body of access control policies inform employees, contractors, and others granted access that they are responsible for all actions carried out with their user IDs, and that they should therefore not permit others to "borrow" their user IDs to carry out any actions?					

Continued

Table 12.9 Continued. IP Protection Program Assessment: Information Security—Access Control

IP Protection Program Assessment Tool: Information Security—Access Control	Current Posture				
	100%	50%	0%	N/A	Remarks
Does your enterprise's body of access control policies inform employees, contractors, and others granted access, that they should not "borrow" the user IDs of others to carry out any actions?					
Does your enterprise's access control system use a formal authorization process to grant privileges for the use of systems, applications, networks, and other resources, and does this authorization process perform the following functions?					
■ Identify all applications, products, and technologies (e.g., databases, operating systems, SAP, etc.) for which the access control system would grant privileges					
■ Identify types of jobs (e.g., purchasing agent, network administrator, human resources manager, administrative assistant)					
■ Identify types of users for all applications, products, and technologies					
■ Allocate user privileges for each type of user for each application, product, and technology using the premise that all privileges are granted for the sole purpose of meeting minimum requirements for the function to be performed and for only the time needed					
■ Utilize a mandatory authorization process for the granting of all privileges					
■ Maintain a record of all allocated privileges					

Continued

Table 12.9 Continued. IP Protection Program Assessment: Information
Security—Access Control

IP Protection Program Assessment Tool: Information Security—Access Control	Current Posture				
	100%	50%	0%	N/A	Remarks
Does your enterprise's access control system allocate privileges only to the information, systems, services, and other resources required to accomplish tasks associated with a user's job responsibilities and allow for the denial of privileges to any information, systems, services, or other resources not required to do so?					
Does your enterprise's access control system limit the number of users granted admin istrative privileges to only those users who require such privileges to accomplish their normal job responsibilities?					
Does your enterprise's access control system grant administrative privileges temporarily for those users who require administrative privileges on an infrequent basis or only under special conditions?					
Does your enterprise's access control system prohibit "hard-coding" or otherwise building user IDs or passwords into software programs developed or modified in-house?					
Do your enterprise's access control policies and procedures provide for the reloading of trusted versions of operating system and security software versions on to any system or resource suspected of having been breached or otherwise compromised, and require that this reloading is done only after the incident has been sufficiently analyzed?					
Do your enterprise's access control policies and procedures provide for the review of all relevant privileges to determine if any					

Continued

www.syngress.com

Table 12.9 Continued. IP Protection Program Assessment: Information Security—Access Control

IP Protection Program Assessment Tool: Information Security—Access Control	Current Posture				
	100%	50%	0%	N/A	Remarks
unauthorized modifications have occurred in the event of a possible breach or other compromise of the system?					
Does your enterprise configure its systems to require positive identification measures (e.g., user IDs and passwords, biometrics, tokens, digital certificates, etc.) of users in order for them to gain access?					
Do your enterprise's access control policies and standards include requirements for strong passwords constituted of the following elements? ■ Password length should be a minimum of seven characters					
■ Passwords should not incorporate the user's first or last name or user ID, or the name of any close relative or popular person					
■ Passwords should not incorporate other easily associated names or words, or a single, unaltered word from a dictionary					
■ Passwords should use numbers and special characters embedded in words, replacing individual letters, rather than placed at the beginning or end of words					
■ Passwords should contain at least three out of four classes of character: uppercase letters (e.g., XYZ), lowercase letters (e.g., xyz), numbers (e.g., 4,5,6), nonalphanumeric characters (e.g., #@$%^)					

Continued

Table 12.9 Continued. IP Protection Program Assessment: Information Security—Access Control

IP Protection Program Assessment Tool: Information Security—Access Control	Current Posture				
	100%	50%	0%	N/A	Remarks
Does your enterprise configure its systems, networks, and other computing resources to require the changing of user passwords on a regular basis (e.g., 90 days or less)?					
Do your enterprise's access control policies and procedures prohibit users from sharing their passwords or disclosing them to others?					
Do your enterprise's access control policies and procedures prohibit users from storing their passwords in batch files, automatic login scripts, macros, function keys, etc., storing them in modem dial-up programs, Internet browsers, or other communications programs, or keeping a hard copy or unencrypted digital record of their passwords?					
Does your enterprise configure its systems and networks to lock out the user account after five or less consecutive failed attempts to login, and keep the user account locked until the person it is assigned to requests a password reset?					
Does your enterprise configure its system, network, and browser sessions to require that the user reauthenticate users after a set period of inactivity (e.g., 20 minutes)?					
Has your enterprise established a multifactor authentication method (e.g., utilizing personal information and a minimum of two questions) to authenticate a user before resetting his or her password?					
Are your enterprise's networks, systems, and directories configured to deactivate network user, system user, and active directory/LDAP					

Continued

www.syngress.com

Table 12.9 Continued. IP Protection Program Assessment: Information Security—Access Control

IP Protection Program Assessment Tool: Information Security—Access Control	Current Posture				
	100%	50%	0%	N/A	Remarks
user accounts that have been inactive for 90 days or more, and keep them locked until the person the account is assigned to (or other authorized person) requests reactivation?					
Does your enterprise's body of access control policies and procedures require written authorization from executive leadership or the appropriate authority within the enterprise's internal security organization before access is granted to those who are not employees, contractors, or other designated insiders?					
Do your enterprise's access control policies and procedures require that temporary employees, contractors, or consultants be granted access only to those systems and networks necessary to perform their limited and defined roles and only for that period of time during which their work will be performed?					
Do your enterprise access control policies and procedures require that all third-party personnel (e.g., technicians performing computer repair, software upgrade, or other maintenance) must sign a confidentiality agreement prior to receiving access to the enterprise's information, systems, or services?					
Do your enterprise's access control policies and procedures prohibit the sale, transfer, or installation of the enterprise's systems, software, information, documentation, or assets to third parties unless the action has been approved by the appropriate					

Continued

Table 12.9 Continued. IP Protection Program Assessment: Information
Security—Access Control

IP Protection Program Assessment Tool: Information Security—Access Control	Current Posture				
	100%	50%	0%	N/A	Remarks
management authority and is conducted in compliance with all applicable license agreements?					
Does your enterprise advise customers, suppliers, partners, and others with the scope of their responsibilities as defined by contractual relationships?					
Does your enterprise require third parties to secure their systems or networks at levels commensurate with the enterprise's own security requirements prior to connecting them to enterprise's systems or networks?					
Does your enterprise hold the right to conduct surprise audits (i.e., with no advance notice) on third-party systems and networks to evaluate their security measures?					
Does the enterprise hold the right to terminate connections to all third-party systems and networks if it has reason to believe that the third party has not adhered to necessary security requirements, or if for some other reason the third party's systems and networks pose a risk of attack against the enterprise's own?					
Does your enterprise instruct its users to change their passwords whenever they receive any indication that their passwords may have been compromised, and to contact the appropriate personnel in the enterprise's security or IT organizations to inform them of the possible compromise?					
Does your enterprise prohibit its users from exploiting any vulnerabilities or deficiencies					

Continued

www.syngress.com

Table 12.9 Continued. IP Protection Program Assessment: Information Security—Access Control

IP Protection Program Assessment Tool: Information Security—Access Control	Current Posture				
	100%	50%	0%	N/A	Remarks
they discover in the enterprise's information security programs and controls in any way (e.g., to obtain unauthorized access, alter or damage information or information systems, disrupt operations, deny resources to other users, etc.)?					
Does your enterprise's body of policies and procedures require users to report any vulnerabilities or deficiencies they discover in the enterprise's information security programs and controls to appropriate personnel in the enterprise's security or IT organizations?					
Does your enterprise's access control requirement include the following access restrictions?					
■ Control access to system functions with menus					
■ Restrict users' knowledge of information or system functions that they are not authorized to access					
■ Control users' access rights (e.g., read, write, delete, execute, etc.)					
■ Make certain that systems involved with confidential information provide only the output relevant to the user of the output and that this output is accessible only from authorized locations and terminals					
Has your enterprise implemented adequate security controls to prevent unauthorized access to information stored or processed on its systems?					

Continued

Table 12.9 Continued. IP Protection Program Assessment: Information
Security—Access Control

IP Protection Program Assessment Tool: Information Security—Access Control	Current Posture				
	100%	50%	0%	N/A	Remarks
Does your enterprise configure production systems to maintain logs that collect the following types of information?					
■ Session activity, including user IDs, and the date and time of both login and logout					
■ Any changes made to critical application system files					
■ Any additions or changes made to the privileges of users					
■ Start-ups and shutdowns of the system					
■ Failed attempts to access system objects					
Does your enterprise configure any of its systems, database management systems, etc. that store, process, or transmit confidential or critical information to log potential security events, including the following?					
■ System usage outside of normal business hours					
■ Multiple IDs utilized to authenticate from one IP address					
■ Statistically significant dataset returns on queries to tables of confidential information					
■ Concurrent multiple authentications					
Does your enterprise configure its systems and directories to log the creating, deleting, or changing privileges for user IDs and accounts by system administrators or other holders of privileged user IDs?					

Continued

www.syngress.com

Table 12.9 Continued. IP Protection Program Assessment: Information Security—Access Control

IP Protection Program Assessment Tool: Information Security—Access Control	Current Posture				
	100%	50%	0%	N/A	Remarks
Do your enterprise's security and IT organizations regularly review logs of security events looking for security exceptions, anomalies, and inappropriate activities and/ or utilize software that provides automated notification of such exceptions, anomalies, or inappropriate activities?					
Do your enterprise's networks display a login banner that informs all users that they are subject to the policies and standards of the enterprise, that they are subject to monitoring, that their use of network resources constitutes their agreement to be monitored, and that both their online activity and the enterprise's monitoring of their activity are subject to relevant laws and jurisdictions?					
Does your enterprise's body of policies and procedures prohibit the monitoring or observing of any user's online activities unless that user has been notified (e.g., by the login banner) that such activity may indeed be monitored or observed?					
Does your enterprise's body of policies and procedures require that the monitoring or observing of any user's online activities must be approved by either the enterprise's human resources group or its executive leadership, and pursued as an element of an ongoing investigation into possible policy violations or criminal activity?					
Does your enterprise limit knowledge of investigations into a user's online activities to the organization conducting the					

Continued

Table 12.9 Continued. IP Protection Program Assessment: Information
Security—Access Control

IP Protection Program Assessment Tool: Information Security—Access Control	Current Posture				
	100%	50%	0%	N/A	Remarks
investigation, e.g., legal counsel and/or human resources?					
Does your enterprise log all such monitoring for review by management and human resources for potential use as evidence in disciplinary actions or legal proceedings?					
Does your enterprise require users to receive prior, documented authorization by the information technology group to establish any of the following processes, services or resources?					
■ Modem connections to internal networks					
■ Wireless access points					
■ Electronic bulletin boards					
■ Local area networks					
■ Intranet or Internet servers					
■ Multiuser systems for communication					
Does your enterprise place its public Internet servers on subnets to separate them from its internal networks and intranet servers?					
Does your enterprise restrict traffic from public servers to internal network with the use of enterprise-approved routers and firewalls?					
Are the enterprise's firewalls deployed at all access points to nonenterprise networks— at a minimum?					
Are additional firewalls deployed as appropriate between network zones within the overall computing architecture?					

Continued

Table 12.9 Continued. IP Protection Program Assessment: Information
Security—Access Control

IP Protection Program Assessment Tool: Information Security—Access Control	Current Posture				
	100%	50%	0%	N/A	Remarks
Does your enterprise segregate servers, devices, and services in network zones; e.g., untrusted DMZ, semi-trusted DMZ, data center and internal active directory, global WAN, guest networks, and wireless networks?					
Does your enterprise configure both its public Internet servers and internal intranet to detect attempts at unauthorized access attempts?					
Does your enterprise monitor its networks, firewalls, servers, applications, etc. with Intrusion Detection Systems (IDS) in order to detect and analyze suspicious events, and does the enterprise's IDS monitor, at a minimum, UNIX syslogs, Windows event logs, application logs, denied traffic logs from firewalls, configuration changes to firewalls and other vital warning signs?					
Does your enterprise verify that any systems or network segments that are going to be connected to the enterprise's network have met the following security criteria prior to going forward with the connection?					
■ An enterprise-approved firewall for all Internet connections has been implemented					
■ An enterprise-approved user-authentication system has been implemented					
■ An enterprise-approved access control system has been implemented					
■ An authorized change control process has been implemented					

Continued

Table 12.9 Continued. IP Protection Program Assessment: Information Security—Access Control

IP Protection Program Assessment Tool: Information Security—Access Control	Current Posture				
	100%	50%	0%	N/A	Remarks
▪ System management responsibilities have been clearly defined					
▪ Operations are clearly documented					
Do the wireless networks your enterprise makes available for guests include appropriate security controls, such as those listed in the following example? (Note: Of course, technology advances relentlessly; this example is from the midpoint of this first decade in the 21st century.) ▪ 802.11a, 802.11b, or 802.11g (not 802.11i) wireless protocols					
▪ Strong WEP key (i.e., one that is not easily guessed) that is changed every three months (at minimum)					
▪ Access point placed in its own zone, with a firewall separated from the rest of the enterprise's network					
▪ Access point positioned and aligned to limit transmissions outside of the enterprise's facilities					
▪ Unique client addresses from non-enterprise address spaces					
Do the wireless networks your enterprise makes available for employees, contractors, and other authorized users include appropriate security controls, such as those listed in the following example? (Note: Of course, technology advances relentlessly; this example is from the midpoint of the first decade in the 21st century.) ▪ 802.1g or 802.11a wireless protocols					

Continued

Table 12.9 Continued. IP Protection Program Assessment: Information
Security—Access Control

IP Protection Program Assessment Tool: Information Security—Access Control	Current Posture				
	100%	50%	0%	N/A	Remarks
■ WPA or WPA2, 802.1x/PEAP, and authentication server for encryption and authentication					
■ Access point placed in its own zone, with a firewall separating it from the rest of enterprise's network					
■ Access point positioned and aligned to limit transmissions outside of the enterprise's facilities					
■ Unique client addresses from any nonenterprise address space					
Does your enterprise instruct employees and other authorized users to implement security precautions for wireless communications from public places, including the following measures?					
■ Use only WEP for access via public networks					
■ Do not conduct transactions (e.g., purchases) via untrusted wireless networks					
■ Turn off wireless and infrared adaptors on PDAs and laptops when these devices are not in use					
■ Use enterprise user ID and password only on the enterprise's own web sites, VPNs, or dial-in programs					
■ Do not engage in business conversations in e-mail or instant messaging without using WEP (at a minimum) or other encryption					

Continued

Table 12.9 Continued. IP Protection Program Assessment: Information Security—Access Control

IP Protection Program Assessment Tool: Information Security—Access Control	Current Posture				
	100%	50%	0%	N/A	Remarks
Does your enterprise implement an enterprise-approved Virtual Private Network (VPN) and/or a dial-up solution to enable remote access for employees and other authorized users?					
Does your enterprise instruct employees using laptops, PDAs, smartphones, and other mobile computing devices to implement the following security controls?					
■ Available power on password features should be activated					
■ Available data encryption features if devices contain confidential information					
■ Utilize removable storage media as appropriate					
■ Conduct periodic backups of vital information					
■ Never loan mobile computing devices to others					
■ Never leave mobile computing devices unattended unless secured or safely stored					
■ Eradicate all data from mobile devices before disposing of them					

Table 12.10 assesses an enterprise's use of systems development and maintenance policies as part of an IP Protection Program Assessment Tool for information security.

Table 12.10 IP Protection Program Assessment Tool: Information Security—Systems Development and Maintenance Policies

IP Protection Program Assessment Tool: Information Security—Systems Development and Maintenance Policies	Current Posture				
	100%	50%	0%	N/A	Remarks
Does your enterprise include the identification and documentation of any security requirements in the overall requirements phase of all system development projects?					
Does your enterprise include the identification and documentation of all security requirements and controls in the overall requirements phase of any system development project?					
Does your enterprise include system security requirements as an element in the overall business case for any new information systems?					
Does your enterprise follow generally accepted secure coding principles and practices in the development and maintenance of its systems?					
Does your enterprise follow generally accepted secure coding principles and practices in the development and maintenance of its systems?					
Does your enterprise use commercial information security products for processes and functions such as identity management, authentication, access control, encryption, and security administration instead of developing custom solutions?					
Does your enterprise use shared security services available in operating systems, network operating systems, database management systems, access control					

Continued

Table 12.10 Continued. IP Protection Program Assessment Tool: Information Security—Systems Development and Maintenance Policies

IP Protection Program Assessment Tool: Information Security—Systems Development and Maintenance Policies	Current Posture				
	100%	50%	0%	N/A	Remarks
packages, firewalls, gateways, routers, active directory, LDAP, etc., rather than developing custom functionality to deliver security within the enterprise's computing environment?					
Does your enterprise exercise control over the ability to access, update, or duplicate the source code, executable code, and system files for its development, test, and production environments?					
Does your enterprise keep its source code and files for development, test, and production in separate locations, and also maintain a log recording all updates to these libraries?					
Does your enterprise prohibit the implementation of executable code on any operational system unless successful testing has been completed, user acceptance has been confirmed, and updates have been made to corresponding program source libraries?					
Does your enterprise require a minimum of three testing cycles (i.e., unit, integration, and user acceptance testing) on all systems or programs developed in-house, as well as additional testing for mission-critical systems or applications?					
Does your enterprise prohibit the implementation of any software, whether custom developed or packaged, unless it has undergone adequate security testing performed by the internal organization					

Continued

Table 12.10 Continued. IP Protection Program Assessment Tool: Information Security—Systems Development and Maintenance Policies

IP Protection Program Assessment Tool: Information Security—Systems Development and Maintenance Policies	Current Posture				
	100%	50%	0%	N/A	Remarks
(e.g., security or information technology) or authorized third-party responsible for such security testing?					
Does your enterprise sanitize and strip production data of its identity before it is utilized in the software testing process, provided that such use is not prohibited by local laws, and this sanitizing and stripping process include the removal or alteration of confidential or private information unless prior written authorization?					
Has your enterprise established change control and release management procedures for maintaining, copying, and promoting the enterprise's libraries of source and executables?					
Does your enterprise include the following elements in its change control procedures?					
■ Document approval of and agreement to proposed change					
■ Review of standards and architecture relevant to the proposed change					
■ Review security impact of proposed change					
■ Test user acceptance of change					
■ Update system document to include change					
■ Update all relevant training content, operations documentation, and user procedures					
■ Update system change log					

Continued

Table 12.10 Continued. IP Protection Program Assessment Tool: Information Security—Systems Development and Maintenance Policies

IP Protection Program Assessment Tool: Information Security—Systems Development and Maintenance Policies	Current Posture				
	100%	50%	0%	N/A	Remarks
Does your enterprise evaluate and test the potential impact of changing or upgrading operating systems (including the impact on applications and other software already installed) prior to initiating any such update?					
Does your enterprise utilize audit trails, activity logs, and security controls (including the validation of input data, output data, and internal processing) in systems and applications in order to thwart misuse, unauthorized modification, or loss and to prevent the exploitation of known vulnerabilities (e.g., buffer overflow, etc.)?					

Chapter 13

The Intelligent Approach

Introduction

Why should any consideration be given to having an intelligence function within an enterprise? If one exists, what should be the remit of the individual or unit? How should this intelligence component integrate into a holistic program; what should it look like?

First, as with every other component, your organization's commitment, made tangible in budget dollars and warm bodies, will in large part determine the scope and reach of your intelligence program. With a modicum of funding, a great deal can be accomplished, both from an enterprise protection perspective, as well as enhancing the operational side of the equation. Initial seed funds, expended in acquiring the correct talent with the appropriate background, can catapult an enterprise from being largely blind both offensively and defensively, to an enterprise which is seemingly gifted with a high degree of prescience.

In many organizations, there will be a struggle in the convincing of decision-makers that there is need for an intelligence component.

Where such an intelligence team would report within an organization, and how much money it would have in its budget, will vary.

In some organizations, you may win approval for only one warm body, and with that warm body you will have 100 percent more than most organizations. (Few organizations will field a team.)

This individual or team should have a budget ranging from tens of thousands to one-hundred thousand dollars to allow access to relevant third-party information feeds, some sold as intelligence feeds, others as news aggregators, and still others as market research. Couple these feeds with the myriad of other sources and resources available, and one person can be an effective force multiplier, providing that person is properly schooled in the acquisition, distillation, compilation, and presentation of the information, in a succinct manner which addresses the identified audience(s) within the enterprise.

As noted, this individual will monitor the flow of information, call it intelligence in security-related areas such as travel risk, cyber risk, and incidental risk, as well as provide data points for the effective and efficient operation of the enterprise by focusing on various economic factors (e.g., global markets, mergers and acquisitions, research and development, and competitive information).

With an intimate knowledge of your organization's operations, and an understanding of both the strategy and direction that has been plotted by the executive leadership, this individual could provide a variety of intelligence products in the form of monthly, weekly, and daily high-level briefings for executives based on their individual needs.

In addition, the operations-level risk summaries as well as timely ad hoc travel threat advisories will have great utility for the general corporate populace.

Such internal products should include analysis of the risk, threat, opportunities, or challenges on global, regional, or local scales, and of how they specifically relate to the organization's operations or direction, as well as recommendations on how, if possible, to mitigate the risks and threats and overcome the challenges, while taking advantage of any opportunities.

As noted, few organizations are able to staff an intelligence unit consisting of several warm bodies with the fiat to develop a robust program. Most enterprises begin lean and then expand upon establishment of credibility and value added.

In a perfect world, the executive leadership of the organization as a whole would have access to the following types of information, provided via the intelligence function:

- Status updates on competitors
- Market assessments
- Market composition
- Corporate share of the overall market
- Projected market expansions/contractions
- Intellectual property protection assessments
- By country
- Current and pending litigation having a possible effect on the enterprise
- By relevant industry

In a perfect world, they would have a team of individuals designated to focus on discrete portions of the flow from these disparate, proprietary sources, and one individual or one sub-set of the team to break down, analyze, aggregate, and integrate these disparate elements, and then relate the whole to the organization's circumstances and prospects. This end result would in turn become intelligence product to be presented to the corporate leadership.

The intelligence function (i.e., provision of the information the enterprise needs to function efficiently and competitively) is sector dependent, industry dependent within the sector, market dependent, and geographically dependent.

With those parameters, you can determine the amount of investment you want to make in such an intelligence function; e.g., someone who has a company with a market limited to Wisconsin is going to pay attention to all comers in Wisconsin, and maybe in Minnesota, Illinois, and Michigan, but he or she is probably not going to pay much attention to anywhere else, unless the business is vulnerable to competition coming in via the Internet, where geography is not a determinate of success.

With those parameters, you can determine the amount of investment you want to make in such an intelligence function; e.g., someone who has a company with a market limited to Wisconsin is obliged to pay attention to all comers in Wisconsin, and maybe in Minnesota, Illinois, and Michigan, but he or she is probably not going to pay much attention to the activities of similar enterprises anywhere else, unless the enterprise is engaged in business which can be conducted over the Internet.

The Intelligence Function As an Internal Early Warning System

An additional function, which the intelligence component can perform, is adding to protecting the enterprise. In order to provide appropriate analysis, the enterprise and the intelligence director and his or her team should have access to what is the baseline on spectrum of activities, and so forth, so that what isn't baseline can be identified and examined (i.e., the anomalous).

Imagine a control panel with levers zero to ten on all the functions in your company. If everything is running at normal, it should be around five, signified by the color blue. But when something glitches, it should either go down or up from the baseline, i.e., it should go either red or green on the control panel, and that should trigger an inquiry.

Let us say, for example, that manufacturing is producing at two times normal capacity; that would turn green on your control panel. It could be a positive event. But it would trigger an inquiry. Why are we there?

Well, it should correlate to your book to build. Perhaps you have a backlog of orders. But if that production ramps up and the book to build does not reflect any such demand, it might be indicative of a fourth shift pumping out gray market. It is not counterfeit, because it is the real McCoy.

The same is true of sales efforts and the bidding processes. You would look for patterns that deviated from the baseline and then inquire into the contributing factors.

On a daily basis, the intelligence team is monitoring all of these baselines. And of course, they are also looking outside. What is going on with the competitors? What is going on in the business environment?

Many so-called competitive intelligence analysis are really only looking at products versus products. Very few of them actually compare the strategy and direction of companies versus other companies.

Your intelligence guru's team could also be your focal point for putting together the equivalent of the virtual competitor team to test the postulations of the enterprise against the perceived strategies of its competitors. Professional sports teams scout their competition, and in some sports, practice against colleagues emulating the competitor's strategies and tactics to good effect. Why do we see so little of this in the commercial enterprise?

The reality is the market may be growing, but it is finite. There are only so many customer dollars available. It is in your interest to capture as large a share of that market, while protecting your intellectual properties. Your competitor will want to learn your go-to-market plan; you need to protect that data. Your competitor will want to know your research and development figures. Protect that as well. The role playing and scenario techniques serve the enterprise that utilize these methods in a most positive manner, as it forces the enterprise to ask, "what if?" followed by, "now what?"

If Company A (i.e., yours) wishes to evolve a new product that does X and markets it in Location 2, how would Companies B, C, and D react?

Or conversely, Company B wishes to evolve a new product that does X, how does Company A react?

As stated, such scenarios can be analyzed and projected upon. What are your options?

In the real world, governments do the" if this then what" exercise all the time.

If you work in government, you are always looking at the hypothetical. Furthermore, you are not constrained by the outlandish. You just don't spend as much time planning for the lower probabilities. But you have to plan for all events.

In many enterprises that we have looked into, there is no planning for any events at all; and in most of those that do plan for some types of events, the planning is generic and superficial.

In summary, in a perfect world, your intelligence director would be looking at all of these areas and highlighting potential challenges or opportunities. To Sales and Marketing, you could say, "Bingo! It looks like Company B is doing Y, you might want to pay attention." To Manufacturing, you could say, "Bingo! It looks like production is up to x-percent. You might want the anti-counterfeit group to get out there and make sure we do not have a fourth shift pumping out product for the gray market."

There are many things that you can measure to sense abnormality. The rate of employee turnover might tell you something. A sudden surge or decline in the rate of electricity used in a plant might tell you something. What is your run rate?

What Happens to a Million Grains of Sand in a Perfect Storm?

In the "Perfect Storm" conditions of economic espionage (i.e., where we find ourselves here in the early decades of the 21st century), it comes at you from different angles. Coming in with a brute force approach is not only highly alerting, it is also not very productive. But those who take the million grains of sand approach come in under the radar, and their targets do not even notice they are losing anything. Your secrets exist a little at a time, instead of all at once.

Are you losing your intellectual property or your information assets? Do the people within your organization even know the difference?

In the corporate parlance, intellectual property generally means your trademarks and that which you patent. But losing information assets (e.g., your RFIs, your go to market plans, your personnel files, your compensation files, your health files, your benefit structure, your options functions, all of the kinds of information that make the enterprise run) can have just as deleterious effect on your enterprise as losing your patent, perhaps more.

Sometimes the force differentiator between an efficient company and a highly efficient company is how they do their backbone infrastructure and how they handle employees' day-to-day needs.

In our view, that differentiation and how it occurs could be construed as something worthy of protection, because it is your organic culture that makes your enterprise different and better than your competitor's. You want to advertise your efficiency in the way you do business, but you do not want to advertise the content of it. So if in the world of economic espionage, people were focusing on acquiring your methodologies, that's going to be easy, because you advertise them. But if they want to acquire your content, it is your culture that has to prevent them from succeeding. People should be empowered to talk about processes, unless those processes are your differentiation. We are talking about administrative processes, not functional processes (e.g., a process on how to create a widget is worthy of protection, but the fact that you outsource your production of widgets isn't necessarily worthy of protection).

Similarly, in some instances you may want to keep from the public spotlight whom you are using as a contracted manufacturer or outsourced resource. In all cases you must impose upon your external partners the same level of protection you place on your data and processes, make no assumptions. Manage your own expectations; by managing the level of protection expected and then audit, inspect, and adjudicate if found lacking. Generally speaking, that which is measured is accomplished, so an inspection regime found to be not only hollow in implementation, but also in remediation, may place your enterprise at risk.

Some companies have sales successes that are graded as "excellent," when in fact they could have actually got "outstanding," except that unbeknownst to them, they had lost their market plan, and the information it yielded to the competition cut into their sales.

The plan was, "We're going to go in and ask for ten," but the person you are negotiating with knows your break-even point is seven. As they have learned your go-to-market plan via one of your outsourced marketing team, who himself was a contracted resource with his feet planted in both your camp and that of your customer. Your customer does not want to dig into seven, because they know they have the inside track and they want to ensure that they take no action which may put that valuable resource in jeopardy, so they allow you an eight. You're happy and they're very happy because they just saved themselves two. And you are none the wiser, as you never knew they knew what your break-even point was and therefore you negotiated appropriately. They were hardball with you—six, six, six—knowing that there was no deal unless you got them up to seven, but then they allowed you to make a profit by going to eight, and kept you in the game. They knew what was going on all along. That is reality. You need to protect yourself against this reality.

But if you are doing analysis on the methodologies that your customers are using, whether corporate or governmental, and you are measuring it (e.g., by asking "What are the tactics being used here?"), you might pick up an early warning indicator.

The negotiating tactics of a customer might give you a tip-off that they know more about you than you do. Conversely, consistently losing bids might be a tip-off that your competition or your customer is selling your bid information.

In sales, you need to protect your response to quotations, because if put in your competitors' hands it can be used to underbid you, and to manipulate their bid to your detriment. Likewise, if your customer gets a hold of this information, it can also be used to your detriment. The individual instances usually do not constitute far-reaching losses. They are most often incremental losses, particularly in the large-scale service provider industry, or in national infrastructure projects, where the deal includes one buy and options for six more years worth.

When you have, as you do in so many industries today, partners doing your core work (i.e. outsourcing), you end up in a morass in which you must trust your partner to protect your goods and intellectual property just like you would. You must ask yourself, are you achieving expectations with that partner, or not? And indeed, are you exceeding expectations in your dealings with them? In Corning's case, their relationship with their partner is what saved them. It was their partner's valuing of the relationship, and their highly ethical business practices that enabled Corning to be aware that the subterfuge has occurred.

The Partnership Issue Is a Daunting Force-Multiplier, Double-Edged Sword

The investment in the partnership has to be commensurate with the loss that the partner could cause you. This investment is not so much in money, as it is in time spent in building relationship; it is taking the time to build the trust, and thus level the expectations. If, for example, you are relying on a partner for manufacturing and they roll slowly on you, there is a potential downside.

But it could be even worse. If they sell your intellect to a competitor, and suddenly your competitor leapfrogs your advance because they figured out what you did while you were still rolling slow in production, then you win, they win, you lose (i.e., you have won the battle but lost the war).

You have to engage in ongoing Corporate Relationship Management (CRM). Whether you call them partners, or consultants, or they are part of your network in terms of interconnectivity, you have to get in there and maintain the relationship with all of those individuals and entities that interact with your core.

Consultants are of particular concern because they learn from you, they leave you, they jump to another company, and out the door your intellectual property goes.

In sum, you must take steps to know who is working on your behalf. Demand background checks; demand to see the results of the background checks of all aspects of your workforce. Governments do this all the time; they demand individuals with whom they are engaging, and will have access to the respective nation's sensitive data to acquire "security clearance." In most instances, this involves a comprehensive self-declaration of data from the individual, followed by an even more comprehensive background and indices checks by the government entity. The individual is allowed access to the data when and only when the "clearance" is issued.

Far too often, enterprises utilize the Non-Disclosure Agreement (NDA) as if it was an ironclad mechanism by which disclosure or abuse of your data sets is prohibited. The reality is that the NDA allows you a reasonable chance of success in a court of law. But the true reality is that when you appear in the court of law, the damage more than likely has already occurred.

Your NDA is the means by which you keep the toothpaste in the tube. The enforcement of the NDA is the action you take when the toothpaste is on the table; it does not get the toothpaste back in the tube. Therefore, the goal is to avoid the opportunity to allow toothpaste out of the tube.

You must ensure your price points are protected data: audit the data; monitor the deal; monitor the customer negotiating and buying patterns; monitor your outsourced resources; and so forth. All of which is possible, though most are not utilized due to both the level of difficulty, as well as the limited resources.

Chapter 14

Protecting Intellectual Property in a Crisis Situation

Introduction

Business continuity, disaster recovery, and crisis management are vital aspects of your enterprise's overall security program. The primary concerns are, of course, the safety of your people and the rapid resumption of your operations either in the same locale or elsewhere.

But in regard to intellectual property and trade secret theft, another dimension often receives insufficient attention: protection of your data while in the midst of a crisis.

Your IT professionals should have an inventory of all your enterprise's information assets in any given area at any given time.

They should also have a replication of all those assets in a geographically separated area in the event the primary location is destroyed. In a perfect situation this replication would be accomplished via a real-time process configured for automatic switchover.

But it is not simply a question of not losing the information, or of how quickly you can get your information systems up and running again; it is also a question of the potential exposure or misappropriation of information assets that are abandoned or otherwise compromised in the chaos prior to or in the immediate aftermath of an emergency evacuation or the destruction of a building.

If the emergency is an earthquake, you get zero warning.

If the emergency is a hurricane, you get weather reports.

If the emergency is a military incursion, you will probably hear the rattling of sabers.

As your enterprise's champion of intellectual property (IP) and trade secret theft protection, you need to advocate a TEN-SEVEN-FIVE-THREE-ONE-NOW approach. If you had ten days' notice, what could you do to protect your information assets? Now make a list assuming you had only seven days.

Next, working with the seven days' list, you re-prioritize and develop a list of what you could do if you only have five days notice.

Likewise, make a list of what you can do with three days' notice.

With one day's notice, of course, you can do only the minimal. But the planning and prioritizing that goes into the process of working down from ten to one will ensure that you get the most out of that one desperate day.

And, of course, when disaster hits all of a sudden, right *now*, with no warning, it is a matter of self-preservation and assistance to those in your immediate environment.

IP Protection Designing & Planning...

The TEN-SEVEN-FIVE-THREE-ONE-NOW Approach

Here's how it works:

You are responsible for a branch office. You have your asset inventory in hand, including both human and technological assets.

You have 15 desktop computers, all possessing critical intellectual property and new developmental work, such as the designs for the newest widget and so on. You also have three storage servers, one mail server, and one server used to allow employees to create a virtual private network into the branch office when they are working in a mobile mode. You have 15 persons (14 regular staff and one visiting employee from your corporate headquarters).

You now must identify those items which require more than seven days to implement a protective regime (destruction, replication, relocation).

You should develop a list of protection measures you can take with 10 days' notice for the information assets at risk in any particular facility.

Then, working down from the 10-day list, you prioritize and draw up a list of what you can do if you only have seven days' notice.

In Table 14.1 a plan is laid out for the office itself, as well as for its vital IP elements, for example, desktop computers, the storage servers, the communications server, the corporate papers, and the personnel. Each inventoried element has a set of corresponding procedures to be enacted on the basis of amount of time remaining before the incident or disaster.

Table 14.1 Countdown Plan for Protecting Intellectual Property in Crisis Situations

Intellectual Property	Day 10	Day 7	Day 5	Day 3	Day 1	Crisis
Location of the IP (Server, Client, Safe, etc.)	Situation Normal	Items identified as taking 7 or less man-days to address	Items identified as taking 5 man-days to address	Items identified as taking 3 or less man-days to address	Items identified as taking 1 day to address	Crisis – deal with crisis at hand and then address the IP
Desktop Computer #1-15 – CAD diagrams, new development work, PII etc.	Encrypt Hard drive	N/A	Force Replication to HQ's server	Copy hard drive to DVD and encrypt	Secure or destroy hard drive	When safe recover hard drive
Storage Server	Server encrypted Daily replication to HQ server	N/A	N/A	N/A	N/A	When safe inspect server
Communications Server	Begin Alternate Routing protocol	100% data replication to Alt-Route location	Dual mode at Branch and at Alt-Route	Switch-over to Alt-Route	Activate Alt-route	Activate Alt-route

Continued

Table 14.1 Continued. Countdown Plan for Protecting Intellectual Property in Crisis Situations

Intellectual Property	Day 10	Day 7	Day 5	Day 3	Day 1	Crisis
Corporate papers	Scan crucial documents	Continue Scanning	Secure or relocate all important docs according to importance	Secure or relocate all important docs according to importance	Secure all important docs	When safe, secure all important documents
Personnel	Test phone tree and alternate forms of communi-cation	Implement phone tree with situation report work	Non-Essential personnel begin or enact alternate environment plan	Non-Critical personnel begin or enact alternative work environment plan	Remaining personnel enact emergency procedures if safe	Protect self – then property

On the flip side, you also have to develop a plan for re-constitution from day zero to day ten. How long is it going to take to put it all back together? Far too often, the disaster preparedness planning stops when the "crisis" appears to have concluded, and then the reassembly isn't conducted with the same level of planning. Once again, intellectual property is inadvertently put at risk.

You will also want to conduct a damage assessment that addresses, among other issues, whether there was or could have been exposure or compromise of IP or trade secrets.

If there is an earthquake, a zero notice event, and no one is in the office at the time, the lines go down and your servers are sitting there unprotected. You can mitigate the danger to your data using some technological fixes, such as encryption of the server.

If you have a facility in an environment where earthquakes are prevalent but there are no hurricanes, you are less likely to have ten-day scenarios; most of your scenarios will be zero or one-day notice, so maybe you should consider using technology such as encryption to mitigate the fact that you will not get the opportunity to off-load in your most likely emergencies.

Of course, in environments such as Seattle, where you have earthquakes, heavy rains, and flooding, as well as the threat of volcanoes and tsunamis, you have to anticipate and prepare for numerous scenarios.

When you chat with your colleagues about this issue, they will probably look at you as if you were a multi-horned beast. They will protest, "Who has the time to plan for all of that?" Our suggested response: "How can you afford not to?"

One reasonable compromise in such circumstances is to identify those locales most susceptible to day zero events in the disaster vectors—such as political hot spots, war zones, close proximity to fault lines, coastal areas vulnerable to hurricanes and tsunamis, inland areas prone to tornadoes—and address them as a priority.

But if you do not know what your inventory of information assets is, you do not know how long it will take to protect it.

You do not simply have to plan for protecting your data or destroying it; you also need to know how long it takes to do each of these tasks. You must realistically test your plan, within the context of personnel and infrastructure limitations; you won't know if you can do what appears to be "impossible" unless you practice.

Answering these questions and putting a viable plan in place ensures that you are not a victim of haphazard processes, but rather are simply inconvenienced, since you planned ahead and created a solution to a potentially damaging situation.

There is more to it than being able to say, "Everyone is out alive, and we are up and running."

The best crisis management planning demands that you think outside the box, and when you factor in protecting intellectual property during a crisis situation, you must stretch your mind even more.

NOTE

A building housing a conglomerate's headquarters, in a developing country, burst into flames in the middle of the night.

The fire brigade showed up and began to fight the flames. These were robust, physically imposing individuals, who fearlessly engaged the fire.

As the fire began to come under control, but while it still was unsafe to re-enter the building, a second wave of "firefighters" arrived, looking similar to the first brigade. However, the attentive might have noticed that some of them were not as "fit." These individuals had trouble scaling the ladder into the building and didn't appear terribly happy to have been placed in this situation by their superiors.

The second wave of responders turned out not to be firefighters after all. They had bribed their way into the building in an attempt to obtain items of value (presumably documents and other important papers not destroyed by the fire) under circumstances in which the rightful owners could not notice and would assume that they had been destroyed rather than stolen.

If someone is targeting your intellectual property, and is watching your company closely, it is quite possible that that person would take advantage of your misfortune, particularly if your protection program were otherwise robust. Table 14.2 is an example of an IP protection program assessment for business continuity and crisis management.

Table 14.2 IP Protection Program Assessment—Business Continuity
and Crisis Management

IP Protection Program Assessment—Business Continuity and Crisis Management	Current Posture					
	100%	75%	50%	25%	N/A	Remarks
Does your enterprise have a formal Crisis Management Team (CMT), with a designated CMT Director, CMT Deputy Director, and CMT representative for all functions, facilities, regions, and/or divisions, as appropriate?						
Does your enterprise have a documented crisis management plan, which is regularly reviewed and updated?						
Is your enterprise's crisis management plan tested regularly (for example, quarterly or annually), and does this testing include drills and exercises based on plausible scenarios?						
Does your enterprise's crisis management team maintain emergency contact numbers for all team members, delegated back-ups, and all other personnel who would be called to act in an emergency capacity?						
Does your enterprise have a designated crisis management command center?						
Is your enterprise's crisis management command center equipped with all necessary communications						

Continued

Table 14.2 Continued. IP Protection Program Assessment—Business Continuity and Crisis Management

IP Protection Program Assessment—Business Continuity and Crisis Management	Current Posture					
	100%	75%	50%	25%	N/A	Remarks
devices, TVs and radios, IT infrastructure, independent power supplies, and emergency supplies (water, rations, medical supplies, etc.)?						
Does your enterprise have an established Business Continuity Team?						
Does your enterprise have a formal Business Continuity Plan?						
Does your enterprise's business continuity plan identify alternate sites, as appropriate, for facilities in the event of an emergency or other natural disaster?						
Does your enterprise's business continuity plan factor in all information technology (i.e., systems and data) requirements should it be necessary to get up and running at an alternative site?						

Chapter 15

How to Sell Your Intellectual Property Protection Program

Introduction

Without executive commitment, your intellectual property protection program won't go anywhere. Without a meaningful, tangible executive mandate, the populace within the enterprise will blow you off. You may be the recipient of some pleasant indulgence and some seemingly sincere lip service in the initial phases, but sooner or later your program will end up in the dustbin of institutional memory. People will say, "Oh yeah, someone tried that once. Nothing ever came of it, why would we want to make that mistake a second time?"

No one is going to change corporate culture, or "make more work" for his or her team, unless it is unmistakably clear that this is the will of the chief executive and the message is being consistently and repeatedly pushed downward throughout the enterprise. In sum, this initiative has to flow from the top down; otherwise it is doomed to failure.

Our task is further complicated by the fact that no executive, whether C-level or at the entry level to the executive suite, is ever going to say, "No, security isn't important to us, we don't do everything possible to protect our intellectual property," publicly or internally. Board members, shareholders, clients, business partners, industry analysts, consumer advocates, perhaps even the public at large would soon be clamoring for their heads. No, executives will always list the security of the enterprise's people and intellectual property as one of his or her top priorities.

That means you are looking for something deeper. You are looking for a real commitment, a genuine understanding. You want to see the light switch go off, and you want that bright bulb to be seen from everywhere, from every cubicle, every assembly line, every test lab, and every conference room. Then and only then will you have what you desire: an integrated security program designed to protect the enterprise's lifeblood, the intellectual property.

In order to have a successful security program, both senior and mid-level management must understand the value of the security program and use this value as a differentiator in their outreach to clients, customers, partners, and vendors. So how do we get from zero support by any within the enterprise to acceptance and embracement of the concept by management?

You need a mandate with teeth in it, muscle behind it, and mechanisms to project this mandate. To get such a mandate, you have to deliver a stellar presentation with an irrefutable, irresistible pitch. The chief executive or the executive staff must come away from your pitch both informed and engaged. More importantly, they must come away from your pitch understanding what is required.

In this chapter, we will go through a five-slide presentation, one by one, and inspect the various elements of each slide, examining what goes into each of the elements and how one slide leads to the next.

The slide presentation aims to assist you in your own presentation to your corporation's leadership team, whether that is the executive suite, the board, or key principals, such as the CEO, CFO, and COO.

The immediate goal of such a presentation is to win executive commitment for your IP protection program. The ultimate goal is to change or enhance the corporate culture, so that every time employees speak of their activities, security of the intellectual property and of the enterprise as a whole is a "forethought" and not an afterthought. Employees will understand the overall value to the enterprise of having their research, development, manufacturing, sales, personnel, marketing, and the firm's products secured. To assist in this regard, as discussed in prior chapters, properly research and position the established body of policies and standards, as well as other resources, for them to rely on in the pursuit of an integrated, holistic security environment.

You are going to need to do your homework. You are going to have to take the concepts and principles outlined in this chapter, and the sample presentation it documents, and turn it all into a pitch and a presentation that is properly calibrated to your corporate culture, accurately reflects the facts on the ground in your business environment, and offers a reasonable and achievable path to success. It is often said that when Wall Street looks at a publicly traded conglomerate, it is like looking at an American Quarter Horse and the prospects for the horse's success in the quarter-mile sprint. The reality is, your perspective must be that of the endurance race horse, prepared for the 50-mile ride. This journey through the process will entail both fact-finding and thinking outside the box. Success rarely comes pre-packaged.

The fact that you are able to have this conversation is a very good sign that you, the implementer, have a reasonable expectation of success; now you have to demonstrate that your expectations can be actualized.

If you follow the logic, the analytical process, and the argumentation suggested here, you will improve your chances significantly. Remember, as Thomas Edison said, "Hell, there are no rules here—we are trying to accomplish something."

Questions to Ask and People to Approach

There are five questions, or perhaps more accurately, five areas of inquiry which require exploration and development of answers. These are:

1. What is your business differentiation from your competitors?

2. Who do you have to protect your intellectual property and differentiators from?

3. What are the probabilities in terms of likely vectors of threat, what would they target within your enterprise, and what would these adversaries have as their objectives?

4. If they succeeded in their objective (theft, tampering, destruction), what would the consequences be to the overall enterprise?

5. What countermeasures would be cost-effective and business-enabling, vice prohibitively expensive and disabling?

Notice in the second half of the title for this section, after "questions to ask," we said "and people to approach" rather than "and who you need to answer them." That is because it is unlikely that very many, if any, of the executives, managers, and individual contributors will have thought about what you are endeavoring to aggregate, analyze, and articulate.

The obvious business differentiators may be on the tip of everybody's tongue, but you have to go deeper and cast a wider net. It is not enough to know that your corporation has the best product in a direct comparison to the competition or that the firm's advertising agency assisting the marketing and sales entities is more professional, experienced, and in-tune with the target audience for the products being sold and developed.

You must put your closed-ended questions into the dust bin and focus on the open-ended inquiries to get to the items worthy of protection. You have to look for the undetected, the unseen, and the unconsidered to grasp the situation in an accurate manner.

You certainly need to ask executives about what differentiates the enterprise from its competitors, but also ask your engineers, your programmers, your operations people, your sales and marketing professionals, your human resources professionals, maybe even your customer service or procurement people. While it clearly depends on the nature of your business, it is paramount that your engagement is as all-inclusive as possible.

What differentiates your business could be how you make your product, what goes into it, who makes it for you, or where it is made. If, for example, your firm assisted a partner to enable the partner to make your product more efficiently, then perhaps that methodology is worthy of protection. Think of Henry Ford and his use of the assembly line in the automotive industry. Had he kept the concept and implementation of the assembly line "secret" would he have had competition on his heels as soon as he did? What other industries would not have evolved as quickly? It is a business decision to either protect or share methodologies.

What differentiates your product could be what you sell, how you sell it, who sells it for you. If you sell all your own products and have your own integrated work force, you may have greater control over the protection of your IP than if you used outside entities such as distributors, channel partners, vendors, or contracted sales forces.

What differentiates your product could be all of the above, and more. And it is this "more" which you must strive to identify.

All across the enterprise, there are people you will have to approach on your fact-finding mission who won't have thought much about the issues you are inquiring into beyond the cursory observation that they are good at what they do and are proud of their efforts and results. Therefore, they will have to be brought along; you will have to pluck it out of their heads or extrapolate it from their responses. What you are looking for is what differentiates your enterprise and its products and who would benefit from stealing it or causing it to fail.

You will also have to go outside the enterprise, to the World Wide Web, government resources, third party intelligence aggregators, industry analytic resources, individual subject matter experts, and more—particularly in regard to answering the second and third questions: who do you have to protect from and what bad could come from the successful compromise of the enterprise's intellectual property.

Let's look at each of these five areas of inquiry in more depth.

What Is Your Business Differentiation from Your Competitors?

What makes you different? Your people? Your processes? Your R&D? Your differentiation points are what you are declaring as worthy of protection.

> Human resources policies and procedures, such as hiring practices, could make your enterprise unique. What about your compensation regime?

Retention policy and leadership development could also be a source of differentiation, as well as future personnel needs and projections.

Research and development capabilities, level of investment, locale of investment, methodologies, personnel headcount, equipment allocation, and topics could be differentiators.

Manufacturing as a whole could be a differentiator. If you outsource, how do you integrate the third-party's methodologies into your own? The Boeing Company had for years dictated to its manufacturing partners how components would be built and how these components would be integrated into its aircraft—it was the company's differentiator. In 2007, Boeing introduced their newest aircraft, the Boeing 787 "Dreamliner," and with this introduction, Boeing also introduced a paradigm shift away from dictating methodologies to collaborative and consultative engagement.[1]

Marketing and Sales also have data worthy of examination and perhaps will be a differentiator as well. As noted previously, is your level of investment in advertising and marketing campaigns indicative of other metrics within the enterprise? Are your marketing efforts in a given market based on your competition's expected success in the market and designed to support your own success? How about your sales figures, margins, discounts, client lists? All of these individually or collectively could differentiate you from your competition and thus are worthy of addressing as a potential differentiator.

Whom Do You Have to Protect These Differentiators From?

What are your points of vector, such as individual, competitor, organized criminal cartels, or state elements? Or is your enterprise threatened to some degree by all of them? The first step is to determine who would benefit from learning about any of these differentiators.

Individuals This vector is often characterized as the "insider-threat," but that is also a mischaracterization on the whole. That is not to say that the bona fide insider isn't in a better position to capitalize on your data, etc., but that individuals outside the enterprise can use the previously identified methodologies to garner your intellectual property as a force multiplier for their individual efforts. Take for example the situation in China, which according to 2007 statistics has identified 86% of all software as counterfeit.[2] This isn't just a theft of a company's intellectual property in the creation of the counterfeit, from the individual perspective, but it is the cost savings in going down this path as the individual as they prepare to enter the competitive marketplace—if an individual doesn't have similar infrastructure expenses as a similar enterprise, their cost of entry is reduced considerably. So we advocate looking from within and monitoring, auditing, and enforcing the need-to-know principal with your workforce, whether staff or contracted, but also being mindful of the individual not associated in any manner with your enterprise who may be looking for a quick point of entry into your market or the market of another.

Competitors It is unfortunate, but the world is not a level playing field with respect to free-market competitive engagements. And thus competitors will fall into two categories: those who will exploit any edge, legal or illegal, and those who will only engage in legal activities to take you and your enterprise to task in the market place. You must defend against both. The former will invest and engage at whatever level they believe is required to garner the desired results. The latter will engage and exploit anything you project or inadvertently provide via public disclosure and their ability to extrapolate. For example, it is totally appropriate to engage trade show staff in conversation and lead the conversation down any rabbit-trail to drill for details on a company's products. In this way, an ethical competitor may engage in ethical business practices advocated by the Society of Competitive Intelligence Professionals (SCIP),[3] whereas others may exceed this ethical brief and attempt to coerce information from your staff with financial inducements or other under-the-table arrangements. In both cases, your inappropriately protected data lands in the hands of your competitor.

Criminal elements These organizations have one goal—monetization. If there is a way they can manipulate your data systems to their financial advantage, through customer support, order mechanisms, or simply inducing an individual to share your intellectual property so that they may sell it to the aforementioned unscrupulous competitor, they usually will make the attempt.

State entity As noted in previous chapter(s), it is almost impossible to stop a state entity when the nation's resources have been allocated to compromise your intellectual property. That said, that does not mean that the boxing axiom does not apply—one does not lead with one's chin. You need to be on top of which state entities may be interested in your technology and why. For example, will your technology assist an indigenous firm who is your direct competitor? How is your technology being used by a geo-political competitor? It would surprise no one that during the Cold War, the former Soviet Union was very interested in the many commercial items used by the United States' military forces; that same level of interest is being played out today from the Chinese perspective. Take for example the case of Chi Mak and Tang Wai Mak, both accused and indicted for sharing their employer's data with the People's Republic of China (PRC),[4] data which would be of use to the PRC's military.

What Are the Probabilities in Terms of Likely Attackers, Targets, and Objectives?

Remember the formula Keith Rhodes provided in our Virtual Roundtable of Experts?

Risk = Threat * Vulnerability * Impact

The Threat = Adversary + Capability + Intent

The Vulnerability = Opportunity, and the Impact = Asset Value

Ask yourself, "Who would want it?" For example, we make sandals. The probability that any government would want to take our sandals is low; unless we have come up with something like a way to make a plastic sandal that would be market-shattering, and then perhaps they would want that information. Maybe we need to protect our fancy machinery or chemical processes. If I am a milk bottler, then perhaps I do not have to protect myself so much from state power, I just have to have a general Hazardous Analysis Critical Control Point (HACCP) program and a clean environment that would allow me to protect from everything (six years ago only three people in the USA were teaching it). Then the real things I need to protect are my customer lists and my discounts. Or perhaps your HR activities project more than it may seem: Is your enterprise advertising an expansion into a given country via their employment advertisements, and thus signaling to the competition a move in research and development or an increase coming downstream in sales and marketing? This may benefit the competitor. Could it benefit the organized criminal elements? What of the individuals you will be hiring in this locale? Are they subjected to the same background checks as the rest of the enterprise? If not, then perhaps the criminal elements can manipulate your hiring practices so that they can monetize their inside knowledge. What of the state entities? Do they have an interest in who is hired by your enterprise?

If the Competition Obtained or Tampered with Your Intellectual Property, What Harm Would Be Done?

In mid-2007, counterfeit Colgate toothpaste was front and center in the news, with large quantities of the counterfeit product finding its way into the United States. Colgate appropriately warned the consumer of the existence of the counterfeit product, a product that actually damaged your teeth in contrast to the true Colgate product, and also provided the consumer a means to identify the true Colgate product. So, were these actions sufficient? Were these actions the full extent of what could have been accomplished given the circumstances? The situation begs several questions: How many consumers took the time to review the guidance? How many other consumers simply tossed out their Colgate and bought a competitor's brand? So in this example, it is clear that the monetization of the Colgate brand by unscrupulous criminal elements placed a stellar brand at risk. Could the company have done something different?

What if you sell a product used in the sophisticated arms purchased by a nation's defense forces, and an adversarial nation caused your product to malfunction or to act in a manner different than what you had envisioned? Are you protecting your research and development methodologies, checking and rechecking for unadulterated operability, or otherwise guaranteeing to your customer that what you sell operates as advertised and only as advertised?

What Security Measures Would Be Cost-Effective and Business-Enabling?

You must demonstrate that good security enables good risk taking. Your analysis has identified and articulated both business differentiators and risks that threaten to co-opt or otherwise nullify them, so now you have to offer ways to mitigate the risks. But just as importantly, the plan has to make business sense.

For example, in order to make this differentiator reasonably secure, it costs $5. If we don't do this, we put $1 million at risk. It is a clear business decision. It is worth a $5 investment to protect $1 million.

But if it takes a $1 million dollar investment in security to protect $10, then you have to make a business decision.

And once you make that decision, either way, all of your available resources designed to protect your intellectual property must line up behind this decision. Even if it may not be the right one from your perspective, the fact that your security regime is present allows for the risk taking by the business elements, and a business decision is a business decision. There is no room for standing back and second-guessing or undermining that business decision. If the enterprise has decided that it is worth taking the risk for the good of the business—for example, if we are successful, and we believe we will be, we will be able to jump ahead of our competition—then all your security resources have to align to protect the enterprise within the new paradigm that has been created by the business decision to move forward in spite of the risk. You can't just walk away from it and say, "I am done now." The security regime designed to protect the enterprise and its intellectual property is always in a dynamic state and thus must be flexible enough to step forward as a full partner as the business dynamics adjust to the market place.

So you have to think through these issues ahead of time. You cannot wait for the executives to do the math for you. You have to do it for yourself first, and then demonstrate it to the executives. By doing so, you accomplish two vital feats: not only do you solve the problem of how best to protect that particular differentiator, or collection of differentiators, you have also demonstrated that security, personified by you and your efforts, is a business enabler, not a business impeder, and that security protects profit instead of draining it away.

Let us go through each of the five figures in this chapter and explore what they are meant to communicate and the desired effect they are meant to achieve. Let's now discuss Figure 15.1.

Figure 15.1 Intellectual Property Protection Program—the Agenda

Intellectual Property Protection Program

- Agenda:
  - Identification of intellectual property and associate risks
  - Implementation plan and established milestones
  - Socialization process
  - Executive commitment to execute program

Notes on Figure 15.1

The overall protection program for a corporation's intellectual property starts with a confirmation of what the information, processes, etc. are and where they reside within the corporation's footprint, and also identifies the risk to that same property. This is your agenda—it fulfills the first tenet of executive briefings: you are identifying and presenting the cadence of the briefing and the content of the briefing. Your executive should now be well prepared to actively listen. Now let's discuss Figure 15.2.

Figure 15.2 Intellectual Property Identification and Risk Identification

Intellectual Property Identification and Risk Identification

- Intellectual property locales:
- Identified risks
- Implications of loss:
- Business value of protecting intellectual property

Notes on Figure 15.2

First you must identify the locales where intellectual property may reside:

Executives and Board Members

You may wish to highlight, for example, those topics which are discussed in the board room, such as meeting agendas, board meeting minutes, compensation committee minutes, and more.

You may also wish to highlight the information your executive team would have natural access to, but which may not be accessible by the rank-and-file of the company. Some examples of these types of data would be discussion on potential mergers and acquisitions, changes in the strategic vision of the company, new partnerships, geographic expansion plans, direction of the firm in out-years, and more.

Research and Development

Consideration should be given to identifying exemplars such as new product designs, unregistered inventions, pending patents, awarded patents, new innovations, researched dead-ends, research successes, new materials, new developmental and testing methodologies, schematics, and so on. In addition, the individuals who make up the company's research and development department may also be potential holders of intellectual property, to include their unique and irreplaceable base of knowledge.

Manufacturing

Your manufacturing entity has unique methodologies and materials. In addition, the enterprise's supply chain, from start to finish, includes partners, vendors, and sub-contractors. Additionally, finished goods, unfinished goods, goods storage, raw materials, and so forth should be considered for review as possible sources of the firm's intellectual property.

Sales and Marketing

Information resident in the sales and marketing arena may include the firm's go-to market plan, pending and historic bids, profit margin and discount margins, inside and outside sales methodologies and organizations; public relations campaigns, and reseller networks, to include channels and distributors.

Additional areas of potential interest could be corporate branding (present and future), conference and trade show presentations and participation, client list, customer lists, and order sheets.

Specifics located in the competitive intelligence group may include product comparisons, marketing guidance, and results of table-top exercises which detail the results of the hypothetical competitor strategy comparison exercise. For example: How would Accenture beat our Ernest and Young in a head-to-head competition for a given bid? How would your enterprise fare in a head-to-head with your primary competitor?

Human Resources

Areas retaining intellectual property within the scope of human resources may include the firm's hiring processes, files/databases containing personal identifying information, employee health issues, performance evaluations, vacation schedules, individual salary compensation, EEO files, benefits, and so on.

Additionally, knowledge of the firm's processes, such as how the background investigation process works, what is included, how cases are adjudicated, etc., may allow an individual to craft a scenario to beat your processes.

Operations

Data found within the operations entity of most companies would include costs, margins, budgetary data, information technology infrastructure, business continuity plans and test results, physical security, information security policies, transportation, equipment procurement (to include channels used), problem mitigation methodologies, data destruction protocol including degauss and shredding regimes, and contractor identification (if one is used).

Risk Identification

Risk can come at you from only two vectors—inside and outside. Inside risk is almost completely in your control, whereas outside risk is almost completely out of your control. Each of the identified intellectual property items should be charted with all known inside/outside risks. In both cases, data/information leakage is a very real risk; inadvertent publication of confidential information can occur in both inside and outside environments, data can be physically stolen, electronic surveillance can be done of your personnel and facilities. One methodology that may be of assistance is rating the risk to intellectual property based on geography, as detailed in Table 15.1. It will allow you to rank your intellectual property in order of risk.

Table 15.1 Risk Levels 1–5

Risk level 1–5	Factors
1 = Lowest	Little or no technological threat: first generation public switched telephone network, with limited national infrastructure, some protection to intellectual property rights exists and laws do not hinder the ability to protect yourself
2 = Low	Low technological threat: developing national infrastructure, competitors present, minimal protection to intellectual property rights, laws and regulations which may preclude the ability to protect yourself are not present
3 = Moderate	Moderate technological threat: developing national infrastructure, competitors present in force, foreign official presence potential threat, moderate protection to intellectual property rights, laws concerning the ability to protect yourself are present but not enforced

Continued

Table 15.1 Continued. Risk Levels 1–5

Risk level 1–5	Factors
4 = High	Advanced technological threat: developed national infrastructure, competitors present in force, foreign official presence confirmed by nations with track record of assisting competitors, intellectual property rights, protection is the norm, laws and regulations may preclude the ability to use Cisco technology to protect yourself
5 = Highest	Confirmed advanced technological threat: advanced national infrastructure, competitors present in force, foreign official presence confirmed assisting competitors in this locale or domestic official presence known to pose intellectual property threat, intellectual property rights protection regime exists, but is problematic, laws and regulations preclude the ability to use Cisco technology to protect yourself

Implications of IP loss

When you lose your intellectual property, the potential ramifications should be identified for inclusion in your presentation, to show the cost to the enterprise, which is not always fiscal loss. Knowing what you need to protect, the risks involved, as well as the ramifications of losing the intellectual property, allows you to respond to market opportunities with speed, strength, and agility.

- Research & Development
  - Loss of competitive advantage
  - Loss of market leadership
  - Litigation probability
- Manufacturing
  - Counterfeit risk
  - Loss of customer confidence
- Sales & Marketing
  - Loss of customers
  - Brand reputation

- Human Resources

  - Loss of employees

  - Brand degradation

  - Potential legal quagmire

Now let's move on to Figure 15.3.

Figure 15.3 Plan Execution Road Map

Execution Roadmap

- Implementation plan
- Potential inhibitors
- Identified milestones

Notes on Figure 15.3

Implementation Plan

Discuss where the rollout of the plan will occur, the cadence, and so forth. It is important to know where you start, where you will finish, and how often you are going to review and repeat the educational processes and audits.

Potential Inhibitors

Identify internal points of resistance to change in intellectual property protocol, potential competitor action which may cause you to adjust your intellectual property protection schema, events which may render your plan moot, and environmental (global), political, or legal factors which could derail your plan, such as partner, vendor, or contractor failures.

Identified Milestones

Socialization schedule: When are you going to message to whom, where and how, and obtain audit and feedback

Identified timeline points for review of process and rollout and redirection opportunities

Expected budget, burn-rate, and potential costs not included in the burn-rate analysis

Headcount required; identification of key personnel, dedicated and shared resources, and conflict resolution regime for acquisition of shared resources

Logistical considerations, if any

Partners, vendors, and/or other outside resources required to achieve success

We'll now discuss Figure 15.4.

Figure 15.4 Socialization of IP Protection Program to the Enterprise

Socialization of IP Protection Program to the Enterprise
- Senior executive messaging
- Group level messaging
- First line manager messaging
- Feedback process
- Measuring, adjusting and re-messaging

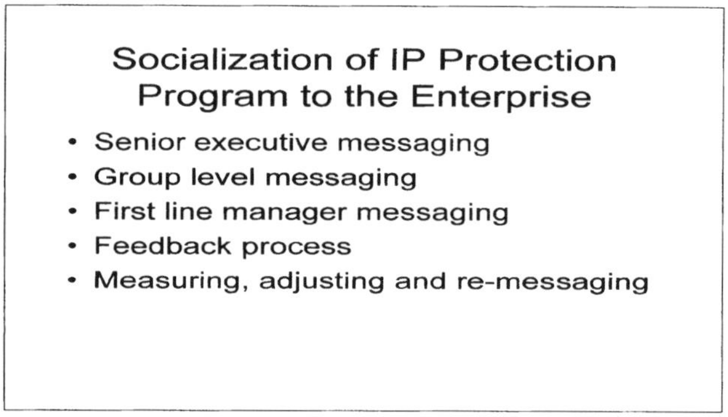

Notes on Figure 15.4

Using the aforementioned awareness platform, share the upside and downside of each individual engaging in the protection of the firm's intellectual property within each of the various business areas.

Demonstrate the value of the intellectual property to be protected in a monetary unit of measure and a man-hour unit of measure, and be sure to tie into this portion of the presentation the identified milestones and expectations.

Create a core message, which will be retooled, oriented, and calibrated for each of the various business units by the executive and management team so as to ensure the message resonates with the receiving audience—the firm's individual employees.

Ensure that there is available an employee and executive feedback methodology so as to allow a sharing of results across the enterprise to adjust, redirect, or message anew as appropriate.

Identify the required policies to be created, via recommendations, position papers, and formal policy evolution—this is a linear thought process.

We'll now discuss Figure 15.5.

Figure 15.5 Executive Staff—Execute Commit

Executive Staff – Execute Commit

- Executive
  - Backing
  - Messaging
  - Policy and exception policy defined
  - Review at milestones and course correct.

- Business value statement

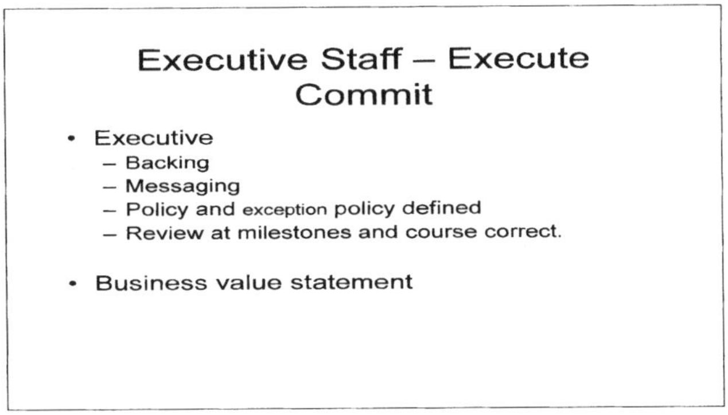

Notes on Figure 15.5

Executive Commitment

Backing—stakeholders identified—be it the CEO, COO, CIO, etc.

Overview of the sharing of messaging amongst the different identified strata by the appropriate executives

Policy identification and policy exception process

Business Value Statement

Good security of the intellectual property risks enables educated risk taking with respect to business opportunities with the knowledge and expectation that the security apparatus will align behind the business unit taking the approved risk.

Notes

1. www.mscsoftware.com/events/vpd2003/na/agenda.cfm

2. "Piracy from China: How Microsoft, Ralph Lauren, Nike And Others Can Cope." SeekingAlpha.com. April 9, 2007. http://retail.seekingalpha.com/article/31723

3. www.scip.org/

4. http://cicentre.com/Documents/DOC_Chi_Mak.html

Chapter 16

Conclusion

Protect Your IP

The threat to your intellectual property is real. But the ability to protect your intellectual property from these threats is within your grasp.

Learn from the examples offered in this book. Those in positions of responsibility in many of the firms mentioned in Part 1 had discussed the issue, and thought they had a comprehensive program, but they didn't. Those in positions of responsibility in these firms hadn't been mindful enough of the full spectrum of risks and threats.

Take the elements of the holistic program we have offered, adapt them to your environment, champion their adoption, and then move forward aggressively.

Most importantly, don't fall into the trap of initiating changes, creating policies, and then forgetting about them. As the ancient Greek philosopher Heraclitus said, "You cannot step into the same river twice." The world is a dynamic market place. And part of what this dynamism means is that the challenges you face will continue to evolve, and your solutions will continue to be challenged, over and over (sometimes successfully). Adapt, adapt, adapt. Your adversaries do.

For example, even as we wrapped up this text for our publisher, there are emerging trends and intensifying currents.

The level of malware and spam entering the portals of enterprises has approached more than 90% of the total volume; that is, greater than 90% of all e-mail arriving at the e-mail servers of enterprises can be characterized as trash.

Consider the art of "Phishing." It has reached the utmost level of professionalism. The attention to detail reflected in such attacks has evolved from that of amateurs to that of a seasoned professional. The language used has evolved from the stilted and grammatically incorrect to the linguistically impeccable. The text of the latest attacks resonates with the reader, making the attacks much more effective against the uninformed.

And just as we focused on the targeted Trojan in our exploration of the Haepharati case, here we note that the one-off Trojan has now permeated a number of industries, targeting individuals at all levels and on a global basis.

Encourage your work force to remain vigilant. We shall continue to monitor the changes in both methodology and sponsorship, and update both in the next edition.

Until then, keep your secrets safe, and your fortunes will not evaporate before your eyes.

We thank you for allowing us to share our thoughts with you, and we are secure in the knowledge that we have provided you with a boost toward self-preservation in the global marketplace.

Baseline Controls for Information Security Mapped to ISO

Tables A.1 through A.10 list 20 baseline controls for each of 10 vital areas of information security, mapped to ISO:

- Personnel Security

- Physical Security

- Business Process Controls

- End-User Controls

- Network Security Controls

- Internet Security Controls

- Web Security Controls

- Telecommunications and Remote Access Controls

- E-commerce Security Controls

- Wireless and Mobile Computing Security Controls

Table A.1 Baseline Controls for Personnel Security

Description	ISO 17799:2005
Personnel Policies and Practices	
1. Overall, management policies and practices demonstrate a genuine concern for personnel welfare, professional development, security, and safety (ISO 17799 3.1).	5.1
2. "Adherence to security policies and procedures" is a measured line item in annual individual personnel reviews (ISO 17799 6.1).	8.1
3. Salaries and fringe benefits are kept competitive with those of other companies in the area and the industry.	
4. All newly hired network and system users are given an initial security briefing, followed by periodic IP refreshers and targeted in-depth training (ISO 17799 6.2).	8.2.2
5. Employees handling sensitive or confidential information are covered by a fidelity bond (ISO 17799 6.1.2).	8.1.3
6. A prospective employee's academic, personal, and employment references are checked with special attention given to gaps in employment history and independent background investigations for employees performing mission-critical job responsibilities (ISO 17799 6.1.2).	8.1.2

Continued

Table A.1 Continued. Baseline Controls for Personnel Security

Description	ISO 17799:2005
7. Procedures exist and are followed for communication between personnel and security administration groups to ensure prompt removal of obsolete users' IDs (ISO 17799 9.2).	8.3.3
8. Each manager is aware of and questions any changes in personnel lifestyle or behavior patterns (such as personal or financial problems, dress, schedule, work habits, quality of work, demeanor) and is prepared to conduct a formal investigation (ISO 17799 6.1).	8.2.1
9. Employee identification cards include the employee's signature, photograph, issue date, a control or employee number, and are protected against alteration (e.g., lamination), and are worn by all employees (ISO 17999 7.3).	11.2.1
10. Business associates on site for extended periods are issued photo IDs and required to wear them at all times (ISO 17799 7.3).	11.5.2
11. Exit interviews are conducted with terminated employees to recover portable computers.	8.3.1
12. Employees discharged for cause are escorted from the premises immediately.	8.3.1
13. Employees take yearly vacations that provide at least one week with little network or system interaction.	8.2.1
14. Detailed job descriptions are given to all employees who use organizational information and/or communications resources and include a clear statement of security responsibilities (ISO 17799 6.1).	8.1.1
15. The mission statement for the IP area has been published and is visibly supported by executive management (ISO 17799 3.1).	6.1.3
16. A single individual (e.g., CISO) has been designated at the organization-wide level for IP (ISO 17799 4.1).	6.1.1
17. Employees and business associates have been notified about how they should report suspected violations or vulnerabilities (ISO 17799 6.3).	13.1.1
18. The organization would seek to prosecute employees, business associates, or any others found guilty of a premeditated criminal act against the organization (ISO 17799 6.3).	13.2

Continued

www.syngress.com

Table A.1 Continued. Baseline Controls for Personnel Security

Description	ISO 17799:2005
19. Sufficient in-house expertise is maintained (through training, professional certification, etc.) to demonstrate what is actually going on inside the organization's information systems (ISO 17799 7.1).	13.2.3
20. Confidentiality agreements have been signed by all personnel and business associates and copies are maintained based on the organization's records management program (ISO 17799 6.1.3.).	6.1.5

Table A.2 Baseline Controls for Physical Security

Description	ISO
1. Access to data centers, server centers, network communications centers, tape/disk libraries, forms storage areas, on-site vaults, etc., is denied to personnel other than those who have a business need to enter those areas; any exceptions are logged and investigated (ISO 17799 7.1).	9.1.1
2. Outside signs, the building directory, and publicly-available information do not make reference to computer centers or their locations (ISO 17799 7.1).	9.1.1
3. Visitors are logged in and out and escorted within data centers, server centers, and areas where non-public information is processed (ISO 17799 7.1).	9.1.6
4. Employees have been trained to challenge any stranger, unescorted visitor, or person not wearing an ID badge in non-public areas (ISO 17799 7.1).	9.1
5. Servers are kept in protected areas, and are accessible only by authorized individuals (ISO 17799 7.2).	9.2.1
6. Audit and/or IP departments conduct random, after-hours inspections of work areas and report findings to management (ISO 17799 7.3).	9.1.3
7. Magnetic media are stored and secured in accordance with the classification of the data and with manufacturers' suggested standards (ISO 17799.73).	9.1.4

Continued

Table A.2 Continued. Baseline Controls for Physical Security

Description	ISO
8. Guards at entrances and exits randomly check briefcases, boxes, or portable PCs to prevent unauthorized items from coming in or leaving (ISO 17799 7.1).	9.1.1
9. Fire detectors and an automatic extinguishing system are installed on the ceiling, below raised flooring, and above dropped ceilings in computer rooms and tape/disk libraries (ISO 1799 7.2).	9.1.4
10. Hand fire extinguishers are strategically placed throughout the work site and employees are well-trained in their use (ISO 17799 7.2).	9.1.4
11. Rooms containing connector panels, network hardware, and modems are locked to prevent unauthorized access, and they are periodically checked to ensure cleanliness, thus minimizing the risk of potential hazards such as fire (ISO 17799 7.1).	9.1.5
12. A continuous and effective computer room house-keeping program is practiced, and it includes special attention to the under-floor area (ISO 17799 7.1).	9.1.5
13. Documents containing non-public information are not discarded in whole, readable form; they are cross-shredded, burned, or otherwise irreparably destroyed (ISO 17799 8.6.2).	9.2.6
14. The operability of electric power generation equipment and standby battery power is tested and verified regularly for all types of computer and communications equipment (ISO 17799 7.2).	9.2.1
15. A well-planned, documented preventive maintenance program is in effect for all environmental and protection systems (ISO 17799 7.3).	9.2.4
16. Data center and server center activity is monitored and recorded on closed-circuit TV and displayed on a bank of real-time monitors (ISO 17799 7.1).	9.1.2
17. There is a constantly occupied central location (for example, a security station) that serves as a focal point for physical security at the worksite (ISO 17799 7.1).	9.1.2

Continued

Table A.2 Continued. Baseline Controls for Physical Security

Description	ISO
18. Employees who travel with portable computers as part of their duties are provided with theft prevention devices and trained how to use the devices (ISO 17799 7.2.5).	9.2.5
19. Organizational sub-units using removable storage devices have a readily available secure location for nights, weekends, and other temporary storage of any such devices containing non-public information (ISO 17799 7.2.5).	9.2.5
20. Each person entering a controlled area must provide his or her own authentication. "Tail-gating" is prohibited by policy and actively discouraged by employees (ISO 17799 7.1).	9.1.1

Table A.3 Business Process Controls

Description	ISO 17799:2005
1. Only authorized personnel are permitted to access or operate hosts and servers on the network (ISO 17799 8.1).	10.1.1
2. IS employees are prohibited from initiating original accounting transactions, receivables, payables, adjustments, corrections, check requests, and non-financial data entries (ISO 17799 9.6).	10.1.3
3. Privileged accounts set up for emergency problem resolution are fully logged to areas inaccessible to the people using the accounts. All such privileged access is reviewed and monitored regularly (ISO 17799 9.5).	11.5.4
4. A secured log of system events including restarts and abnormal conditions is reviewed independent of operating staff on a regular basis (ISO 17799 8.4).	10.10.4
5. There are comprehensive documentation standards. Periodic review of the documentation shows that it closely follows the required standards (ISO 17799 8.6).	10.7.4
6. A formal change control procedure, which includes security testing, is used to manage all software modifications to any software running in production on all platforms (ISO 17799 10.5.1).	10.1.2

Continued

Table A.3 Continued. Business Process Controls

Description	ISO 17799:2005
7. A formal cause analysis is performed and documented for all interruptions of operating systems services (ISO 17799 8.1).	13.2
8. A formal procedure is in place to respond to failed access attempts (ISO 17799 9.4).	11.4.2
9. Authorization to access information is based on preserving the confidentiality, integrity, and availability of the information (ISO 17799 9.1).	11.1.1
10. Access to sensitive data is appropriately authorized on a "need-to-know," least-privilege basis, providing employees and business associates all the access they need to do their jobs, but no more (ISO 17799 9.1).	11.1.1
11. Production and testing environments are separated to preserve the integrity of production data and program code (ISO 17799 9.4).	10.1.4
12. Procedures are documented and implemented to preserve information and data as evidence in legal proceedings (ISO 17799 8.5).	13.2.3
13. There is a records management schedule, developed with the input of legal counsel, records management, and audit, documented and implemented for all organizational information (ISO 17799 8.6).	10.7.3
14. An information classification scheme, based on information criticality, sensitivity, and value, has been developed and implemented (ISO 17799 5.2).	7.2.1
15. Public logon accounts, such as "Guest" or "Anonymous" that are not audit-accountable to a specific individual, are reviewed and, if inappropriate, are not permitted (ISO 17799 8.5).	11.2.1
16. New applications are reviewed (including "code review" where applicable) for compliance with security policy prior to implementation in production (ISO 17799 10.5).	12.5.1
17. Application and system resources (including source code, executable code, object directories, and more) are secured against unauthorized access and modification (ISO 17799 10.4).	12.5.3

Continued

Table A.3 Continued. Business Process Controls

Description	ISO 17799:2005
18. If risk analysis warrants, encryption is used to protect non-public information (particularly on equipment used outside of the organization-controlled office environment) (ISO 17799 10.3).	12.3.1
19. There are appropriate policies, procedures, and standards documented and implemented for encryption key use, management, and recovery (ISO 17799 10.3).	12.3.2
20. An adequately staffed and properly trained Emergency Response Team, empowered to deal with incidents such as electronic network intrusions or denial of service attacks, has either been established internally or contracted from outside (ISO 17799 6.3).	13.2.1

Table A.4 End-User Controls

Description	ISO
1. An organizational policy on copyright compliance has been implemented and all employees and business associates have been made aware of it (ISO 17799 12.1).	15.1.2
2. A standard operating environment has been established and a list of acceptable hardware and software has been published. This standard is updated regularly (ISO 17799 8.1).	10.1.1
3. Appropriate measures are taken to protect unattended workstations (ISO 17799 9.3).	11.3.2
4. Where appropriate, the organization uses anti-theft devices (anchors, cables, etched logos, warning stickers, etc.) (ISO 17799 9.3).	11.3.2
5. The organization repeatedly stresses to users the importance of backups and provides them simple, effective ways to create backups (ISO 17799 8.4).	10.5.1
6. The organization provides all users with regularly updated anti-virus protection information and software to prevent, detect, and recover from attacks by computer viruses and other malicious code (ISO 17799 8.3).	10.4.1

Continued

Table A.4 Continued. End-User Controls

Description	ISO
7. The organization has documented and implemented an emergency response process to respond to end-users quickly and effectively when computer-related or information security incidents occur (ISO 17799 6.3).	13.1.1
8. There are workstation standards in place to protect against environmental hazards. Compliance to these standards is required (ISO 17799 9.3).	9.2.1
9. "Power-up" passwords or other extra safeguards for workstations are required (ISO 17799 9.3).	11.3.1
10. Each workstation is connected to some form of surge protector and uninterruptible power supply (ISO 17799 7.2).	9.2.1
11. Network and computer systems users are required to authenticate themselves each time they sign-on (ISO 17799 9.2).	11.1.1
12. There is a formal, on-going security awareness program implemented and procedures are regularly followed to measure its effectiveness (ISO 17799 6.2).	8.2.2
13. Employees and business associates receive regular communications (e.g., a quarterly newsletter) alerting them to risks and vulnerabilities involved in computing, educating them about their role in information protection, and reminding them of the importance of basic tasks such as back-up anti-virus scanning and choosing strong passwords (ISO 17799 6.2).	8.2.2
14. There are annual observances of internationally recognized events such as Computer Security Day (November 30th), Virus Awareness Day (September 8th), and Emergency Response Day (May 10th) as well as other security awareness functions (such as video presentations and guest speakers from law enforcement) throughout the year (ISO 17799 6.2).	8.2.2
15. Security awareness posters reminding users about important information protection issues (such as software piracy and password control) are displayed in hallways, lunch rooms, or other common areas\ (ISO 17799 6.2).	8.2.2
16. End-users are provided with practical items (note pads, screen savers, mugs, mouse pad, key chains, etc.) that carry security awareness messages as reminders to promote information protection within their own work areas (ISO 17799 6.2).	8.2.2

Continued

Table A.4 Continued. End-User Controls

Description	ISO
17. There are periodic reviews of end-users' work areas to monitor compliance with the information protection program (ISO 17799 7.3).	11.3.3
18. End-users must sign an Internet usage and responsibility agreement prior to gaining any type of Internet access, acknowledging that they understand what they may do (for example, only access the Internet for legitimate work-related purposes) and may not do (for example, no downloading of games, no "spamming") with their on-line privileges (ISO 17799 9.4).	11.4.1
19. As part of their on-going security awareness training, end-users are instructed on how to detect and thwart "social engineering" attacks as well as competitive intelligence probes (such as bogus marketing surveys) whether launched via telephone, e-mail, or other medium (ISO 17799 6.2).	8.2.2
20. All security incidents end-users detect are reported to the appropriate individual or department, documented, and reviewed (ISO 17799 6.3).	13.1.1

Table A.5 Network Security Controls

Description	ISO
1. A network security policy governing internal and external (Internet, business partners, etc.) connections has been implemented (ISO 17799 8.2).	10.6.2
2. Each individual wishing to access the network is authenticated individually using strong passwords, two-factor authentication, or biometric authentication methods (ISO 17799 9.2).	11.2.2
3. In addition to the normal authorization process, an additional level of authentication is required for remote access to the network (ISO 17799 9.8).	11.2.2
4. The organization maintains an inventory listing all significant components that make up the network (ISO 17799 5.1).	7.1.1
5. Transmission of sensitive information between security domains in the network or outside the organization's network are encrypted using a corporate-approved encryption method (ISO 17799 10.3).	12.3.1

Continued

Table A.5 Continued. Network Security Controls

Description	ISO
6. Data encryption is used to protect highly sensitive and legislatively-required information and data during network transmission and while in storage (ISO 17799 10.3).	12.3.1
7. Before an individual is given access to the network, he or she must sign a document indicating understanding and agreement to abide by network security rules and policies (ISO 17799 6.2).	8.2.2
8. Controls on passwords for network access include recommendations for choice (size, composition, etc.), forced change intervals, prevention of reusing recent passwords, and account lock out upon reaching a violation threshold of 3-5 consecutive unsuccessful authentication attempts (ISO 17799 9.2).	11.2.3
9. Downloads of shareware or other programs or data from the public domain or outside bulletin boards are either forbidden or made to a quarantined workstation not connected to the network (ISO 17799 10.4).	12.4.1
10. Prior to conducting electronic data interchange (EDI), trading partners sign mutual agreements specifying appropriate behavior and implementation of security controls on each other's networks (ISO 17799 8.7).	10.8.2
11. Electronic mail security features are activated and must be used. E-mail users are aware that privacy of e-mail is not guaranteed, and that e-mail may be monitored at any time (ISO 17799 8.7.4).	10.8
12. Network and computer users are automatically timed out and logged off after a specified period of inactivity (ISO 17799 9.5).	11.5.5
13. Network operating system security controls are fully implemented and used (ISO 17799 9.5).	11.4.6
14. Security controls within the applications running on organizational systems have been implemented and are being used to complement the network operating system security (ISO 17799 10.2).	11.6
15. A warning banner appears at logon to each network system and device, notifying all individuals attempting to log on that the organization reserves the right to monitor all network traffic and information and that law enforcement will be contacted if criminal activity is suspected or detected (ISO 17799 9.5).	11.5.1

Continued

Table A.5 Continued. Network Security Controls

Description	ISO
16. Disaster recovery plans for department networks and the organizational backbone have been developed and are tested in conjunction with other elements of the entire business continuity plan (ISO 17799 11.1).	14.1.1
17. No computer system or device may connect to the organization's network, or to another connected computer system, without compliance to published organizational standards and appropriate authorization (ISO 17799 9.4).	11.4.1
18. The connections between the corporate network and external networks (Internet, business partner networks, etc.) are protected by a properly configured and monitored firewall(s), and tunneling is used to protect connections between remote sections of the enterprise to create a virtual private network (VPN) (ISO 17799 9.4).	11.4.1
19. A mobile computing policy based on risk analysis that meets the security needs of the organization has been implemented and is enforced (ISO 17799 9.8).	11.7.1
20. Intelligent hubs or routers, or fully functioning firewalls, are used to separate domains within the network (ISO 17799 9.4.6).	11.4.5

Table A.6 Internet Security Controls

Description	ISO
1. There is a policy that governs which Internet services will be available to employees and business associates (ISO 17799 9.4).	11.4.1
2. There are policies that govern employee and business associate use of Internet access privileges (ISO 17799 9.4).	11.4.2
3. Firewalls are used to implement and enforce Internet policies (ISO 17799 9.4.6).	11.4.5
4. Firewalls are used, where deemed appropriate by risk analysis, within the intranet (for example, between major organizational domains) (ISO 17799 9.4.6).	11.4.6
5. Firewalls log all traffic passing through them; logs identify hosts or users, Web sites visited, names of files transferred (optional), and amount of data transferred (ISO 17799 9.7).	10.10.2

Continued

Table A.6 Continued. Internet Security Controls

Description	ISO
6. Audit logs on firewalls are routinely collected, scanned for violations, and attempted violations of policy summarized in a report, distributed to appropriate management, and archived for at least six months (ISO 17799 9.7).	10.10.3
7. If the policy requires that Internet users be identifiable, Internet users must be authenticated before being permitted to access resources on the other side of Internet firewalls (ISO 17799 9.2).	11.2.1
8. Access to firewall administration functions is tightly controlled, protected, and logged (ISO 17799 8.1).	10.1.3
9. Firewall hardware and software are kept in physically secure areas (ISO 17799 7.2).	9.2.1
10. External users wishing to access internal resources through the firewall must use strong authentication (such as one time passwords) (ISO 17799 9.2).	11.2.4
11. Strong encryption is used to protect external communications that contain non-public information (ISO 17799 10.3).	12.3.1
12. Security resources on the Internet (vendor security mailing lists, CERT and CIAC advisories, etc.) are subscribed to and patches and updates recommended by these sources are installed as soon as possible on all Internet accessible systems (ISO 17799 8.1).	10.1.1
13. Firewalls are covered by a service-level agreement from the vendor, and firewall patches/updates applied as quickly as possible (ISO 17799 8.5).	10.6.2
14. All software downloaded from the Internet is scanned for viruses and other malicious code following the same policy/ procedures as diskettes and CDs brought into the organization (ISO 17799 8.3).	12.4.1
15. All source code obtained from the Internet undergoes a code review before use (ISO 17799 10.5).	12.5.1
16. All applications and systems directly accessible from the Internet have their security audited rigorously and regularly (ISO 17799 12.2).	10.10.1
17. There is a clearly documented and implemented incident handling policy and emergency procedures for dealing with system and network attacks (ISO 17799 6.3).	13.1.1

Continued

Table A.6 Continued. Internet Security Controls

Description	ISO
18. Incident handling procedures are tested regularly in a realistic manner (for example, conducting disaster recovery drills) (ISO 17799 6.3).	14.1.5
19. Management must approve all policies and procedures that permit Internet commerce activities (ISO 17799 3.1).	11.1.1
20. Internal network traffic is monitored to verify that controls are working correctly and that no unexpected activity is taking place (ISO 17799 9.7).	10.10.1

Table A.7 Web Security Controls

Description	ISO
1. There is a minimally configured Web server system (bastion host). (The more complex the server, the greater the likelihood that software bugs, which may expose the system, exist) (ISO 17799 8.1).	10.1.1
2. Web servers with publicly-accessible content are not placed on the internal network, but on a separate network protected by a firewall (often called a DMZ), and CGI or ASP scripts are used to make requests from databases or e-commerce systems on the internal network (ISO 17799 9.4.6).	11.4.5
3. Server side "includes," which may execute arbitrary system commands or CGI scripts, are not used unless approved by IP or similar appropriate authorities (ISO 17799 10.2).	12.5.1
4. Access to the Web server operating system and application code is restricted to only those with a business need (ISO 17799 10.4)	12.4.1
5. Strong passwords, preferably one-time passwords, are used for every log-on account (ISO 17799 9.2).	11.2.3
6. Operating system shells/interpreters that are not necessary or used are removed (ISO 17799 9.5).	11.7.1
7. Web server logs are checked regularly and frequently for suspicious activities (unusually long argument lists for CGI or ASP scripts may indicate a break-in attempt) (ISO 17799 9.7).	10.10.2

Continued

Table A.7 Continued. Web Security Controls

Description	ISO
8. Correct file and directory ownership/permissions/ACLs are used in compliance with systems administration standards (server root writable by administrator only, documents by content administrators only, etc.) (ISO 17799 10.4).	12.4.1
9. Configuration and log files are accessible only by administrators with responsibilities that require such access (ISO 17799 10.4).	10.10.2
10. Automatic directory listings on Web servers are not used (ISO 17799 10.4).	12.4.1
11. Symbolic links on Web servers are not used (for example, PathAlias is used instead) (ISO 17799 10.2).	12.5.2
12. Documented policies and procedures are implemented to strictly control Web content (for example, no pages added without inspection). Such policies disallow user-maintained directories (~user) (ISO 17799 10.1).	12.1.1
13. The Web server is run as a non-administrative user (nobody) when possible (NOTE: cannot be done for some NT systems) (ISO 17799 10.4).	12.4.1
14. Hierarchy can be shared with an FTP server only if no writes are permitted to non-administrative users (ISO 17799 10.4).	10.6.1
15. When Web server document and information access must be restricted, a combination of IP address and user authentication is used (ISO 17799 9.6).	10.6.1
16. A corporate-approved encryption method (e.g., SSL) is used for the transmission of sensitive information (personal information, credit card numbers, etc.) during electronic commerce (ISO 17799 10.2).	12.3.1
17. CGI scripts are stored in the cgi-bin or Scripts directory. Interpreters, such as Perl or command.com, are never stored in the cgi-bin or Scripts directory (ISO 17799 10.4).	12.4.1
18. C programs are used for CGI scripts if possible. CGI and ASP scripts are always carefully examined and reviewed prior to production regardless of the source. Individuals who attempt to input to CGI scripts must be validated (ISO 177999 10.4).	12.5.1

Continued

Table A.7 Continued. Web Security Controls

Description	ISO
19. POST instead of GET is used to prevent user input of forms from appearing in logs and forwarding URL records (ISO 17799 10.2).	12.2.2
20. Risks analysis and management approval is used to determine information to log. Access to Web server logs is strictly controlled to only those with a business need (ISO 17799 9.7).	10.10.3

Table A.8 Telecommunications and Remote Access Security Controls

Description	ISO
1. There is a documented and implemented policy on the use of organizational telecommunications resources and telecommuting requirements (ISO 17799 9.8).	11.7.1
2. Security, application, and network personnel actively work to improve the efficiency and ease of use of security measures for dial-in users through simplifying messages, minimizing required sign-ons, coordinating password changes, etc. (ISO 17799 9.8).	11.7.2
3. Non-modifiable and access-controlled logs of system restarts, rerun time, all remote accesses and abnormal conditions or events during remote access is reviewed independent of the operations department on a regular basis to detect patterns of reliability and security problems (ISO 17799 9.8).	10.10.3
4. When repeated dial-in attempts to use invalid passwords or illegal procedures cause an ID to get suspended, security contacts both the owner of that ID, and the owner's manager. The ID must stay suspended until the ID owner is contacted (ISO 17799 9.8).	11.5.1
5. Database designs and structures provide for limiting access and functions to specifically authorized programs and individuals, and these features have been implemented for critical functions, sensitive records, and data elements reachable via dial-in (ISO 17799 10.4).	12.4.1

Continued

Table A.8 Continued. Telecommunications and Remote Access Security Controls

Description	ISO
6. For all remotely-accessible mission-critical applications, there is an audit trail diagram and/or description clearly indicating how a transaction may be traced through the system (ISO 17799 10.2).	10.10.1
7. When possible and applicable, the main security program (mainframe package, network OS, etc.) is used to control dial-in access to specific applications; extra security features in communication servers and within applications augment, but do not replace, the main security program (ISO 17799 9.8).	12.4.1
8. Special procedures and audited IDs exist for application and network remote troubleshooting activity (ISO 17799 9.8).	11.4.4
9. Employees authorized for Internet and remote access are made aware of the organization's non-public information; specifically, what they can and cannot discuss in forums, chat groups, and with friends and family (ISO 17799 6.2).	8.2.2
10. Managers are responsible for reviewing telephone bills each month to discover potential toll fraud, prevent unnecessary loss, and prepare for prosecution (ISO 17799 4.1).	13.1.1
11. Messages and transactions coming in via phone lines are serially numbered, time stamped, and logged for audit investigation and backup purposes (ISO 17799 8.4).	10.10.2
12. Users of organizational voice-mail systems change the default passwords on their voice-mail boxes as soon as the accounts are issued (ISO 17799 9.3).	11.2.4
13. Organizational users of cellular phones are briefed that cellular conversations may be unencrypted and/or trivial to intercept, therefore no sensitive information can be discussed on this type of circuit (ISO 17799 6.2).	8.2.2
14. Employees with organizational calling cards use card-insert or card-swipe phones where possible; failing that, they conceal the card number they are entering to prevent compromise by "shoulder surfing" or filming by phone fraudsters (ISO 17799 6.2).	8.2.2
15. When people leave the organization, their calling cards are disabled and the passwords on their voice-mail accounts and dial-in accounts are changed immediately (ISO 17799 8.5).	8.3.2

Continued

www.syngress.com

Table A.8 Continued. Telecommunications and Remote Access Security Controls

Description	ISO
16. Non-public data stored on portable computers (notebooks, handhelds, laptops, etc.) is encrypted using a standardized, corporate-approved product, and portable computer users have been trained in how to appropriately use the encryption solution (ISO 17799 10.3).	12.3.1
17. Portable computer users are provided with the requisite software and a dial-in number or some other easy-to-use mechanism allowing them to back-up appropriate information to a server or to media they carry (ISO 17799 9.8).	11.7.1
18. Employees and business associates must sign some form of equipment control document when taking or returning a portable computer; a copy of the signed document is kept on file (ISO 17799 9.8).	12.3.1
19. Portable computer users who travel are trained regularly on the security exposures they face and actions they must take to minimize risk (ISO 17799 6.2).	8.2.2
20. The organization seeks to prosecute employees or outsiders found guilty of a premeditated criminal act against the organization (ISO 17799 12.1).	13.2.1

Table A.9 E-commerce Security Controls

Description	ISO
1. A detailed and up-to-date business continuity plan for e-commerce Web server computer outages has been developed and implemented (ISO 17799 11.1).	14.1.1
2. A recovery plan for e-commerce Web server computer outages is tested on a regular basis, utilizing realistic exercises more detailed than table-top scenarios (ISO 17799 11.1).	14.1.4
3. A computer emergency response team (internal CERT) has been designated, trained and regularly drilled to deal with problems like hacker intrusions (ISO 17799 6.3).	13.2.1
4. An uninterruptible power supply system (UPS) is employed to provide necessary power in case of a power outage that lasts several hours or longer (ISO 17799 7.2).	14.1.1

Continued

Table A.9 Continued. E-commerce Security Controls

Description	ISO
5. Network communications using telephone lines are supported by lines to two or more central telephone company offices (ISO 17799 7.2).	9.2.1
6. A mirror Web site provides geographical diversity for contingency planning purposes as well as increased performance.	14.1.1
7. Redundant equipment such as RAID (redundant array of integrated disks) ensures that a single hardware fault or failure will not bring the e-commerce system down (ISO 17799 7.2).	9.2.1
8. E-commerce systems are physically isolated from other computers in a data center room via locked wire cages, separate locked rooms, etc. (ISO 17799 7.2).	9.2.1
9. Internet e-commerce systems are protected from hackers with a verified effective firewall, and the most recent version of this firewall is installed (ISO 17799 8.7).	10.8.1
10. Access controls are used to limit what individual employees and business associates can read, write, or execute based on actual business need (ISO 17799 9.2).	11.2.2
11. Credit card numbers, and other non-public information, sent over Internet communications lines are encrypted using SSL or a stronger corporate-approved encryption process (ISO 17799 10.3).	12.3.1
12. Backup tapes are encrypted and stored off-site in a locked container, room, and/or facility (ISO 17799 8.6).	11.1.1
13. A fraud detection system is used to catch suspicious credit card orders before the order is submitted or fulfilled (ISO 17799 10.2).	
14. A publicly-accessible verified digital certificate is provided for all customers to verify that they have reached a legitimate server (ISO 17799 10.2).	12.3.1
15. All communications between corporate network systems and servers that make up the Internet commerce suite are encrypted and supported by digital certificates (ISO 17799 10.3).	12.3.1
16. A network and Web server intrusion detection system provides instant notification to appropriate personnel of hacker attacks and related problems (ISO 17799 6.3).	10.10.1

Continued

www.syngress.com

Table A.9 Continued. E-commerce Security Controls

Description	ISO
17. A network management system provides real-time information to appropriate personnel about system load, response time, system down time, and other performance issues (ISO 17799 8.5).	10.6.1
18. A vulnerability identification system identifies configuration and set-up problems before hackers can exploit them (ISO 17799 8.5).	10.6.2
19. Staff with access to the e-commerce operating code and data pass background checks prior to beginning their job responsibilities (ISO 17799 6.1.2).	8.1.1
20. E-commerce privacy and security policies have been developed and posted on the e-commerce Web site(s) (ISO 17799 8.7).	10.8.1

Table A.10 Wireless and Mobile Computing Security Controls

Description	ISO
1. A formal documented policy has been developed, approved, implemented, and communicated that addresses the risks of working with mobile computing devices (ISO 17799 9.8).	11.7.1
2. Personnel and business associates using mobile computing devices are provided tools and must follow standards for physically protecting the devices (ISO 17799 7.2).	9.2.5
3. Personnel and business associates are provided corporate-approved methods and tools for encrypting non-public information stored on mobile computing devices (ISO 17799 10.3).	12.3.1
4. Information access controls are implemented for information stored on mobile computing devices, and to control the access mobile computing devices have to information while they are connected to the corporate network and computer systems (ISO 17799 9.6).	11.1.1
5. Procedures have been developed and implemented to ensure centralized synchronization on the corporate network of information on mobile computing devices (ISO 17799 9.8).	12.4.1

Continued

Table A.10 Continued. Wireless and Mobile Computing Security Controls

Description	ISO
6. Procedures have been developed and implemented to track and monitor the individuals using mobile computing devices to access or process business information (ISO 17799 9.8).	10.10.2
7. Procedures exist to immediately disable mobile computing device connections to the network when personnel terminate (ISO 17799 9.8).	8.3.3
8. Procedures exist to reclaim mobile computing devices when personnel change job responsibilities, go on strike, terminate, etc. (ISO 17799 9.8).	8.3.2
9. Tools are used to scan for viruses and malicious code on mobile computing devices (ISO 17799 8.3).	10.4.1
10. The organization has identified and communicated the mobile computing devices authorized to use with the corporate network and for business processing (ISO 17799 6.2).	11.7.1
11. Employees and business associates back up mobile computing device data, using an approved corporate method, on a regular basis to avoid loss of valuable corporate information (ISO 17799 8.4.1).	11.7.1
12. Mobile computing devices used in the course of corporate business are subject to audits just like any other electronic device, even if employee-owned (ISO 17799 12.2).	11.7.1
13. Power-on passwords must be used on all mobile computing devices containing corporate information (ISO 17799 9.3).	11.2.4
14. Passwords must be used to enable data transfers to and from the corporate network and mobile computing devices (ISO 17799 9.8).	11.7.1
15. Strong link or end-to-end encryption methods (SSL, VPNs, etc.) are used to protect wireless information transmissions (ISO 17799 9.8).	12.3.1
16. Access controls are used to identify wireless network users and authorize or deny access according to prescribed guidelines (ISO 17799 9.4).	11.4.2

Continued

Table A.10 Continued. Wireless and Mobile Computing Security Controls

Description	ISO
17. A policy has been developed, implemented, and communicated addressing wireless networking security issues, including procedures to ensure wireless ranges for your organization do not overlap with another organization's wireless transmissions (possibly exposing your non-public information), and measures have been implemented to prevent unauthorized individuals from accessing and using your wireless network (ISO 17799 9.4).	11.4.1
18. A secured room is provided to house the physical wireless computer devices (ISO 17799 7.2).	9.2.1
19. Wireless network products are considered on the basis of the security mechanisms they provide prior to purchasing such products (ISO 17799 8.5).	10.6.1
20. Passwords used on mobile computing devices must be different from passwords used to authenticate to the organization network (ISO 17799 9.3).	11.3.1

Leveraging Your Tax Dollar

So how does a corporation leverage their tax dollars to ensure they are deriving all possible benefit and perhaps more importantly, government perspective and knowledge in their efforts to protect their intellectual property? We've compiled a list of potential avenues of pursuit that may produce the value-added.

Domestic The Department of Justice and the Department of Homeland Security are both first stops for current trends on what threats are being experienced across the country, as both have visibility into gross data sets. Both have outreach programs designed specifically to provide information to individuals and corporations on a variety of topics and cadences.

International Should you need an international focus, the Department of Commerce has an entire Bureau dedicated to leveling the playing field and helping the corporate entity in protecting their intellectual property. The Department of State also publishes a plethora of data sets that may be of interest.

With the above as the backdrop, the following should serve as a primer on those U.S. Government entities that may be able to provide any U.S. corporation with assistance. Experience has shown that each of the governmental entities identified welcome contact from the private sector and will respond should a corporation initiate contact with a request for assistance.

Domestic
Department of Justice (DOJ)

Within the DOJ there are a large number of Bureaus, Divisions, and Programs, all of which support the overall mission of the DOJ and produce information and analysis which may be of use to your firm. The following are those most likely to be of interest to a corporate security office.

- Bureau of Customs and Border Protection (BCBP)
- Bureau of Immigration and Customs Enforcement (ICE)
- INTERPOL—U.S. National Central Bureau
- Antitrust Division Asset Forfeiture Program
- Attorney General
- Bureau of Alcohol, Tobacco, Firearms, and Explosives
- Bureau of Justice Assistance (OJP)

- Bureau of Justice Statistics (OJP)
- Civil Division
- Civil Rights Division
- Criminal Division
- Drug Enforcement Administration
- Executive Office for Immigration Review
- Federal Bureau of Investigation
- National Criminal Justice Reference Service (OJP)
- National Drug Intelligence Center
- National Institute of Justice (OJP)
- Office of the Chief Information Officer
- Office of Information and Privacy
- Office of the Inspector General
- Office of Intelligence Policy and Review
- Office of Intergovernmental and Public Liaison
- Office of Justice Programs
- Office of Legal Counsel
- Office of Legal Policy
- Office of Legislative Affairs
- Office of Professional Responsibility
- Office of Public Affairs
- Professional Responsibility Advisory Office
- U.S. Attorney
- U.S. Marshals Service

Of those noted previously in this section, the U.S. Attorney and the Federal Bureau of Investigation would be among the recommended first stops. Within each of the 56 FBI division offices exist a variety of office entities (squads) specifically focused on topical areas of interest: Counterintelligence, Economic Espionage, and

High-Technology Cyber Crime. In addition, if cyber-crime is a topic of interest, then within the DOJ's Criminal Division is the Computer Crime and Intellectual Property Section (CCIPS). On request, any and all of these entities can provide briefings tailored to specific needs/threats.

Department of Homeland Security (DHS)

As with the DOJ, the DHS has a large number of entities. The following are believed to be the most pertinent to the interests of the corporate security perspective. The descriptions were extracted directly from the DHS Web site.

- **Directorate for Preparedness** Works with state, local, and private sector partners to identify threats, determine vulnerabilities, and target resources where risk is greatest, thereby safeguarding our borders, seaports, bridges, highways, and critical information systems.

- **Directorate for Science and Technology** The primary research and development arm of the Department. It provides Federal, state, and local officials with the technology and capabilities to protect the homeland.

- **Directorate for Management** Responsible for Department budgets and appropriations, expenditure of funds, accounting and finance, procurement, human resources, information technology systems, facilities, equipment, and the identification and tracking of performance measurements.

- **Office of Intelligence and Analysis** Responsible for using information and intelligence from multiple sources to identify and assess current and future threats to the United States.

- **Office of Operations Coordination** Responsible for monitoring the security of the United States on a daily basis and coordinating activities within the Department and with Governors, Homeland Security Advisors, law enforcement partners, and critical infrastructure operators in all 50 States and more than 50 major urban areas nationwide.

- **Federal Emergency Management Agency (FEMA)** Prepares the nation for hazards, manages Federal response and recovery efforts following any national incident, and administers the National Flood Insurance Program.

- **Transportation Security Administration (TSA)** Protects the nation's transportation systems to ensure freedom of movement for people and commerce.

- **Customs and Border Protection** Responsible for protecting our nation's borders in order to prevent terrorists and terrorist weapons from entering the United States, while facilitating the flow of legitimate trade and travel.

- **Immigration and Customs Enforcement (ICE)** The largest investigative arm of the Department of Homeland Security, responsible for identifying and shutting down vulnerabilities in the nation's border, economic, transportation, and infrastructure security.

- **Federal Law Enforcement Training Center** Provides career-long training to law enforcement professionals to help them fulfill their responsibilities safely and proficiently.

- **U.S. Coast Guard** Protects the public, the environment, and U.S. economic interests in the nation's ports and waterways, along the coast, on international waters, or in any maritime region as required supporting national security.

- **U.S. Secret Service** Protects the President and other high-level officials and investigates counterfeiting and other financial crimes, including financial institution fraud, identity theft, computer fraud, and computer-based attacks on our nation's financial, banking, and telecommunications infrastructure.

- **Homeland Security Advisory Council** Provides advice and recommendations to the Secretary on matters related to homeland security. The Council is comprised of leaders from state and local government, first responder communities, the private sector, and academia.

- **National Infrastructure Advisory Council** Provides advice to the Secretary of Homeland Security and the President on the security of information systems for the public and private institutions that constitute the critical infrastructure of our nation's economy.

- **Interagency Coordinating Council on Emergency Preparedness and Individuals with Disabilities** Established to ensure that the Federal government appropriately supports safety and security for individuals with disabilities in disaster situations.

As with the DOJ, the DHS has a variety of missions, all focused on securing the United States, and thus may be of minimal utility if the locus of attention is not within the United States. A common thread between criminal cases originating from within the DOJ and the DHS is the U.S. Attorney's office as the prosecuting office. Again, a relationship with the U.S. Attorney's office will be time well invested.

If electronic financial crime is topical, the USSS and their Electronic Crimes Branch capabilities will be of interest.

The important point to carry forward when dealing with Federal entities, be they law enforcement or other departments/agencies, is that while they may have turf issues, these are not your issues—it is at this nexus where the relationship with the U.S. Attorney keeps the corporate entity out of any "turf" discussion, as there is only one prosecutor.

International

Focus on the international milieu requires interaction with a separate set of U.S. government agencies and capabilities.

Department of Commerce (DOC)

- Trade Compliance Center
- Country Market Research
- Advocacy Center—leveling the playing field

Department of State (DOS)

- Office of Commercial and Business Affairs
- International—country background notes
- U.S. Embassy index
- Consular Affairs
- Diplomatic Security Overseas Security Advisory Council

Within the U.S. Department of Commerce, there are entire offices that are specifically chartered with leveling the playing field for U.S. industries. When an unscrupulous business practice is uncovered, reporting this event to members of Congress concurrently with the Department of Commerce will ensure your situation receives attention. Similarly, the Department of State, the foreign policy arm of the United States, offers a plethora of information for the asking and invites membership in their Diplomatic Security—Overseas Security Advisory Council, an efficient manner in which a corporate entity can keep tabs on what the U.S. Government is telling its citizens resident in a given locale. This is important, as the U.S. Government adheres closely to a "no double standard" rule on threat advisories—if U.S. government personnel are being warned, then all U.S. citizens are warned, thus obviating the need for a "special relationship" to stay atop of country specific warnings; not all governments adhere to such a policy.

Notes on Cyber Forensics

Here are some notes on cyber forensics that Jim Christy provided for us during his participation in Virtual Roundtable, featured in Part 1: The Challenge.

Digital Evidence: Volume

The world is going digital and so are important sources of evidentiary material for cyber investigators.

On average, each U.S. household owns 25 electronic products. Included on that list are laptop computers, cell phones, personal digital assistants (PDAs), and digital cameras, all items with utilities adaptable to criminal activity. Investigative planning, search warrant affidavit preparation, and crime scene exploitation must account for these and other electronic devices because they can be the tools of a crime that hold large amounts of incriminating evidence.

The electronics industry grows 11% annually because, as it has throughout its history, it continues to produce products whose features and performance rise while their costs decline. For example, the first computer hard drive, developed 50 years ago by IBM, was the size of two large refrigerators, weighed 2,000 pounds, was leased to customers for $250,000 annually (2006 dollars), and held 5 megabytes of information on 50 24-inch disks. Today, the hard drive in a laptop computer is 2.5 inches in diameter, weighs a few ounces, and, for about $100, can hold 60 GB of data.

The hard drive size, weight, and cost comparisons are impressive, but let's consider the information storage capability of the latest technology. How much potential evidentiary material could be on that laptop?

Based on 80 characters per page line, 60 lines per printed page, 4,800 characters per page, and 5,000 pages per file drawer, some basic math produces an estimate that one gigabyte of storage capacity equals the amount of information kept in 8.3 five-drawer file cabinets. Therefore, a laptop with a 60 gigabyte drive can hold 498 file cabinets, or 2,490 file drawers, of information.

The pervasiveness and utility of other digital electronics products makes them, like a laptop, important sources of evidence. Cell phones, owned by two-thirds of the people in the United States, can have one gigabyte (8.3 cabinets) of internal storage capacity. This gives the user a large space to save information from the many functions, such as camera, PDA, GPS, Web browsing, and e-mail, that cell phones now perform.

As individual devices, PDAs and digital cameras may come with 32MB of internal storage, a smaller amount than cell phones but not insignificant. Using the same formula referred to earlier, they are potentially holding 1.5 file drawers of information.

But, let's not forget about the storage media that attach to digital electronic products to enhance performance capabilities and attract customers. Memory cards come in several different shapes and, although the largest is only slightly more than 1.5" long, they may hold 4GB (33 cabinets) of information.

Thumb drives are all just a few inches long and have the same type of connector. They are sold with various amounts of storage capacity, some ranging as high as 16GB (133 cabinets).

And, there are three basic types of compact disks (CDs): standard CDs measure about 4.75" in diameter and store 650 or 700 megabytes (5.5 cabinets); mini-CDs measure 3" in diameter and hold 180 megabytes (almost 1 cabinet); and business card CDs, their name describing their size, have 40 megabytes (1.5 file drawers).

The bottom line is, law enforcement and cyber investigators should plan for seizing all types of electronic devices and digital media when pursuing a case. All of these products have some amount of internal storage capacity that equals a significant amount of information.

Moreover, advances in the electronics industry have led to the production of many small-sized items that have an immense amount of storage capacity. It may require a diligent search to find these removable, easily concealed items, but the potential rewards for uncovering this digital evidence are great.

Digital Evidence: Searches/Legal

DNA evidence can put a subject at the crime scene. Digital evidence can go beyond that and provide answers to the traditional who, what, when, where, why, and how questions.

Since most crime scenes now involve some sort of digital evidence, it is extremely critical to have a person with the expertise addressing unforeseen digital media collection issues, and ensuring successful seizure of computer media.

There are several legal points to remember when collecting digital evidence. First, make certain the search warrant includes electronic devices, digital media, digital cameras, and anything else that might hold digital evidence.

For example, you might list such items as computers, printers, cell and wireless phones, answering machines, PDAs, pagers, global positioning system (GPS) receivers, and cameras, along with their respective chargers and data cables. Don't forget other types of media that digitally store information. These include smart cards, memory cards, memory sticks/thumb drives, electronic game players, compact disks (CDs), and digital video disks (DVDs).

Second, be sure to collect important documentation related to digital media evidence. Look for such items as computer manuals, printed material, user notes, passwords, and encryption keys. Without this information, examiners will have to use digital forensic methods to recover the data—methods that can be time consuming and may not always be successful. Digital media service provider information can also be very valuable. Satellite, cell phone, cable, and pager billing records can add significantly to a case.

Finally, follow traditional criminal investigative procedures as they relate to digital evidence. Photograph the computer. Label the wires. Sketch a diagram of the wire connections. These will help examiners duplicate the computer's configuration. And, collect fingerprints. As with any case, this will help tie the wrongdoer to the crime.

Digital Evidence: Cell Phones

Criminal and counterintelligence investigators ... where are your cell phones? As digital evidentiary material, that is. They're screwed into ears everywhere (of your subjects and witnesses), but seldom seized as part of your cases, relatively speaking.

More than two-thirds of the people living in the United States own cell phones, the most common electronics device in the world. And those phones do more than dial numbers. Expanded memory cards give them added storage space for such functions as cameras, organizer tools, music players, and GPS receivers.

The Defense Cyber Crime Center (DC3)'s Defense Computer Forensic Laboratory (DCFL) only examined 52 cell phones and 17 personal digital assistants (PDAs) from April 2005 until Oct 2006 when it began tracking these objects as digital media items. Given the ubiquitous presence of these electronic devices in the lives of almost everyone—including criminals—these numbers are surprisingly low. This observation is consistent with the experience of supervisors of the FBI's Computer Analysis Response Team (CART) program, in terms of cell phones seized and referred for examination.

From the DC3's perspective, more cell phones and PDAs should be appearing as evidence in digital forensic exams. They are invariably "tools of the crime," as the conveniences and real-time exchange of information they provide ideally suits the motivation and interest of criminals.

Whether it's a cell phone or PDA, the device can contain data of enormous probative value. DCFL examiners have been very successful at extracting a wide variety of data from cell phones, including: contact lists (phone book), call records (out-going, in-coming, and missed calls), pictures, and videos. Information found on PDAs is dependent upon the user's purpose for the device; however, most commonly scheduling, appointment, calendar, contacts, and e-mail data are recoverable.

We worry that the relative number of referrals possibly indicates a deficit in investigative planning (and search warrant affidavit prep) and crime scene exploitation—which should include the seizure of a greater range of digital devices that can be tools of the crime (digital cameras, GPS systems, etc). It may be that field investigators aren't tying cell phones to their search, or are simply doing a "Kojak field test" by looking at the last number dialed.

If so, they risk missing a rich load of data that can identify co-conspirators, accessories to the crime, or (depending on the nature of the crime) previously unknown victims, or generate other fruitful leads, and more.

Digital Evidence: Accreditation

Digital Forensics is the forensic examination and exploitation of digital media. Today there is a proliferation of electronic devices that contain digital information about everything we do. These devices have become integrated into our daily lives and therefore we have become dependent on digital devices such as cell phones, pagers, PDAs, computers, laptops, alarm systems, badge access systems, video games systems, GPS units, watches, video cameras, ATMs, and so on.

These devices contain information digitally stored in e-mail, bank records, word processing documents, calendars, spreadsheets, contact lists, alarm codes, pictures, and more.

For investigative purposes both civilly and criminally, the exploitation of these digital devices forensically is in a very nascent stage even for the federal government. As recently as the Fall of 2003, the American Society of Crime Laboratory Directors/ Laboratory Accreditation Board (ASCLD/LAB) accepted Digital Forensics as a new forensics discipline just like the traditional forensics disciplines of ballistics, DNA, serology, hand writing, questioned documents, toxicology, tool marks, etc., and approved standards for the processing of digital evidence.

Just like the crime labs you see on every television network today, there are digital devices that need to be exploited forensically to prove or disprove allegations. The difference between what you see on TV and reality is the time and expense to process digital evidence.

The days of looking through someone's file cabinet or desk drawer for evidence are fading. People today are storing their information on computers and portable wireless devices. That means that a run-of-the-mill investigator can no longer review evidence on site and discover the evidence relevant to their investigation. Today those electronic devices must be seized or forensically copied at the source and then examined/exploited in a laboratory environment with specialized tools and highly trained experts. Only these specialized tools can make the information visible for review to determine if it is relevant or not.

And now ASCLD/LAB has established standards for the forensic processing of these devices. There are approximately 312 crime labs that have been accredited in North America by ASCLD/LAB. Today, only 12 labs are accredited to process digital forensics. All of these labs are government labs. There are no private sector accredited digital forensics labs today.

At least 3 states have passed legislation that prohibits the introduction of forensics evidence (both digital and non-digital evidence) into their courts unless processed by an accredited forensic crime lab. Several states are considering this legislation but have not passed it due to the fact that they don't currently have access to an accredited forensics lab.

Definitions

- **Digital Forensic Examinations** Perform the scientific process of discovering information that is probative to an investigation or administrative matter using an approved methodology that would withstand the rigor of the legal process.

- **Digital Forensic Examination Reports** The easy-to-read report created as a result of the Digital Forensics Examination. This report must be able to be read and comprehended by both non-technical readers as well as readers with a technical background.

- **Expert witness testimony** Testimony in a court or administrative hearing by a witness, who by virtue of education, profession, publication, or experience, is believed to have special knowledge of their subject beyond that of the average person, sufficient that others may officially and legally rely upon their opinion.

- **On-site evidence acquisition** The physical copying or seizing of computer media that could possibly be of evidentiary value based on a legal authority including consent.

Digital Evidence: Digital Forensics Intelligence

The Defense Cyber Crime Center (DC3) established a new intelligence discipline in 2005 to support cyber investigations and digital forensics. Everyone is familiar with the foreign intelligence and criminal intelligence disciplines. In the recent past, a new Cyber

Intelligence discipline was established to focus on computer intrusion investigations. If you were to place these three intelligence disciplines in a Venn diagram, where they all overlap, what we define as Digital Forensics Intelligence would be created. It's the tools, techniques, and procedures (TTPs) that subjects use to obfuscate data, and the TTPs we use in law enforcement to uncover evidence. Sometimes evidence is obfuscated by technology itself.

We have found that many of our examiners happen to be introverted, maybe the nature of the beast. In the past, an experienced examiner may have encountered a new challenge, performed their own research, solved the problem, and moved on to the next case. A month later, an inexperienced examiner may have encountered the same problem, performed their own research, and not solved the challenge. There was no process to capture the corporate knowledge.

DC3 has established standard operating procedures that create and sustain a perpetual knowledge management system for analyzing, collecting, and disseminating the refined TTPs of digital forensic examinations.

The DFI Team is currently comprised of a senior traditional intelligence analyst and a senior digital forensics examiner. The DFI Team designed and built the DFI Portal, an intranet Web site where DC3's entire staff could access a storehouse of information. By the end of 2006, the DFI Portal held more than 1,000 documents and DC3 personnel had used the Portal's search engine approximately 2,000 times. It was so successful that DC3 felt that all federal, state, and local law enforcement agencies (LEAs) could benefit from such a system. Today, most state and local LEAs can not afford more than a handful of examiners, and training for these examiners is usually nascent.

DC3 and Oklahoma State University (OSU) have teamed in a joint initiative to create the National Repository of Digital Forensic Intelligence (NRDFI). Representatives from Oklahoma State's Center for Telecommunications and Network Security (CTANS) met with the DFI Team and plans were outlined to create a DFI knowledge management portal aimed at linking cyber investigators from the various criminal investigative agencies.

The following are examples of the types of searchable information that will populate the NRDFI.

- List of "Tips-n-Tricks"
- Test and Validations reports of tools
- Training course manuals

- White papers

- Newsletters

- Technical presentations

- Actual copies of government-developed tools

- Legal library

OSU has been able to acquire some minimal funding and has assigned a full-time programmer to develop the NRDFI proto-type. DC3 has migrated all unclassified material to be shared with all participating LE agencies. OSU is currently looking for federal, state, and local LEAs that would like to beta test the system.

In addition, when reviewing electronic crime, there are many aspects that must be reviewed for new methodologies, new discovery techniques, etc. The Anti-Phishing Working Group, a non-profit organization, hosts an annual research conference for those involved in the research of electronic crime. In addition, in the United States, the National Institute of Justice funds research in the field of electronic forensics in support of the United State's local, regional, state, and national law enforcement entities, many of which have literally no resources available to support their e-forensic efforts.

What areas should be reviewed? We suggest that the enterprise IT department be schooled in the anatomy of "Phishing" and "Pharming," as well as the intricacies of professionally prepared software which is created to separate funds, data, or intellect from an individual, and by extension the enterprise. One organization which the forensic team in any enterprise should belong to is the High Technology Criminal Investigators Association (HTCIA), which has regional chapters around the globe and holds educational seminars and conventions on a regular cadence.

In addition, the legal and financial departments must be up to speed on both the legal precedence and fraud prevention methodologies, and the enterprise as a whole must be sensitive to the deleterious effects which a legal or fiscal imbroglio will have on the corporate brand and/or reputation—both worthy of protection in the grand scheme of intellectual property protection and loss prevention.

As important is the need to be on top of the countermeasures and acceptable digital forensic tools which are allowed to be used in various courts of law. How sad to find that your IP has been stolen, and then the first employee to the data mishandles the data and thus it isn't acceptable in court and is open to conjecture as to whether or not the data was corrupted by the "forensic" process.

Appendix D

U.S. International
Trade Commission
Section 337 Process

The US International Trade Commission (USITC) Section 337 process is designed to provide companies a means to protect their intellectual property rights.

Section 337 investigations (www.usitc.gov/trade_remedy/int_prop/inv_his.htm) conducted by the U.S. International Trade Commission most often involve claims regarding intellectual property rights, including allegations of patent infringement and trademark infringement by imported goods. Both utility and design patents, as well as registered and common law trademarks, may be asserted in these investigations. Other forms of unfair competition involving imported products, such as infringement of registered copyrights, mask works or boat hull designs, misappropriation of trade secrets or trade dress, passing off, and false advertising, may also be asserted. Additionally, antitrust claims relating to imported goods may be asserted. The primary remedy available in Section 337 investigations is an exclusion order that directs Customs to stop infringing imports from entering the United States. In addition, the Commission may issue cease-and-desist orders against named importers and other persons engaged in unfair acts that violate Section 337. Expedited relief in the form of temporary exclusion orders and temporary cease and desist orders may also be available in certain exceptional circumstances. Section 337 investigations, which are conducted pursuant to 19 U.S.C. § 1337 and the Administrative Procedure Act, include trial proceedings before administrative law judges and review by the Commission.

As of mid-2007, there were 613 registered investigations spanning the last 30 years, indicative of the high bar required in having a petition accepted by the USITC, with 42 of these cases remaining active. Table D.1 provides the investigation number, status, and title for most of these cases. Provision of the entire list is to give you an immediate understanding that if you are the victim of intellectual property loss, and need to protect your market share in the United States, precedent and procedures exist to assist you in doing so.

Table D.1 USITC Section 337 Investigations

Investigation Number	Status	Investigation Title
610	Pending	Certain Endodontic Instruments
609	Pending	Certain Buffer Systems and Components Thereof Used in Container
608	Pending	Certain Nitrile Gloves
607	Pending	Semiconductor Devices, DMA Systems, and Products Containing Same
606	Pending	Personal Computers and Digital Display Devices
605	Pending	Semiconductor Chips with Minimized Chip Package Size and Products
604	Pending	Sucralose, Sweeteners Containing Sucralose, and Related
603	Pending	DVD Players and Recorders and Certain Products Containing Same
602	Pending	GPS Devices and Products Containing Same
601	Pending	3G Wideband Code Division Multiple Access (WCDMA) Handsets and
600	Pending	Rechargeable Lithium-Ion Batteries, Components Thereof, and
599	Pending	Lighting Control Devices Including Dimmer Switches and/or
598	Pending	Unified Communications Systems, Products Used With Such Systems,
597	Pending	Bassinet Products
596	Pending	GPS Chips, Associated Software and Systems, and Products
595	Pending	Dynamic Random Access Memory Devices and Products Containing Same
594	Pending	Lighting Products, Components Thereof, and Products Containing
593	Pending	Digital Cameras and Component Parts Thereof

Continued

Table D.1 Continued. USITC Section 337 Investigations

Investigation Number	Status	Investigation Title
592		NAND Flash Memory Devices and Components Thereof, and Products
591		Wireless Conference Calling Devices, Components Thereof, and
590	Pending	Coupler Devices for Power Supply Facilities, Components Thereof,
589	Pending	Switches and Products Containing Same
588	Pending	Digital Multimeters, and Products with Multimeter Functionality
587	Pending	Connecting Devices For Use With Modular Compressed Air
586	Pending	Stringed Musical Instruments and Components Thereof
585		Engines, Components Thereof, and Products Containing Same
584		Alendronate Salts and Products Containing Same
583	Pending	Wireless Communication Devices, Components Thereof, and Products
582	Pending	Hydraulic Excavators and Components Thereof
581		Inkjet Ink Supplies and Components Thereof
580		Peripheral Devices and Components Thereof and Products Containing
579	Pending	Nickel Metal Hydride Consumer Batteries, Components Thereof, and
578	Pending	Mobile Telephone Handsets, Wireless Communication Devices, and
577	Pending	Wireless Communication Equipment, Articles Therein, and Products
576		Portable Digital Media Players and Components Thereof
575	Pending	Lighters

Continued

Table D.1 Continued. USITC Section 337 Investigations

Investigation Number	Status	Investigation Title
574	Pending	Equipment for Telecommunications or Data Communications Networks,
573		Portable Digital Media Players
572		Insulin Delivery Devices, Including Cartridges Having Adaptor
571	Pending	L-Lysine Feed Products, Their Methods of Production and Genetic
570		Flash Memory Chips, Flash Memory Systems, and Products Containing
569	Pending	Endoscopic Probes for Uses in Argon Plasma Coagulation Systems
568		Products and Pharmaceutical Compositions Containing Recombinant
567	Pending	Foam Footwear
566		Chemical Mechanical Planarization Slurries and Precursors to Same
565	Pending	Ink Cartridges and Components Thereof
564	Pending	Voltage Regulators, Components Thereof and Products Containing
563		Portable Power Stations and Packaging Therefor
562		Incremental Dental Positioning Adjustment Appliances and Methods
561		Combination Motor and Transmission Systems and Devices Used
560		NOR and NAND Flash Memory Devices and Products Containing Same
559	Pending	Digital Processors and Digital Processing Systems, Components
558	Pending	Personal Computer/Consumer Electronic Convergent Devices,
557		Automotive Parts

Continued

www.syngress.com

Table D.1 Continued. USITC Section 337 Investigations

Investigation Number	Status	Investigation Title
556		High-Brightness Light Emitting Diodes and Products Containing
555		Devices for Determining Organ Positions and Certain Subassemblies
554		Axle Bearing Assemblies, Components Thereof, and Products
553		NAND Flash Memory Devices and Products Containing Same
552		Flash Memory Devices and Components Thereof, and Products
551		Laser Bar Code Scanners and Scan Engines, Components Thereof and
550	Pending	Modified Vaccinia Ankara ("MVA") Viruses and Vaccines and
549		Ink Sticks for Solid Ink Printers
548		Tissue Converting Machinery, Including Rewinders, Tail Sealers,
547		Personal Computers, Monitors and Components Thereof
546		Male Prophylactic Devices
545		Laminated Floor Panels
544		Hand-Held Mobile Computing Devices, Components Thereof And
543		Baseband Processor Chips and Chipsets, Transmitter and Receiver
542		DVD/CD Players and Recorders, Color Television Receivers and
541		Power Supply Controllers and Products Containing Same
540		Automotive Grilles
539		Tadalafil or Any Salt or Solvate Thereof, and Products Containing

Continued

Table D.1 Continued. USITC Section 337 Investigations

Investigation Number	Status	Investigation Title
538		Audio Processing Integrated Circuits, and Products Containing
537		Weather Stations and Components Thereof
536		Pool Cues with Self-aligning Joint Assemblies and Components
535		Network Communications Systems for Optical Networks and
534		Color Television Receivers and Color Display Monitors, and
533		Rubber Antidegradants, Components Thereof, and Products
532		Automotive Fuel Caps and Components Thereof
531		Network Controllers and Products Containing Same
530		Electric Robots and Component Parts Thereof
529		Digital Processors, Digital Processing Systems, Components
528		Foam Masking Tape
527		Digital Image Storage and Retrieval Devices
526		NAND Flash Memory Circuits and Products Containing Same
525		Semiconductor Devices and Products Containing Same
524	Pending	Point of Sale Terminals and Components Thereof
523		Optical Disk Controller Chips and Chipsets and Products
522		Ink Markers and Packaging Thereof
521		Voltage Regulator Circuits, Components Thereof and Products
520		Digital Image Storage and Retrieval Devices

Continued

Table D.1 Continued. USITC Section 337 Investigations

Investigation Number	Status	Investigation Title
519		Personal Computers, Monitors, and Components Thereof
518		Ear Protection Devices
517		Shirts With Pucker-Free Seams and Methods of Producing Same
516		Disc Drives, Components Thereof, and Products Containing Same
515		Injectable Implant Compositions
514		Plastic Food Containers
513		Electronic Devices, Including Power Adapters, Power Converters,
512		Light-Emitting Diodes and Products Containing Same
511		Pet Food Treats
510		Systems for Detecting and Removing Viruses or Worms, Components
509		Personal Computers, Server Computers, and Components Thereof
508		Absorbent Garments
507		Medical Devices Used to Compact Inner Bone Tissue and Products
506		Optical Disk Controller Chips and Chipsets and Products
505		Gun Barrels Used In Firearms Training Systems
504		Signature Capture Transaction Devices and Component Parts
503		Automated Mechanical Transmission Systems for Medium-Duty and
502		Automobile Tail Light Lenses and Products Incorporating Same
501	Pending	Encapsulated Integrated Circuit Devices and Products Containing

Continued

Table D.1 Continued. USITC Section 337 Investigations

Investigation Number	Status	Investigation Title
500		Purple Protective Gloves
499		Audio Digital-to-Analog Converters and Products Containing Same
498		Insect Traps
497		Universal Transmitters for Garage Door Openers
496		Home Vacuum Packaging Machines
495		Breath Test Systems for the Detection of Gastrointestinal
494		Automotive Measuring Devices, Products Containing Same, And
493		Zero-Mercury-Added Alkaline Batteries, Parts Thereof, and
492		Plastic Grocery and Retail Bags
491		Display Controllers and Products Containing Same
490		Power Amplifier Chips, Broadband Tuner Chips, Transceiver Chips,
489		Sildenafil or Any Pharmaceutically Acceptable Salt Thereof, Such
488		Screen Printing Machines, Vision Alignment Devices Used Therein,
487	Pending	Agricultural Vehicles and Components Thereof
486		Agricultural Tractors, Lawn Tractors, Riding Lawnmowers, and
485		Truck Bed Ramps and Components Thereof
484		Machine Vision Systems, Parts and Components Thereof and Products
483		Tool Handles, Tool Holders, Tool Sets, and Components Therefor
482		Compact Disc and DVD Holders

Continued

www.syngress.com

Table D.1 Continued. USITC Section 337 Investigations

Investigation Number	Status	Investigation Title
481		Display Controllers with Upscaling Functionality and Products
480		Panel Fasteners, Products Containing Same, and Components Thereof
479		Coamoxiclav Products, Potassium Clavulanate Products, and Other
478		Ground Fault Circuit Interrupters and Products Containing Same
477		Ammonium Octamolybdate Isomers
476		Radios and Components Thereof
475		Electronic Educational Devices and Components Thereof
474		Recordable Compact Discs and Rewritable Compact Discs
473		Video Game Systems, Accessories, and Components Thereof
472		Semiconductor Devices and Products Containing Same
471		Data Storage Systems and Components Thereof
470		Semiconductor Memory Devices and Products Containing Same
469		Bearings and Packaging Thereof
468		Microlithographic Machines and Components Thereof
467		Canary Yellow Self-Stick Respositionable Note Products
466		Organizer Racks and Products Containing Same
465		Semiconductor Timing Signal Generator Devices, Components
464		Video Cassette Devices and Television/Video Cassette Combination

Continued

Table D.1 Continued. USITC Section 337 Investigations

Investigation Number	Status	Investigation Title
463		Power Saving Integrated Circuits and Products Containing Same
462		Plastic Molding Machines with Control Systems Having Programmable
461		Clay Target Throwing Machines And Components Thereof
460		Sortation Systems, Parts Thereof, and Products Containing Same
459		Garage Door Operators Including Components Thereof
458		Digital Display Receivers and Digital Display Controllers and
457		Polyethylene Terephthalate Yarn and Products Containing Same
456		Gel-filled Wrist Rests and Products Containing Same
455		Network Interface Cards and Access Points for Use in Direct
454		Set-Top Boxes and Components Thereof
453		Programmable Logic Devices And Products Containing Same
452		Personal Watercraft and Components Thereof
451		CMOS Active Pixel Image Sensors and Products Containing Same
450		Integrated Circuits, Processes For Making Same, And Products
449		Abrasive Products Made Using a Process for Making Powder
448		Oscillating Sprinklers, Sprinkler Components, and Nozzles
447		Aerospace Rivets and Products Containing Same

Continued

Table D.1 Continued. USITC Section 337 Investigations

Investigation Number	Status	Investigation Title
446		Ink Jet Print Cartridges and Components Thereof
445		Plasma Display Panels and Products Containing Same
444		Semiconductor Light Emitting Devices, Components Thereof, and
443		Flooring Products
442		Closet Flange Rings
441		Field Programmable Gate Arrays and Products Containing Same
440		4-Androstenediol
439		HSP Modems, Software and Hardware Components Thereof, and
438		Plastic Molding Machines With Control Systems Having Programmable
437		Synchronous Dynamic Random Access Memory Devices and Modules and
436		WAP-Compatible Wireless Communication Devices, Components
435		Integrated Repeaters, Switches, Transceivers, and Products
434		Magnetic Resonance Injection Systems and Components Thereof
433		Safety Eyewear and Components Thereof
432		Semiconductor Chips With Minimized Chip Package Size And Products
431		Synchronous Dynamic Random Access Memory Devices,
430		Integrated Repeaters and Products Containing the Same
429		Bar Clamps, Bar Clamp Pads, and Related Packaging, Display, and

Continued

Table D.1 Continued. USITC Section 337 Investigations

Investigation Number	Status	Investigation Title
428		Integrated Circuit Chipsets, Components Thereof and Products
427		Downhole Well Data Recorders and Components Thereof
426		Spiral Grilled Products Including Ducted Fans and Components
425		Amino Fluoro Ketone Compounds
424		Cigarettes and Packaging Thereof
423		Conductive Coated Abrasives
422		Two-Handle Centerset Faucets and Escutcheons, and Components
421		Enhanced DRAM Devices Containing Embedded Cache Memory Registers,
420		Beer Products
419		Excimer Laser Systems for Vision Correction Surgery and
418		Rodent Bait Stations and Components Thereof
417		Code Hopping Remote Control Systems, Including Components and
416		Compact Multipurpose Tools
415		Mechanical Lumbar Supports and Products Containing Same
414		Semiconductor Memory Devices and Products Containing Same
413		Rare-Earth Magnets and Magnetic Materials and Articles Containing
412		Video Graphics Display Controllers and Products Containing Same
411		Organic Photoconductor Drums and Products Containing the Same
410		Coated Optical Waveguide Fibers and Products Containing Same

Continued

Table D.1 Continued. USITC Section 337 Investigations

Investigation Number	Status	Investigation Title
409		CD-ROM Controllers and Products Containing Same - II
408		Recombinantly Produced Hepatitis B Vaccines and Products
407		Remodulating Channel Selectors and Systems Containing Same
406	Pending	Lens-Fitted Film Packages
405		Automotive Scissors Jacks
404		SDRAMs, DRAMs, ASICs, RAM-and Logic Chips, Microprocessors,
403		Acesulfame Potassium and Blends and Products Containing Same
402		Integrated Circuits and Products Containing Same
401		CD-ROM Controllers and Products Containing Same
400		Telephonic Digital Added Main Line Systems, Components Thereof,
399		Fluid-Filled Ornamental Lamps
398		Multiple Implement, Multi-Function Pocket Knives and Related
397		Dense Wavelength Division Multiplexing Systems and Components
396		Removable Electronic Cards and Electronic Card Reader Devices and
395		EPROM, EEPROM, Flash Memory, and Flash Microcontroller
394		Screen Printing Machines, Vision Alignment Devices Used Therein,
393		Ion Trap Mass Spectrometers and Components Thereof
392		Digital Satellite System (DSS) Receivers and Components Thereof

Continued

Table D.1 Continued. USITC Section 337 Investigations

Investigation Number	Status	Investigation Title
391		Toothbrushes and the Packaging Thereof
390		Transport Vehicle Tires
389		Diagnostic Kits for the Detection and Quantification of Viruses
388		Dynamic Random Access Memory Controllers and Certain Multi-Layer
387		Self-Powered Fiber Optic Modems
386		Global Positioning System Coarse Acquisition Code Receivers and
385		Random Access Memories, Processes for the Manufacture of Same,
384		Monolithic Microwave Integrated Circuit Downconverters and
383		Hardware Logic Emulation Systems and Components Thereof
382		Flash Memory Circuits and Products Containing Same
381		Electronic Products, Including Semiconductor Products,
380		Agricultural Tractors Under 50 Power Take-off Horsepower
379		Starter Kill Vehicle Security Systems
378		Asian-Style Kamaboko Fish Cakes
377		Microprocessors Having Alignment Checking and Products Containing
376		Variable Speed Wind Turbines and Components Thereof
375		Clog Style Articles of Footwear
374		Electrical Connectors and Products Containing Same
373		Low-Power Computer Hard Disk Drive Systems and Products

Continued

Table D.1 Continued. USITC Section 337 Investigations

Investigation Number	Status	Investigation Title
372		Neodymium-Iron-Boron Magnets, Magnet Alloys, and Articles
371		Memory Devices with Increased Capacitance and Products Containing
370		Salinomycin Biomass and Preparations Containing Same
369		Health and Beauty Aids and Identifying Marks Therein
368		Rechargeable Nickel Metal Hydride Anode Materials and Batteries,
367		Facsimile Machines
366		Microsphere Adhesives, Process For Making Same, and Products
365		Audible Alarm Devices for Divers
364		Curable Fluoroelastomer Compositions and Precursors Thereof
363		Multibrand Infrared Remote Control Transmitters
362		Methods of Assembling Plastic Ball Valves and Components Thereof
361		Portable On-Car Disc Brake Lathes and Components Thereof
360		Devices For Connecting Computers Via Telephone Lines
359		Dielectric Miniature Microwave Filters and Multiplexers
358		Recombinantly Produced Human Growth Hormones
357		Sports Sandals and Components Thereof
356		Integrated Circuit Devices, Processes For Making Same, Components
355		Vehicle Security Systems and Components Thereof

Continued

Table D.1 Continued. USITC Section 337 Investigations

Investigation Number	Status	Investigation Title
354		Tape Dispensers
353		Lens Panels For Lighting Fixtures, Kits Containing Same, and
352		Personal Computers With Memory Management Information Stored In
351		Removable Hard Disk Cartridges and Products Containing Same
350		Sputtered Carbon Coated Computer Disks and Products Containing
349		Diltiazem Hydrochloride and Diltiazem Preparations
348		In-Line Roller Skates With Ventilated Boots And In-Line Roller
347		Anti-Theft Deactivatable Resonant Tags and Components Thereof
346		Magnetic Switches For Coaxial Transmission Lines and Products
345		Anisotropically Etched One Megabit and Greater DRAMs, Components
344		Cutting Tools For Flexible Plastic Conduit and Components Thereof
343		Mechanical Gear Couplings and Components Thereof
342		Circuit Board Testers
341		Static Random Access Memories, Components Thereof and Products
340		Specimen Container Systems and Components Including Alignment
339		Commercial Food Portioners, Components Thereof, Including
338		Bulk Bags and Process For Making Same
337		Integrated Circuit Telecommunication Chips and Products

Continued

www.syngress.com

Table D.1 Continued. USITC Section 337 Investigations

Investigation Number	Status	Investigation Title
336		Single In-Line Memory Modules and Products Containing Same
335		Dynamic Sequential Gradient Compression Devices and Component
334		Condensers, Parts Thereof and Products Containing Same, Including
333		Woodworking Accessories
332		Translucent Ceramic Orthodontic Brackets
331		Microcomputer Memory Controllers, Components Thereof and Products
330		Computer System State Save/Restore Software and Associated Backup
329		Vacuum Cleaners
328		Bathtubs and Other Bathing Vessels and Materials Used Therein
327		Food Trays With Lockable Lids
326		Scanning Multiple Beam Equalization Systems For Chest Radiography
325		Static Random Access Memories and Integrated Circuit Devices
324		Acid-Washed Denim Garments and Accessories
323		Monoclonal Antibodies Used For Therapeutically Treating Humans
322		Microporous Nylon Membrane and Products Containing Same
321		Soft Drinks and Their Containers
320		Rotary Printing Apparatus Using Heated Ink Composition,
319		Automotive Fuel Caps and Radiator Caps and Related Packaging and
318		Anti-Knock Ignition Systems and Automobiles or Automobile

Continued

Table D.1 Continued. USITC Section 337 Investigations

Investigation Number	Status	Investigation Title
317		Internal Mixing Devices and Components Thereof
316		Power Transmission Chains, Chain Assemblies, Components Thereof,
315		Plastic Encapsulated Integrated Circuits
314		Battery-Powered Ride-On Toy Vehicles and Components Thereof
313		Spunbond Nonwoven Fabric: Process, Apparatus, and Components
312		Dynamic Random Access Memories, Static Random Access Memories,
311		Air Impact Wrenches
310		Pyrethroids and Pyrethroid-Based Insecticides
309		Athletic Shoes With Viewing Windows
308		Key Blanks For Keys Of High Security Cylinder Locks
307		Catalyst Components and Catalysts For The Polymerization of
306		Bath Accessories and Component Parts Thereof
305		Aramid Fiber Honeycomb, Unexpanded Block or Slice Precursors Of
304		Pressure Transmitters
303		Polymer Geogrid Products and Processes Therefor
302		Self-Inflating Mattresses
301		Imported Artificial Breast Prostheses and the Manufacturing
300		Doxorubicin and Preparations Containing Same
299		Food Treatment Ovens, Component Parts Thereof And Processes

Continued

Table D.1 Continued. USITC Section 337 Investigations

Investigation Number	Status	Investigation Title
298		Low Friction Drawer Supports, Components Thereof, and Products
297		Cellular Radiotelephones and Subassemblies and Component Parts
296		Phenylene Sulfide Polymers and Polymer Compounds and Products
295		Novelty Teleidoscopes
294		Carrier Materials Bearing Ink Compositions To Be Used In A Dry
293		Crystalline Cefadroxil Monohydrate
292		Methods of Making Carbonated Candy Products
291		Insulated Security Chests
290		Wire Electrical Discharge Machining Apparatus and Components
289		Concealed Cabinet Hinges and Mounting Plates
288		Straight Knife Cloth Cutting Machines
287		Strip Lights
286		Track Lighting System Components, Including Plugboxes
285		Chemiluminescent Compositions and Components Thereof and Methods
284		Electric Power Tools, Battery Cartridges and Battery Chargers
283		Electronic Dart Games
282		Venetian Blind Components
281		Recombinant Erythropoietin
280		High Geometric Surface Area Catalysts and Components Thereof
279		Plastic Light Duty Screw Anchors
278		Programmable Digital Clock Thermostats

Continued

Table D.1 Continued. USITC Section 337 Investigations

Investigation Number	Status	Investigation Title
277		Marine Automatic Pilots
276		Erasable Programmable Read Only Memories, Components Thereof,
275		Nonwoven Gas Filter Elements
274		Toggle Clamps for Clamping, Fixturing Procesessing, and Original
273		Cellular Mobile Telephones and Subassemblies and Components Parts
272		Electronic Chime Modules
271		Buoyant Metallized Balloons
270		Noncontact Tonometers
269		Picture-In-A-Picture Video Add-On Products and Components Thereof
268		High Intensity Retroreflective Sheeting
267		Minoxidil Powder, Salts & Compositions For Use in Hair Treatment
266		Reclosable Plastic Bags and Tubing
265		Dental Prophylaxis Methods, Equipment and Components Thereof
264		Mail Extraction Desks and Components Thereof
263		Office Filing Cabinets
262		Hard Sided Molded Luggage Cases
261		Ink Jet Printers Employing Solid Ink
260		Feathered Fur Coats and Pelts, and Process For The Manufacture
259		Battery-Powered Smoke Detectors
258		Moldable/Extrudable Polyetheresteramide Copolymers
257		Electronic Wall Stud Finders
256		Cryogenic Ultramicrotome Apparatus and Components Thereof

Continued

Table D.1 Continued. USITC Section 337 Investigations

Investigation Number	Status	Investigation Title
255		Garment Hangers
254		Small Aluminum Flashlights and Components Thereof
253		Electrically Resistive Monocomponent Toner and "Black Powder"
252		Heavy Duty Mobile Scrap Shears
251		Electronic Chromatogram Analyzers and Components Thereof
250		Ventilated Motorcycle Helmets
249		Aircraft Carbon Disc Brakes & Replacement Carbon Discs
248		Plastic Fasteners & Processes for the Manufacture Thereof
247		Sickle Guards Intended For Use In Mowing Machines
246		Xenon Lamp Dissolver Slide Projectors and Components Thereof
245		Low-Nitrosamine Trifluralin Herbicides
244		Insulated Security Chests
243		Luggage Products
242		Dynamic Random Access Memories, Components Thereof, and Products
241		Prefabricated Bow Forms
240		Laser Inscribed Diamonds and the Method of Inscription Thereof
239		Non-Contact Laser Precision Dimensional Measuring Devices and
238		Vacuum Cleaner Foot Switches
237		Miniature Hacksaws
236		Portable Bag Sewing Machines and Parts Thereof
235		Human-Powered Vehicles with Combination Steering, Braking and

Continued

Table D.1 Continued. USITC Section 337 Investigations

Investigation Number	Status	Investigation Title
234		Upper Body Protector Apparatus for Use in Motosports
233		Pharmaceutical Closures
232		Glass Firescreens for Fireplaces
231		Soft Sculpture Dolls, Popularly Known as "Cabbage Patch Kids,"
230		Unitary Electromagnetic Flowmeters with Sealed Coils
229		Nut Jewelry and Parts Thereof
228		Fans with Brushless DC Motors
227		One Piece Cold Forged Bicycle Cranks
226		Mass Spectrometers and Components Thereof
225		Multi-Level Touch Control Lighting Switches
224		Cellulose Acetate Hollow Fiber Artificial Kidneys
223		Key Telephone Systems and Components Thereof
222		Automotive Visor/Illuminated Mirror Packages
221		Apparatus for Disintegration of Urinary Calculi
220		Spring Retainers for Garage Door Hardware
219		Porch, Patio and Lawn Gliders
218		Automatic Bowling Machine Printed Circuit Boards
217		Expansion Tanks
216		Ceramic Drainage Foils
215		Double-Sided Floppy Disk Drives and Components Thereof
214		Frozen Beverage Dispensing Machines

Continued

Table D.1 Continued. USITC Section 337 Investigations

Investigation Number	Status	Investigation Title
213		Fluidized Bed Combustion Systems
212		Convertible Rowing Exercisers
211		Electrical Connectors
210		Motor Graders with Adjustable Control Consoles and Components
209		Aluminum Frame Fabric-Covered Luggage and Components Thereof
208		Shoe Stiffener Components
207		Automotive Transmission Shifters
206		Surgical Implants for Fixation of Bone Fragments
205		Dialyzers Using Telescoping Connectors for Fluid Lines
204		Pull-Type Golf Carts and Wheels Thereof
203		Floppy Disk Drives & Components Thereof
202		Telephone Base Housings & Related Packaging & Printed Materials
201		Products with Gremlin Character Depictions
200		Ink Jet Printing Systems
199		Anodes for Cathodic Protection and Components Thereof
198		Portable Calculators
197		Compound Action Metal Cutting Snips and Components Thereof
196		Apparatus for Installing Electrical Lines and Components Thereof
195		Cloisonne Jewelry
194		Aramid Fiber
193		Rowing Machines and Components Thereof
192		Spring Balanced Arm Lamp Heads
191		Stretch Wrapping Apparatus and Components Thereof

Continued

Table D.1 Continued. USITC Section 337 Investigations

Investigation Number	Status	Investigation Title
190		Softballs and Polyurethane Cores Thereof
189		Optical Waveguide Fibers
188		Fluidized Supporting Apparatus and ComponentsThereof
187		Glass Construction Blocks
186		Tennis Rackets
185		Rotary Wheel Printing Systems
184		Foam Earplugs
183		Indomethacin
182		Fluidized Supporting Apparatus
181		Meat Deboning Machines
180		X-Ray Intensifier Tubes
179		Spherical Roller Bearings and Components Thereof and Tools and
178		Vinyl-Covered Foam Blocks
177		Film Web Drive Stretch Apparatus & Components Thereof
176		Outboard Motors and Components Thereof
175		Metal and Wire Shelf Products and Accessories
174		Woodworking Machines
173		Valves
172		Shearing Machines
171		Glass Tempering Systems
170		Bag Closure Clips
169		Process for the Manufacture of Skinless Sausage Casings and
168		Combination Punch Press and Laser Assemblies and Components
167		Single Handle Faucets
166		Computerized Jacquard Pattern Cutting Systems

Continued

www.syngress.com

Table D.1 Continued. USITC Section 337 Investigations

Investigation Number	Status	Investigation Title
165		Alkaline Batteries
164		Modular Structural Systems
163		Nutating Valve Actuators and Components Thereof
162		Cardiac Pacemakers and Components Thereof
161		Trolley Wheel Assemblies
160		Composite Diamond Coated Textile Machinery Components
159		Poultry-Cut Up Machines
158		Plastic Light Duty Screw Anchors
157		Office Desk Accessories and Related Products
156		Minutiae-Based Automated Fingerprint Identification Systems
155		Liquid Crystal Display Watches with Rocker Switches
154		Dot Matrix Line Printers and Components Thereof
153		Microprocessors, Related Parts and Systems
152		Plastic Food Storage Containers
151		Apparatus for Flow Injection Analysis and Components Thereof
150		Self-Stripping Electrical Tap Connectors
149		Radar Detectors and Accompanying Owner's Manuals
148 (148/169)		Processes for the Manufacture of Skinless Sausage Casings and
147		Papermaking Machine Forming Sections for the Continuous
146		Canape Makers
145		Rotary Wheel Printers

Continued

Table D.1 Continued. USITC Section 337 Investigations

Investigation Number	Status	Investigation Title
144		Direct Current Brushless Axial Flow Fans
143		Amorphous Metal Alloys and Amorphous Metal Articles
142		Electronic Chromatogram Analyzers and Components Thereof
141		Copper-Clad Stainless Steel Cookware
140		Personal Computers and Components Thereof
139		Caulking Guns
138		Automatic Turret Rewinders
137		Heavy-Duty Staple Gun Tackers
136		Marine Hardware and Accessories
135		Direction-Reversing Musical Crib Toys
134		Treadmill Joggers
133		Vertical Milling Machines and Parts, Attachments and Accessories
132		Hand-Operated, Gas-Operated Welding, Cutting and Heating
131		Variable Character Display Devices
130		Braiding Machines
129		Limited-Charge Cell Culture Microcarriers
128		Cupric Hydroxide Formulated Fungicides and Cupric Hydroxide
127		Amino Acid Formulations
126		Handbags, Luggage and Briefcases
125		Grooved Wooden Handle Kitchen Utensils and Gadgets
124		Textile Spinning Frames and Automatic Doffers Therefor
123		CT Scanner and Gamma Camera Medical Diagnostic Imaging Apparatus

Continued

Table D.1 Continued. USITC Section 337 Investigations

Investigation Number	Status	Investigation Title
122		Miniature, Battery-Operated All-Terrain, Wheeled Vehicles
121		Plastic-Capped Decorative Emblems
120		Silica-Coated Lead Chromate Pigments
119		High Precision Solenoids and Components Thereof
118		Sneakers with Fabric Uppers and Rubber Soles
117		Automotive Visors
116		Drill Point Screws for Drywall Construction
115		Power Woodworking Tools, Their Parts, Accessories and Special
114		Minature Plug-In Blade Fuses
113		Log Splitting Pivoted Lever Axes
112		Cube Puzzles
111		Vacuum Cleaner Brush Rollers
110		Methods for Extruding Plastic Tubing (Plastic Bags)
109		Multi-Sequential Coded Radio Pagers
108		Vacuum Bottles and Components Thereof
107		Ultrafiltration Membrane Systems and Components Thereof,
106		Airtight Cast-Iron Stoves ("Stoves III")
105		Coin-Operated Audiovisual Games and Components Thereof (viz.,
104		Card Data Imprinters and Components Thereof
103		Stabilized Hull Units and Components Thereof and Sonar Units
102		Wheel Locks and Components Thereof
101		Hot Air Corn Poppers and Components Thereof

Continued

Table D.1 Continued. USITC Section 337 Investigations

Investigation Number	Status	Investigation Title
100		Thermal Conductivity Sensing Gem Testers and Components Thereof
99		Molded-In Sandwich Panel Inserts and Methods for their
98		Screw Jacks and Components Thereof, Including Cold-Worked Pinion
97		Steel Rod Treating Apparatus and Components Thereof
96		Modular Pushbutton Switches and Components Thereof
95		Surface Grinding Machines and Literature for the Promotion
94		Wet Motor Circulating Pumps and Components Thereof
93		Universal Joint Kits, Components Thereof, and Trunnion Seals Used
92		Airtight Wood Stoves ("Stoves II")
91		Mass Flow Devices and Components Thereof
90		Airless Paint Spray Pumps and Components Thereof
89		Apparatus for the Continuous Production of Copper Rod
88		Spring Assemblies and Components Thereof, and Methods for Their
87		Coin-Operated Audio-Visual Games and Components Thereof
86		Shell Brim Hats
85		Slide Fastener Stringers and Machines and Components Thereof for
84		Chlorofluorohydrocarbon Drycleaning Process Machines and

Continued

Table D.1 Continued. USITC Section 337 Investigations

Investigation Number	Status	Investigation Title
83		Adjustable Window Shades and Components Thereof
082A		Headboxes and Papermaking Machine Forming Sections for the
82		Headboxes and Papermaking Machine Forming Sections for the
81		Hollow Fiber Artificial Kidneys
80		Plastic Bouquet Holders
79		Cathode Sputter Coated Glass Transparencies
78		Poultry Disk Picking Machines and Components Thereof
77		Computer Forms Feeding Tractors and Components Thereof
76		Food Slicers and Components Thereof
75		Large Video Matrix Display Systems and Components Thereof
74		Rotatable Photograph and Card Display Units and Components
73		Compressed Air Powered Tire Changers, and Components Thereof
72		Turning Machines and Components Thereof
71		Anaerobic Impregnating Compositions and Components Thereof
70		Coat Hanger Rings
69		Airtight Cast-Iron Stoves ("Stoves I")
68		Surveying Devices
67		Inclined Field Acceleration Tubes and Components Thereof
66		Plastic Molding Apparatus and Components Thereof
65		Precision Resistor Chips (see 063)

Continued

Table D.1 Continued. USITC Section 337 Investigations

Investigation Number	Status	Investigation Title
64		High Voltage Circuit Interrupters and Components Thereof
63		Precision Resistor Chips
62		Rotary Scraping Tools
61		Compact Cyclotrons With a Pre-Septum
60		Automatic Crankpin Grinders
59		Pump Top Insulated Containers
58		Fabricated Steel Plate Products From Japan
57		Cattle Whips
56		Thermometer Sheath Packages
55		Novelty Glasses
054B		Multicellular Plastic Film
054A		Multicellular Plastic Film
54		Multicellular Plastic Film
53		Swivel Hooks and Mounting Brackets
52		Apparatus for the Continuous Production of Copper Rod
51		Cigarette Holders
50		Synthetic Gemstones
49		Attache Cases
48		Alternating Pressure Pads
47		Flexible Foam Sandals
46		Telescopic Sight Mounts
45		Combination Locks
44		Roller Units
43		Centrifugal Trash Pumps
42		Electric Slow Cookers
41		Ceramic Tile Setters
40		Monumental Wood Windows
39		Luggage Products

Continued

Table D.1 Continued. USITC Section 337 Investigations

Investigation Number	Status	Investigation Title
38		Food Slicers
37		Skateboards and Platforms Therefor
36		Plastic Fastener Assemblies
35		Molded Golf Balls
34		Numerically Controlled Machining Centers and Components Thereof
33		Light Shields for Sonar Apparatus
32		Dot Matrix Impact Printers
31		Steel Toy Vehicles
30		Display Devices for Photographs and the Like
29		Welded Stainless Steel Pipe and Tube
28		Knitting Machines and Throat Plates Therefor
27		Chicory Root – Crude and Prepared
26		Solder Removal Wicks
25		Above-Ground Swimming Pools
24		Exercising Devices
23		Color Television Receiving Sets
22		Reclosable Plastic Bags
21		Dry Wall Screws
20		Bismuth Molybdate Catalysts
19		Glass Fiber Optic Devices and Instruments Equipped with Glass
18		Monolithic Catalytic Converters
17		Record Players Incorporating Straight Line Tracking Systems
16		Angolan Robusta Coffee
15		Overlapping Digital Movements
14		High Fidelity Audio and Related Equipment
13		Liquid Propane Heaters

Continued

Table D.1 Continued. USITC Section 337 Investigations

Investigation Number	Status	Investigation Title
12		Automatic Tobacco Leaf Graders
11		Electronic Printing Calculators
10		Ultra-Microtome Freezing Attachments
9		Hydraulic Tappets II
8		Piezoelectric Ceramic Electric Wave Filters
7		Electronic Audio and Related Equipment
6		Eye-Testing Instruments Incorporating Refractive Principles
5		Chain Door Locks
4		Expanded, Unsintered Polytetrafluoroethylene in Tape Form (PTFE)
3		Doxycycline
2		Convertible Game Tables
1		Electronic Pianos

Appendix E

U.S. Trade Representative's 2007 Special 301 Watch List

The Executive Summary of the 2007 "Special 301" report is an annual review of the global state of intellectual property rights (IPR) protection and enforcement, conducted by the Office of the United States Trade Representative (USTR) pursuant to Special 301 provisions of the Trade Act of 1974 (Trade Act). The 2007 Special 301 review process examines IPR protection and enforcement in 79 countries. Following extensive research and analysis, USTR designates 43 countries in this year's Special 301 report in the categories of Priority Watch List, Watch List, and/or Section 306 Monitoring status. The report, produced annually in April, is worthy of adding to every library. This report also highlights, specifically, the role of China and Russia as the number one and two violators of intellectual property protections. Table E.1 lists countries on the priority watch list and the watch list.

Table E.1 The Priority Watch List and the Watch List

Priority Watch List	Watch List
Argentina	Bangladesh
Canada	Belarus
Chile	Brazil
Costa Rica	Bulgaria
Dominican Republic	Colombia
Egypt	Ecuador
India	Greece
Israel	Hungary
Mexico	Indonesia
People's Republic of China	Italy
Russian Federation	Kazakhstan
Saudi Arabia	Kuwait
Thailand	Lebanon
Turkey	Lithuania
Ukraine	Malaysia
Venezuela	Nigeria
	Pakistan
	Peru
	Philippines
	Poland

Continued

Table E.1 Continued. The Priority Watch List and the Watch List

Priority Watch List	Watch List
	Romania
	South Korea
	Spain
	Taiwan
	Tajikistan
	Turkmenistan
	Uzbekistan
	Vietnam

U.S. Department of Justice Checklist for Reporting a Theft of Trade Secrets Offense

United States Department of Justice

CHECKLIST FOR REPORTING
A THEFT OF TRADE SECRETS OFFENSE

If you or your company has become the victim of a theft of trade secrets offense, the U.S. Department of Justice asks that you please fill out the information indicated below and contact a federal law enforcement official to report the offense.

NOTE ON CONFIDENTIALITY: Federal law provides that courts "shall enter such orders and take such action as may be necessary and appropriate to preserve the confidentiality of trade secrets, consistent with the requirements of the Federal Rules of Criminal and Civil Procedure, the Federal Rules of Evidence, and all other applicable laws" 18 U.S.C. § 1835.

Prosecutors utilizing any of the information set forth below will generally request the court to enter an order to preserve the status of the information as a trade secret and prevent its unnecessary and harmful disclosure.

Background and Contact Information

1. Victim's Name:

2. Primary Location and Address:

3. Nature of Primary Business:

4. Law Enforcement Contact:

   Phone: Fax:

   Email: Pager/Mobile:

Description of the Trade Secret:

5. Generally describe the trade secret (e.g., source code, formula):
   Provide an estimated value of the trade secret identifying ONE of the methods and indicating ONE of the ranges listed below:

   Method
   ___Cost to develop the Trade Secret;
   ___Acquisition Cost (identify date and source of acquisition); or
   ___Fair Market Value if sold.

Estimated Value:

___Under $50,000;

___Between $50,000 and $100,000;

___Between $100,000 and $1 million;

___Between $1 million and $5 million; or

___Over $5 million.

Identify a person knowledgeable about valuation, including that person's contact information:

General Physical Measures Taken to Protect the Trade Secret

6. Describe the general physical security precautions taken by the company, such as fencing the perimeter of the premises, visitor control systems, using alarming or self-locking doors, or hiring security personnel.

7. Has the company established physical barriers to prevent unauthorized viewing or access to the trade secret, such as "Authorized Personnel Only" signs at access points? (See below if computer-stored trade secret.) ___YES ___NO

8. Does the company require sign in/out procedures for access to and return of trade secret materials? ___YES ___NO

9. Are employees required to wear identification badges? ___YES ___ NO

10. Does the company have a written security policy? ___YES ___NO

   - How are employees advised of the security policy?

   - Are employees required to sign a written acknowledgment of the security policy? ___YES ___NO

   - Identify the person most knowledgeable about matters relating to the security policy, including title and contact information.

11. How many employees have access to the trade secret?

12. Was access to the trade secret limited to a "need to know" basis? ___YES ___NO

Confidentiality and Non-Disclosure Agreements

13. Does the company enter into confidentiality and non-disclosure agreements with employees and third-parties concerning the trade secret? ___YES ___NO

14. Has the company established and distributed written confidentiality policies to all employees? ___YES ___NO

15. Does the company have a policy for advising company employees regarding the company's trade secrets? ___YES ___NO

Computer-Stored Trade Secrets

16. If the trade secret is computer source code or other computer-stored information, how is access regulated (e.g., are employees given unique user names and passwords)?

17. If the company stores the trade secret on a computer network, is the network protected by a firewall? ___YES ___NO

18. Is remote access permitted into the computer network? ___YES ___NO

19. Is the trade secret maintained on a separate computer server?

    ___YES ____NO

20. Does the company prohibit employees from bringing outside computer programs or storage media to the premises? ___YES ___NO

21. Does the company maintain electronic access records such as computer logs?

    ___YES ___NO

Document Control

22. If the trade secret consisted of documents, were they clearly marked "CONFIDENTIAL" or "PROPRIETARY"? ___YES ___NO

23. Describe the document control procedures employed by the company, such as limiting access and sign in/out policies.

24. Was there a written policy concerning document control procedures and, if so, how were employees advised of it? ___YES ___NO

25. Identify the person most knowledgeable about the document control procedures, including title and contact information.

Employee Controls

26. Are new employees subject to a background investigation? ___YES ___NO

27. Does the company hold "exit interviews" to remind departing employees of their obligation not to disclose trade secrets? ___YES ___NO

Description of the Theft of Trade Secret

28. Identify the name(s) or location(s) of possible suspects, including the following information:

    - Name (Suspect #1):

    - Phone number:

    - Email address:

    - Physical address:

    - Employer:

    - Reason for suspicion:

    - Name (Suspect #2):

    - Phone number:

    - Email address:

    - Physical address:

    - Employer:

    - Reason for suspicion

29. Was the trade secret stolen to benefit a third party, such as a competitor or another business? ___YES ___NO
    If so, identify that business and its location:

30. Do you have any information that the theft of the trade secret was committed to benefit a foreign government or instrumentality of a foreign government? ___YES ___NO
    If so, identify the foreign government and describe that information.

31. If the suspect is a current or former employee, describe all confidentiality and non-disclosure agreements in effect.

32. Identify any physical locations tied to the theft of the trade secret, such as where it may be currently stored or used.

33. If you have conducted an internal investigation into the theft or counterfeiting activities, please describe any evidence acquired:

Civil Enforcement Proceedings

34. Has a civil enforcement action been filed against the suspects identified above? ___YES ___NO

    ■ If so, identify the following:

        i.   Name of court and case number:

        ii. Date of filing:

        iii. Names of attorneys:

        iv. Status of case:

    ■ If not, is a civil action contemplated?

        What type and when?

35. Please provide any information concerning the suspected crime not described above that you believe might assist law enforcement.

Index

Syngress: *The Definition of a Serious Security Library*

Syn•gress (sin–gres): *noun, sing.* Freedom from risk or danger; safety. See *security.*

Syngress IT Security Project Management Handbook

Susan Snedaker

The definitive work for IT professionals responsible for the management of the design, configuration, deployment and maintenance of enterprise-wide security projects. Provides specialized coverage of key project areas including Penetration Testing, Intrusion Detection and Prevention Systems, and Access Control Systems.

ISBN: 1-59749-076-8

Price: $59.95 US $77.95 CAN

Combating Spyware in the Enterprise

Paul Piccard

Combating Spyware in the Enterprise is the first book published on defending enterprise networks from increasingly sophisticated and malicious spyware. System administrators and security professionals responsible for administering and securing networks ranging in size from SOHO networks up to the largest enterprise networks will learn to use a combination of free and commercial anti-spyware software, firewalls, intrusion detection systems, intrusion prevention systems, and host integrity monitoring applications to prevent the installation of spyware, and to limit the damage caused by spyware that does in fact infiltrate their networks.

ISBN: 1-59749-064-4

Price: $49.95 US $64.95 CAN

Practical VoIP Security

Thomas Porter

After struggling for years, you finally think you've got your network secured from malicious hackers and obnoxious spammers. Just when you think it's safe to go back into the water, VoIP finally catches on. Now your newly converged network is vulnerable to DoS attacks, hacked gateways leading to unauthorized free calls, call eavesdropping, malicious call redirection, and spam over Internet Telephony (SPIT). This book details both VoIP attacks and defense techniques and tools.

ISBN: 1-59749-060-1

Price: $49.95 U.S. $69.95 CAN

SYNGRESS®

Syngress: *The Definition of a Serious Security Library*

Syn·gress (sin-gres): *noun, sing.* Freedom from risk or danger; safety. See *security*.

Cyber Spying: Tracking Your Family's (Sometimes) Secret Online Lives

Dr. Eric Cole, Michael Nordfelt,
Sandra Ring, and Ted Fair

Have you ever wondered about that friend your spouse e-mails, or who they spend hours chatting online with? Are you curious about what your children are doing online, whom they meet, and what they talk about? Do you worry about them finding drugs and other illegal items online, and wonder what they look at? This book shows you how to monitor and analyze your family's online behavior.

ISBN: 1-93183-641-8

Price: $39.95 US $57.95 CAN

Stealing the Network: How to Own an Identity

Timothy Mullen, Ryan Russell, Riley (Caezar) Eller,
Jeff Moss, Jay Beale, Johnny Long, Chris Hurley, Tom Parker, Brian Hatch

The first two books in this series "Stealing the Network: How to Own the Box" and "Stealing the Network: How to Own a Continent" have become classics in the Hacker and Infosec communities because of their chillingly realistic depictions of criminal hacking techniques. In this third installment, the all-star cast of authors tackle one of the fastest-growing crimes in the world: Identity Theft. Now, the criminal hackers readers have grown to both love and hate try to cover their tracks and vanish into thin air...

ISBN: 1-59749-006-7

Price: $39.95 US $55.95 CAN

Software Piracy Exposed

Paul Craig, Ron Honick

For every $2 worth of software purchased legally, $1 worth of software is pirated illegally. For the first time ever, the dark underground of how software is stolen and traded over the Internet is revealed. The technical detail provided will open the eyes of software users and manufacturers worldwide! This book is a tell-it-like-it-is exposé of how tens of billions of dollars worth of software is stolen every year.

ISBN: 1-93226-698-4

Price: $39.95 U.S. $55.95 CAN

SYNGRESS®

Syngress: *The Definition of a Serious Security Library*

Syn·gress (sin-gres): *noun, sing.* Freedom from risk or danger; safety. See *security.*

Phishing Exposed

Lance James, Secure Science Corporation,
Joe Stewart (Foreword)

If you have ever received a phish, become a victim of a phish, or manage the security of a major e-commerce or financial site, then you need to read this book. The author of this book delivers the unconcealed techniques of phishers including their evolving patterns, and how to gain the upper hand against the ever-accelerating attacks they deploy. Filled with elaborate and unprecedented forensics, Phishing Exposed details techniques that system administrators, law enforcement, and fraud investigators can exercise and learn more about their attacker and their specific attack methods, enabling risk mitigation in many cases before the attack occurs.

ISBN: 1-59749-030-X

Price: $49.95 US $69.95 CAN

Penetration Tester's Open Source Toolkit

Johnny Long, Chris Hurley, SensePost,
Mark Wolfgang, Mike Petruzzi

This is the first fully integrated Penetration Testing book and bootable Linux CD containing the "Auditor Security Collection," which includes over 300 of the most effective and commonly used open source attack and penetration testing tools. This powerful tool kit and authoritative reference is written by the security industry's foremost penetration testers including HD Moore, Jay Beale, and SensePost. This unique package provides you with a completely portable and bootable Linux attack distribution and authoritative reference to the toolset included and the required methodology.

ISBN: 1-59749-021-0

Price: $59.95 US $83.95 CAN

Google Hacking for Penetration Testers

Johnny Long, Foreword by Ed Skoudis

Google has been a strong force in Internet culture since its 1998 upstart. Since then, the engine has evolved from a simple search instrument to an innovative authority of information. As the sophistication of Google grows, so do the hacking hazards that the engine entertains. Approaches to hacking are forever changing, and this book covers the risks and precautions that administrators need to be aware of during this explosive phase of Google Hacking.

ISBN: 1-93183-636-1

Price: $44.95 U.S. $65.95 CAN

SYNGRESS®

Syngress: *The Definition of a Serious Security Library*

Syn·gress (sin-gres): *noun, sing.* Freedom from risk or danger; safety. See *security*.

Cisco PIX Firewalls:
Configure, Manage, & Troubleshoot

Charles Riley, Umer Khan, Michael Sweeney

Cisco PIX Firewall is the world's most used network firewall, protecting internal networks from unwanted intrusions and attacks. Virtual Private Networks (VPNs) are the means by which authorized users are allowed through PIX Firewalls. Network engineers and security specialists must constantly balance the need for air-tight security (Firewalls) with the need for on-demand access (VPNs). In this book, Umer Khan, author of the #1 best selling PIX Firewall book, provides a concise, to-the-point blueprint for fully integrating these two essential pieces of any enterprise network.

ISBN: 1-59749-004-0

Price: $49.95 US $69.95 CAN

Configuring Netscreen Firewalls

Rob Cameron

Configuring NetScreen Firewalls is the first book to deliver an in-depth look at the NetScreen firewall product line. It covers all of the aspects of the NetScreen product line from the SOHO devices to the Enterprise NetScreen firewalls. Advanced troubleshooting techniques and the NetScreen Security Manager are also covered..

ISBN: 1--93226-639-9

Price: $49.95 US $72.95 CAN

Configuring Check Point
NGX VPN-1/FireWall-1

Barry J. Stiefel, Simon Desmeules

Configuring Check Point NGX VPN-1/Firewall-1 is the perfect reference for anyone migrating from earlier versions of Check Point's flagship firewall/VPN product as well as those deploying VPN-1/Firewall-1 for the first time. NGX includes dramatic changes and new, enhanced features to secure the integrity of your network's data, communications, and applications from the plethora of blended threats that can breach your security through your network perimeter, Web access, and increasingly common internal threats.

ISBN: 1--59749-031-8

Price: $49.95 U.S. $69.95 CAN

SYNGRESS®

Syngress: *The Definition of a Serious Security Library*

Syn·gress (sin-gres): *noun, sing.* Freedom from risk or danger; safety. See *security.*

Syngress: *The Definition of a Serious Security Library*

Syn·gress (sin-gres): *noun, sing.* Freedom from risk or danger; safety. See *security*.

How to Cheat at Designing Security for a Windows Server 2003 Network

Neil Ruston, Chris Peiris

While considering the security needs of your organiztion, you need to balance the human and the technical in order to create the best security design for your organization. Securing a Windows Server 2003 enterprise network is hardly a small undertaking, but it becomes quite manageable if you approach it in an organized and systematic way. This includes configuring software, services, and protocols to meet an organization's security needs.

ISBN: 1-59749-243-4

Price: $39.95 US $55.95 CAN

How to Cheat at Designing a Windows Server 2003 Active Directory Infrastructure

Melissa Craft, Michael Cross, Hal Kurz, Brian Barber

The book will start off by teaching readers to create the conceptual design of their Active Directory infrastructure by gathering and analyzing business and technical requirements. Next, readers will create the logical design for an Active Directory infrastructure. Here the book starts to drill deeper and focus on aspects such as group policy design. Finally, readers will learn to create the physical design for an active directory and network Infrastructure including DNS server placement; DC and GC placements and Flexible Single Master Operations (FSMO) role placement.

ISBN: 1-59749-058-X

Price: $39.95 US $55.95 CAN

How to Cheat at Configuring ISA Server 2004

Dr. Thomas W. Shinder, Debra Littlejohn Shinder

If deploying and managing ISA Server 2004 is just one of a hundred responsibilities you have as a System Administrator, "How to Cheat at Configuring ISA Server 2004" is the perfect book for you. Written by Microsoft MVP Dr. Tom Shinder, this is a concise, accurate, enterprise tested method for the successful deployment of ISA Server.

ISBN: 1-59749-057-1

Price: $34.95 U.S. $55.95 CAN

SYNGRESS®

Made in the USA
Lexington, KY
02 March 2012